ECONOMIC ISSUES, PROBLEMS AND PERSPECTIVES

FOREIGN INVESTMENT

TYPES, METHODS AND IMPACTS

Economic Issues, Problems and Perspectives

Additional books in this series can be found on Nova's website under the Series tab.

Additional e-books in this series can be found on Nova's website under the E-book tab.

Business Issues, Competition and Entrepreneurship

Additional books in this series can be found on Nova's website under the Series tab.

Additional e-books in this series can be found on Nova's website under the E-book tab.

ECONOMIC ISSUES, PROBLEMS AND PERSPECTIVES

FOREIGN INVESTMENT

TYPES, METHODS AND IMPACTS

TORRE DESARE
AND
DANIELE CAPRIOGLIO
EDITORS

Nova Science Publishers, Inc.
New York

For permission to use material from this book please contact us:
Telephone 631-231-7269; Fax 631-231-8175
Web Site: http://www.novapublishers.com

Library of Congress Cataloging-in-Publication Data

Foreign investment : types, methods, and impacts / editors, Torre DeSare and Daniele Caprioglio.
p. cm.
Includes bibliographical references and index.
ISBN 978-1-61470-358-7 (hardcover : alk. paper) 1. Investments, Foreign--Developing countries. 2. Economic development--Developing countries--Case studies. I. DeSare, Torre. II. Caprioglio, Daniele.
HG4538.F637 2011
332.67'3091724--dc23
2011022199

Published by Nova Science Publishers, Inc. † New York

CONTENTS

PREFACE

Many governments are engaged in the attraction and facilitation of foreign direct investment (FDI) into their economies. The reason for this is that foreign-owned firms can generate a variety of positive impacts on their host economies, related to capital investments, employment creation and the generation of export revenues. In this book, the authors present current research in the study of foreign investments, including technology gaps, agglomeration and FDI spillovers; globalization and the rise of logistical foreign direct investments in Italy; comparison of FDI and domestic producer firms; the risk management strategy of foreign direct investment, political risk and corporate social responsibility and the effect of inward FDI on economic growth in the League of Arab States.

Chapter 1 - Recent decades have witnessed a rapid growth of the research field engaged with the empirical identification of spillover effects from Foreign Direct Investment (FDI), where productivity of domestic firms in a host economy is affected by the entrance and operations of foreign owned firms. However, the large body of evidence is very heterogeneous and has fostered limited consensus on the prevalence of positive FDI spillovers. In response to this, recent research is developing alternative research strategies to obtain improved evidence of FDI externalities. One of these strategies concerns the identification of endogenous factors that may influence the occurrence (and perhaps also the nature) of FDI spillovers.

The purpose of this chapter is to provide a survey of FDI spillover studies that try to identify such endogenous factors that affect these externality effects. Previous surveys have focused mainly on the discussion on the overall prevalence of positive FDI spillovers. In comparison, only little attention has been paid to studies that try to identify determinants of FDI spillovers. In particular, the present survey focuses on studies that address the questions whether absorptive capacity of domestic firms is important for FDI spillovers to occur and whether and how agglomerations of economic activity within a host economy influence FDI spillovers.

The main findings of the survey can be summarized as follows. Research on the effect of absorptive capacity of domestic firms uses the level of technological differences between FDI and domestic firms as a direct inverse indicator of absorptive capacity. A closer examination of the use of this technology gap shows however that this interpretation relates only partially to the underlying concept of catch up. This concept holds that, for meaningful spillovers to occur, a sufficient level of absorptive capacity needs to be accompanied by a sufficiently large technology gap. The survey shows that there is substantial empirical evidence that a large technology gap facilitates rather than hinders the occurrence of positive FDI spillovers, suggesting that the commonly used interpretation of the technology gap as direct inverse indicator of absorptive capacity is flawed. Instead, large technological differences are better interpreted as reflecting a substantial scope for positive effects to occur, offering incentives to domestic firms to improve their ability to absorb positive spillovers.

Concerning the effect of agglomeration on FDI spillovers, the large degree of similarity between the mechanisms that create agglomeration economies and channels of FDI spillovers suggests strongly that agglomeration will enhance positive FDI externalities. The limited number of studies that look at this direct relation between agglomeration and FDI spillovers find corroborating evidence of such a positive effect. Clearly, more empirical research on this relationship is called for. Most studies that include assessments of spatial dimensions look at more general geographical dimensions of FDI spillovers. The inclusion of these spatial dimensions is welcome. The evidence shows that the scope for FDI spillovers can be much larger than envisaged originally, as spillovers may occur at the intra- and /or inter-regional level. Having said this, the survey also finds that the majority of the existing evidence on spatial FDI spillovers is characterized by several limitations. In particular, most studies fail to estimate for all types of intra- and inter-regional FDI effects. Furthermore, most studies give insufficient consideration to the variety of relations that may exist between FDI spillovers and geographical distance. FDI spillovers are transmitted via several channels that may be affected differently by distance decay effects. A fuller assessment of the variety of relationships that may exist between spatial spillovers and geographical distance is required to increase the robustness of the evidence on inter-regional FDI externalities.

Chapter 2 - The globalisation of the economy, which has been fostered by the trade barriers reduction and the falling transport, communication and co-ordination costs, has changed the structure of the production processes from being concentrated in few plants to being fragmented in different plants and in different countries and has strongly increased the trade rate. This has fostered a tight increase of exchange flows, affecting the logistics activities, especially transport. Transport, indeed, plays a key role in connecting the different import and export markets and the vertically disaggregated components of production systems, which are widespread in the world. As a consequence, the Foreign Direct Investments (FDI) in logistics have quickly grown: in the last years, the growth rate of FDI in the utilities (energy, gas and water), logistics and communications has more than tripled and outward FDI in the logistics industry equals to 26% of the service total.

The aim of the present chapter is threefold. First, it presents the entity and the characteristics of outward and inward logistics FDI in Italy (section two). This country can be considered an interesting case because it is characterized by a fragmented, small sized transport industry and low value added logistics industry, which has attracted foreign logistics multinational enterprise (MNE) in the integrated logistics. Second, the work investigates in-depth strategies and motivations of the foreign MNE's investment decisions (section three). Specifically, the horizontal, vertical and conglomerate integration strategies are analyzed and the main motivations driving them are discussed. Third, it concerns the main drivers of inward logistics FDI's increase, and generally, the main factor fostering logistics growth: the manufacturing internationalization, which increases the demand for logistics services in the home country and consequently attracts providers from the other countries (section four).

The data on outward and inward FDI in Italy come from the LogINT database, developed by the Laboratory of Economics, Logistics and Territory (LabELT) of DiAP-Polytechnic of Milan in collaboration with the University of Molise, and covers the period 2000 – 2010.

Chapter 3 - This study contributes to the literature on externality impacts that foreign direct investment (FDI) can generate among local suppliers in a host economy. Using unique data from several surveys among firms in the manufacturing sector of Nuevo Leon, Mexico, I present novel qualitative and quantitative evidence on the static and dynamic impact of FDI firms on their Mexican suppliers. Importantly, the data allows me to deal with certain issues and questions that previous research has failed to address satisfactory. In particular, the data makes it possible to compare statistically the operations and impacts of both foreign-owned and domestic producer firms, providing an answer to the question that underlies all research on FDI impacts whether foreign-owned firms actually differ in their impacts from domestic firms. I also use data from an objective sample of actual suppliers in the regional economy to identify the impact of producer firms and to assess whether type of ownership of producer firms matters for this impact.

The main findings can be summarized as follows. First, there are only marginal differences between foreign-owned and Mexican producer firms regarding the level of use of local suppliers. As such, this indicates that type of ownership does not affect the static impact of producer firms. Second, I find several indications that the dynamic impact of foreign-owned firms is significantly larger than the impact of domestic producer firms. FDI firms offer several types of support to their suppliers significantly more frequently. This concerns in particular types of technological support, support that has a direct positive impact on production processes of suppliers. Findings from the survey among local suppliers also indicate that the dynamic impact of foreign-owned firms is larger, as there are significantly more firms among suppliers of FDI firms that indicate to have experienced a large positive impact from their business dealings with their client firms. Related to the finding that FDI firms offer more technological support, the suppliers indicate that it is in particular technological support that is important for generating this large impact. A vast majority of suppliers of FDI firms also indicate that they can use support received from a given client firm to improve their performance to other client firms, indicating the presence of wider positive economic effects from their business dealings with FDI firms.

Third, I conduct a multivariate statistical analysis to identify supplier and business linkage characteristics that influence the likelihood that a supplier experiences a large positive impact. The findings indicate that the level of absorptive capacity of local suppliers facilitates this impact. A large technology gap between a supplier and its client firms, representing a large scope of the potential impact, also fosters the occurrence of a large positive impact of a technological nature. The levels of organizational and technological supportiveness of producer firms are also positively associated with the occurrence of large organizational and technological impacts. Overall, inter-firm linkages characterized by "at arms length" business transactions lower the likelihood that a large impact materializes, suggesting that close relationships between producer firms and suppliers facilitate positive externality effects. Finally, the positive effect of foreign-ownership of producer firms on the creation of large positive impacts among suppliers is maintained in the multivariate analysis. This confirms that the type of ownership of a producer firm clearly matters for the creation of positive dynamic impacts in the regional economy. As such, the findings contain robust indications that FDI firms are a particularly good source of knowledge and technology transfers to their local suppliers, supporting the notion that input-output linkages between FDI firms and domestic firms are a well-suited mechanism for the creation and transmission of positive spillover effects.

Chapter 4 - The conventional view of political risk held by the management of multinational enterprises considers it an exogenous factor. However, recent studies have pointed out that political risk may also provide firms with an opportunity to obtain competitive advantages over their competitors in certain locations. MNEs operating in countries with poor institutional development, high corruption levels or whose governments exercise a high degree of discretionary power may already have or may develop political competitive advantages, in order to manage the political risk and mitigate the market failure of those environments. Those with better political capabilities will be better positioned to take advantage of the market through the proactive use of political risk.

This study reviews the theoretical background behind this particular strategy, which influences both the decision to set up a subsidiary in a given country and the magnitude of Foreign Direct Investment flows. It also offers further evidence on the use of this strategy by Spanish MNEs, as a positive relationship has been identified in recent literature between the degree of internationalization and the level of political risk, measured by several variables including political constraints or corruption indices.

Political risk may therefore be considered not only as a threat but also as an opportunity that plays a key role as a determinant of a firm's internationalization strategy. However, its implications in relation to Corporate Social Responsibility should not be overlooked, as MNEs that resort to corrupt practices sacrifice their social legitimacy and run the risk of losing influence and effectiveness due to the negative impact on their status within the world community.

Chapter 5 - Political risk still plagues foreign investors. Yet one particular kind of business thrives on such risks, namely the political risk assessment industry. The assessments and predictions on offer, however, generally suffer from a number of flaws, which the present chapter seeks to remedy. It does so by way of creating a composite, multidimensional political risk index – POLRISK – which covers 192 countries and territories, and which is based on a variety of publicly available sources. The chapter first presents a brief summary of the theoretical rationale for this multidimensional approach to political risk assessment, along with a description of the methodology employed. It then proceeds to test, by way of a carefully executed time-series cross-section analysis, whether or not multinational companies are influenced by political risk when making investment location decisions. And results show that they are: the relationship between POLRISK and inflows of foreign direct investment (FDI) is consistently positive and significant. Moreover, the new measure performs much better than one of the most widely used commercial political risk indexes, the International Country Risk Guide (ICRG). This perhaps suggests that the political risk assessment industry may not pay sufficient heed to the complexity and multidimensionality of the political risk phenomenon.

Chapter 6 - This study estimates the effect of inward FDI on economic growth for the League of Arab States (LAS) countries over the period 1990-2007. The empirical investigation relies on a dynamic specification using GMM estimation techniques. The empirical results show moderate effect of inward FDI on economic growth where a 10% increase in inward FDI as a share of GDP accelerates economic growth by 0.22% in the short run and 1.07% in the long run. Estimating the effect for different LAS sub-regions reveals positive effect for the *Maghreb* and *Mashreq* countries but not for the Arab Gulf countries and for the Arab LDCs. Finally, the empirical results emphasize the positive effect of human capital in realizing larger benefits from inward FDI in terms of economic growth. However, trade openness and the level of development in financial markets are found not to have such effects.

Chapter 7 - The evidence on the relationship between political freedoms and foreign direct investment (FDI) is mixed. Part of the problem in interpreting results is that past cross-country studies have generally used a large sample of diverse nations and broad measures of political freedoms which do not vary much over time. In this chapter the relationship between political freedoms and FDI in the Central and Eastern European and Former Soviet Union nations is analyzed using recently developed political freedom indexes by Freedom House specific to the transition economies, over the period 1999-2008. By focusing on a specific region of the world which has undergone recent dramatic change in its political institutions, both in terms of positive reforms in certain nations and increased repression in others, a better estimation of the true impact of political freedom can be determined. It is found that greater political freedoms in general discourage FDI. However, not all types of political freedoms significantly hinder FDI. In particular, freedoms related to judicial framework, civil society, and corruption significantly limit FDI, while freedoms related to electoral process and governance do not. Finally, the results for media independence are dependent on specification.

Chapter 8 - Corruption is a key impediment to: foreign direct investment, an accurate measurement of political risk, and a barrier to effective corporate governance. By examining the political structure of Vietnam and the impediments created by corruption, this paper defines some of the difficulties with investing in Vietnam. However, with regard to the sugar industry, some solutions have emerged with companies taking direct control of contracting, offering credit, and the building of infrastructure.

In: Foreign Investment
Editor: Torre DeSare and Daniele Caprioglio
ISBN 978-1-61470-358-7

Chapter 1

TECHNOLOGY GAP, AGGLOMERATION AND FDI SPILLOVERS: A SURVEY OF THE LITERATURE

Jacob A. Jordaan
Deparment of Economics and Business Administration,
VU University Amsterdam, The Netherlands

ABSTRACT

Recent decades have witnessed a rapid growth of the research field engaged with the empirical identification of spillover effects from Foreign Direct Investment (FDI), where productivity of domestic firms in a host economy is affected by the entrance and operations of foreign owned firms. However, the large body of evidence is very heterogeneous and has fostered limited consensus on the prevalence of positive FDI spillovers. In response to this, recent research is developing alternative research strategies to obtain improved evidence of FDI externalities. One of these strategies concerns the identification of endogenous factors that may influence the occurrence (and perhaps also the nature) of FDI spillovers.

The purpose of this chapter is to provide a survey of FDI spillover studies that try to identify such endogenous factors that affect these externality effects. Previous surveys have focused mainly on the discussion on the overall prevalence of positive FDI spillovers. In comparison, only little attention has been paid to studies that try to identify determinants of FDI spillovers. In particular, the present survey focuses on studies that address the questions whether absorptive capacity of domestic firms is important for FDI spillovers to occur and whether and how agglomerations of economic activity within a host economy influence FDI spillovers.

The main findings of the survey can be summarized as follows. Research on the effect of absorptive capacity of domestic firms uses the level of technological differences between FDI and domestic firms as a direct inverse indicator of absorptive capacity. A closer examination of the use of this technology gap shows however that this interpretation relates only partially to the underlying concept of catch up. This concept holds that, for meaningful spillovers to occur, a sufficient level of absorptive capacity needs to be accompanied by a sufficiently large technology gap. The survey shows that there is substantial empirical evidence that a large technology gap facilitates rather than hinders the occurrence of positive FDI spillovers, suggesting that the commonly used interpretation of the technology gap as direct inverse indicator of absorptive capacity is flawed. Instead, large technological differences are better interpreted as reflecting a substantial scope for positive effects to occur, offering incentives to domestic firms to improve their ability to absorb positive spillovers.

Concerning the effect of agglomeration on FDI spillovers, the large degree of similarity between the mechanisms that create agglomeration economies and channels of FDI spillovers suggests strongly that agglomeration will enhance positive FDI externalities. The limited number of studies that look at this direct relation between agglomeration and FDI spillovers find corroborating evidence of such a positive effect. Clearly, more empirical research on this relationship is called for. Most studies that include assessments of spatial dimensions look at more general geographical dimensions of FDI spillovers. The inclusion of these spatial dimensions is welcome. The evidence shows that the scope for FDI spillovers can be much larger than envisaged originally, as spillovers may occur at the intra- and /or inter-regional level. Having said this, the survey also finds that the majority of the existing evidence on spatial FDI spillovers is characterized by several limitations. In particular, most studies fail to estimate for all types of intra- and inter-regional FDI effects. Furthermore, most studies give insufficient consideration to the variety of relations that may exist between FDI spillovers and geographical distance. FDI spillovers are transmitted via several channels that may be affected differently by distance decay effects. A fuller assessment of the variety of relationships that may exist between spatial spillovers and geographical distance is required to increase the robustness of the evidence on inter-regional FDI externalities.

1. Introduction

Multinational enterprises (MNEs) play a central role in the current world economy. By engaging in foreign direct investment (FDI) in a large number of developed and developing host economies, MNEs represent a driving force behind processes of globalization and economic growth. Many governments are actively engaged in attracting new FDI activity into their economies, as the presence and operations of FDI can be linked to a variety of positive economic effects (Caves, 1996; Venables and Barba-Navaretti, 2005). For instance, the entrance of FDI represents a form of capital investment, when a MNE establishes a new affiliate in a host economy or when it makes further investments in an existing affiliate. Also, the entrance of FDI generates important direct employment effects, which may be further enhanced via multiplier effects among supplier and client firms. As FDI is often active on international markets, a host economy is likely to experience increases in export revenues and may also benefit from a growth of exporting activities of domestic firms, when FDI introduces these firms to international markets. Finally, the entrance of FDI often leads to the introduction and dissemination of modern and new technologies. Especially in the case of developing host economies, FDI is often the only or at least main source of new technologies (Dunning and Lundan, 2008; UNCTAD, 2005; Jordaan, 2009).

In the last 20 years, it is especially this last effect that is receiving growing interest. More precisely, the interest focuses on productivity spillovers that can follow from the build up of new technologies in a host economy. As ownership-specific advantages of FDI are often based on modern and/or new technologies (Dunning and Lundan, 2008), the entrance of new foreign-owned firms will enhance the overall level of technology of a host economy. Endogenous growth theory poses long term growth rates to be positively affected by the build up of technology and ideas (Romer, 1994; Grossman and Helpman, 1994), as they share characteristics of public goods. In this context, FDI can be seen as consisting of a bundle of capital stocks, knowledge and technologies (Balasubramanyam et al., 1996; de Mello, 1997). Therefore, the entrance of FDI adds to the stock of knowledge and technologies of a host economy, which may benefit domestic firms through spillover effects. For instance, the presence of a foreign-owned firm may expose domestic firms to a new piece of technology. If the domestic firms absorb this technology successfully, they will be able to increase their productivity or efficiency as a result. This increase in productivity represents a form of positive spillovers or externalities, as the foreign-owned firm is not compensated for this effect (Blomström and Kokko, 1998).

The growing acceptance of the importance of FDI spillovers for technological and economic development of host economies has fostered a rapidly growing body of empirical research that tries to identify and quantify these effects statistically. However, the substantial body of evidence has generated limited consensus (Jordaan, 2009). In several cases, empirical studies have found evidence of a positive relation between the presence of FDI and productivity of domestic firms, which is interpreted as evidence of positive spillovers. Yet, other studies have failed to identify such a positive link or have found evidence suggesting a negative effect of FDI on productivity of domestic firms (see e.g. Aitken and Harrison, 1999)

In response to the heterogeneous nature of the evidence on the prevalence of positive FDI spillovers, recent studies are attempting to identify endogenous factors that may affect these effects. Although there is a variety of factors that may be important, two are particularly noteworthy. First, a number of studies have attempted to link the occurrence of positive FDI spillovers to the level of absorptive capacity of domestic firms. In particular, these studies look at the effect of the technology gap between FDI and domestic firms, whereby this gap is interpreted as a direct inverse indicator of the level of absorptive capacity of domestic firms. Some of these studies do indeed find that positive FDI externalities only appear to materialize in industries or among those domestic firms that are characterized by a small technology gap. However, there is also substantial evidence that large instead of small technological differences promote positive FDI spillovers. This evidence is in direct contrast to the hypothesis on the importance of absorptive capacity of domestic firms and runs counter to the interpretation of the technology gap as direct inverse indicator of the level of absorptive capacity.

The second factor that may influence FDI spillovers is agglomeration or geographical proximity. It is well known from the New Economic Geography (NEG) literature that location patterns of economic activity can be linked to the creation of spatially-confined externalities or agglomeration economies (Jordaan, 2009). For instance, an agglomeration of economic activity can lead to the creation of regional experience and pools of knowledge, fostering the creation and transmission of knowledge spillovers (Duranton and Puga, 2004; Henderson, 2001). This may be particularly the case for knowledge intensive activities such as research and development (R&D) and other types of innovation and knowledge creating activities. From this, it seems straightforward to hypothesize that geographical proximity between FDI and domestic firms can also promote knowledge spillovers, given the interpretation of FDI as a bundle of knowledge and technologies. So far, only a limited number of studies have looked at this direct link between agglomeration and FDI spillovers, however. Instead, there is a related development that appears to be more in line with research that tries to identify knowledge spillovers across geographical space (e.g. Anselin et al., 1997;

Rodriguez-Pose and Crescenzi, 2008). Several recent studies on FDI estimate for the presence of FDI spillovers across geographical space, in an attempt mainly to improve the range of FDI externalities that empirical estimations need to control for.

The purpose of this chapter is to provide a new survey of empirical studies on FDI spillovers. Previous surveys have focused in particular on summarizing and analyzing the body of evidence on the general prevalence of positive FDI externalities, the effects of differences in methodology and the use of cross-sectional versus panel datasets (e.g. Blomström and Kokko, 1998; Hanson, 2001; Lipsey, 2004). In the present survey, I place the focus more on research that looks at the role and effects of absorptive capacity and agglomeration on FDI spillovers. The reason for this is three-fold. First, the heterogeneous nature of the evidence suggest strongly that we need to focus research efforts more on identifying and clarifying the role of determinants of FDI spillovers. Not only will this help with the empirical identification of these effects, it may also advance our understanding of processes that underlie the generation and transmission of these externalities. Second, the contrasting evidence on the importance of absorptive capacity from studies that look at the effect of the technology gap has received only limited attention in the literature. Given that contrasting findings of small or large technological differences promoting positive FDI spillovers have widely different policy implications, a closer examination of the evidence on the effect of the technology gap and the use of the concept of absorptive capacity is called for. Finally, as for the spatial dimensions of spillovers, the clear message from the NEG literature is that agglomeration matters for the creation and dissemination of externalities. The importance of these dimensions is further underlined by findings that spillover effects can also materialize across geographical space. The significance of proximity and geographical space in externality creating processes underline the importance of analyzing the evidence on spatial dimensions of FDI externalities and to assess how current FDI research on these dimensions can be improved and extended.

The chapter is constructed as follows. In section two I discuss the concept of FDI spillovers in more detail and I explain the main channels via which these effects can be generated and transmitted. Section three presents a first look at the empirical evidence, whereby I present a selective overview of findings on the overall prevalence of positive FDI externalities. In section four, I focus on empirical studies that look at the effects of the technology gap, agglomeration and geographical space on FDI spillovers. In section five I summarize the main findings and discuss policy implications.

2. FDI Spillovers: Concept and Channels

2.1. The Concept of FDI Spillovers

MNEs play a central role in the creation of new technologies[1]. Furthermore, by engaging in FDI, these technologies are disseminated to a large number of developed and developing host economies. Not only does this enhance the overall level of technology in these host economies, the level of technological development of domestic firms in these host economies

[1] Although exact statistics are difficult to obtain, MNEs appear to account for at least 65% of total expenditure on business R&D (UNCTAD, 2005).

may also be stimulated. One way how this can occur is via formal technology transfers, where domestic firms purchase technologies from FDI. Alternatively, it is increasingly thought that domestic firms improve their level of technological development through the occurrence of FDI externalities or spillovers.

Externalities can be classified into two types, consisting of technological and pecuniary externalities. Technological externalities occur when 'the actions of one agent directly affect the environment of another agent, i.e. the effect is not transmitted through prices' (Papandreou, 1994, p. 5). To stay with the example discussed earlier, the entrance of FDI may expose a domestic firm to a new piece of technology. The adoption and successful incorporation of the new technology by the domestic firm represents a form of technological externalities, as the domestic firm will not compensate the foreign-owned firm for this effect. In contrast, pecuniary externalities are effects that are transmitted through the market. They are said to arise '...whenever the profits of one producer are affected by the actions of other producers' (Scitovsky, 1954, p. 146). An example of this effect is when a foreign-owned firm purchases inputs from a supplier in a host economy, but demands a price lower than is charged to other firms. The domestic supplier may respond to this price signal by improving its efficiency in order to meet the new lower price. As a result, the presence of the foreign-owned firm has resulted in an improvement in the efficiency level of the domestic firm, but in this case the effect occurred in response to a market (price) signal.

2.2. Channels of FDI Spillovers

There are four main mechanisms or channels via which FDI externalities can occur. These are depicted below in figure 1, alongside an axis indicating whether the externalities are of a technological (non-market) or pecuniary (market) nature. On the far left of the axis are competition effects, which consist of pure pecuniary externalities. In the middle are placed inter-firm linkages and labor turnover, which can be linked to both pecuniary and technological externalities. Finally, on the far right are demonstration effects, which are linked to pure technological externalities.

The competition effect consists of pecuniary externalities. The traditional interpretation of this effect is that the entrance of new FDI generates positive externalities, as it forces domestic firms to become more efficient or productive in response to the increase in competition (Caves, 1996; Blomström and Kokko, 1998). However, recent findings that show a negative relation between the presence of FDI and productivity of domestic firms suggest that the competition effect may alternatively result in negative externalities (Aitken and Harrison, 1999; Venables and Barba-Navaretti, 2005). This can be explained by a so-called market stealing effect, where foreign-owned firms take over part of the market from domestic firms. The volume of production of the domestic firms lowers as a result of this, which, in the presence of scale economies, results in a decreased level of efficiency.

Inter-firm linkages between FDI and suppliers in host economies can be linked to both technological and pecuniary externalities. An example of technological externalities is when a supplier of a foreign-owned firm learns from its client firm. As markets for inputs are often characterized by limited numbers of buyer and supplier firms that are in frequent contact, supply linkages are very conducive to the transmission of ideas and information (UNCTAD, 2001). Also, FDI firms often provide several types of support to their suppliers to improve their operations (Dunning and Lundan, 2008). An example of such support is provided in a recent study by Jordaan (2011a), who investigates supply linkages between FDI firms and local suppliers in the north east of Mexico.

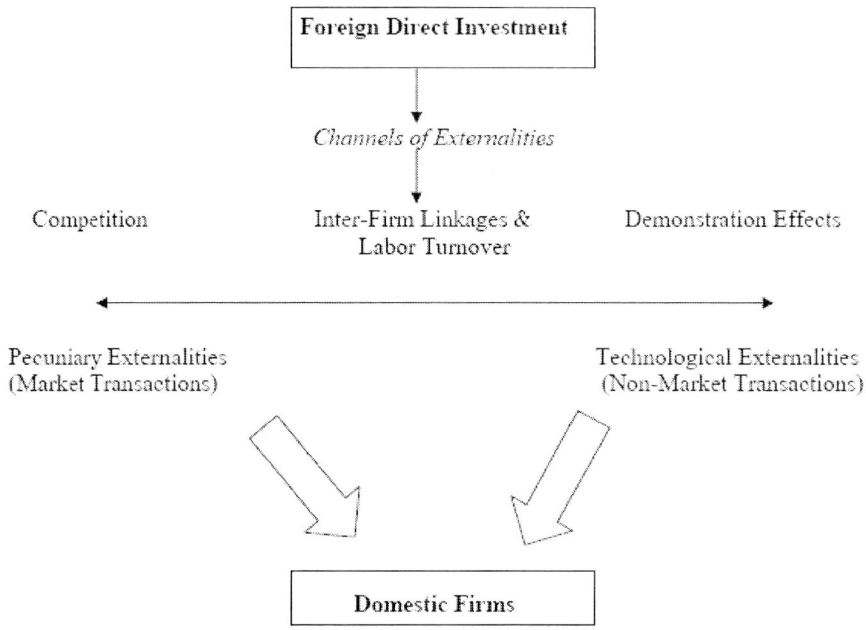

Figure 1. Channels of FDI Spillovers.

Using information from surveys among both types of firm, the findings indicate that foreign-owned firms are involved in a variety of types of support, including assistance with technical production and quality control, the provision or lending of special tools and the training of personnel of suppliers[2]. Of course, FDI firms engage in these supportive linkages to obtain advantages in the form of e.g. cheaper or higher quality inputs. However, as it will be very difficult for foreign-owned firms to obtain complete compensation for the support that they provide their suppliers with, the common assumption is that these supportive linkages usually result in the materialization of positive externalities of some degree (UNCTAD, 2001). This may be particularly so when suppliers can use the support that they receive from one client firm to improve their performance towards other client firms (see Jordaan, 2011a, 2011b).

As for pecuniary externalities via inter-firm linkages, these may occur when a foreign-owned firm exerts pressure on a supplier to lower its prices or improve the quality of its products. If the domestic firm responds to this market pressure by improving its efficiency, this efficiency increase is a form of positive pecuniary externalities (Potter et al., 2002). This type of externalities may also occur when the production of a supplier is subject to increasing returns to scale. When FDI increases its demand for an input, it may be the case that the increase in production volume allows a supplier to reap the benefits from scale economies. If this supplier also produces for other firms in the host economy, this efficiency improvement

[2] See Potter et al. (2002), Javorcik (2008) and UNCTAD (2001) for examples of support between FDI and local suppliers in other host economies.

will have additional positive effects beyond the linkages between the foreign-owned firm and the supplier.

The second channel that can be linked to both technological and pecuniary externalities concerns processes of labor turnover. Technological externalities may arise when a worker substitutes a domestic firm for a foreign-owned firm, allowing the domestic firm to benefit from the experience and skills that the worker gained while working for the foreign-owned firm (Lipsey and Sjöholm, 2004). As for pecuniary externalities, the presence of FDI firms may result in an upward pressure on wage levels in a host economy, which will have a negative effect on profit levels of domestic firms. Positive pecuniary externalities will occur if the wage increase spurs these firms to change their conduct to become more efficient, in response to the upward pressure on wage levels.

Finally, demonstration effects represent a channel of transmission that is linked to pure technological externalities. The entrance and operations of FDI firms may expose domestic firms to new technologies. If the domestic firms are successful in adopting these technologies and incorporating them into their production processes, any resulting productivity improvements represent positive technological externalities (Blomström and Kokko, 1998). Another type of demonstration effect concerns so-called market access spillovers (Görg and Greenaway, 2004). These spillovers occur when domestic firms increase their exporting activities as a result of knowledge and experience that they obtain from the presence of foreign-owned firms that are active on international markets.

3. FDI Spillovers: A First Look at the Evidence[3]

The growing interest in the role of externalities in processes of economic growth has fuelled an increasing interest in the empirical identification of growth and productivity effects of FDI. As FDI can be seen as a central source of new knowledge and technologies, the clear theoretical prediction is that a growing presence of FDI activity will enhance economic growth. However, the empirical evidence on FDI growth effects is far less conclusive. A good example of this is macro-economic research into FDI effects, which estimates the effect of FDI on levels or (average) growth rates of GDP (per capita) for samples of host economies. For instance, de Mello (1999) and Zhang (2001) look at long run positive relations between FDI and GDP growth and find that such relationships do not materialize for several countries in their samples. Alternatively, other studies find in cross-sectional settings that positive FDI growth effects occur only under certain conditions, including the overall level of development of a host economy (Blomström et al., 1994), the level of human capital (Borenzstein et al., 1998) or the presence of good functioning institutions or financial markets (Hermes and Lensink, 2003; Alfaro et al., 2004). Furthermore, cross-sectional estimates of FDI growth effects are riddled with problems including aggregation bias, omitted variable bias and causality issues (Hanson, 2001; Jordaan, 2009). Finding presented by Carkovic and Levine (2005) are particularly important in this context. They estimate FDI growth effects for several different samples of host economies, employing a variety of econometric specifications and controlling for issues of causality and endogeneity. In none of their findings is FDI

[3] In this survey, I focus on empirical findings from FDI productivity studies. For a discussion of studies on FDI wage spillovers, see Lipsey and Sjöholm (2004).

significantly associated with economic growth, indicating the difficulties surrounding the empirical identification of FDI growth effects in macro-economic settings (see Carkovic and Levine, 2005).

The majority of empirical studies on FDI spillovers consist of micro-economic studies, where FDI productivity effects are estimated at the industry or plant level for individual or small numbers of host economies. Caves (1974) represents the first empirical study in this tradition. In an attempt to identify FDI spillovers, Caves estimated determinants of value added per worker for a sample of Australian manufacturing industries, including the share of FDI in industry employment as one of the control variables. The findings show a significant positive association between this industry foreign participation variable and value added per worker, which Caves interpreted as evidence of the presence of positive spillovers. As Blomström and Persson (1983) explain, ' ... if there is a positive relation between the productivity level of domestically-owned plants in an industry and the share of foreign participation in the same industry (ceteris paribus), the foreign investment does raise the productivity of domestically owned plants through spillover efficiency' (Blomström and Persson, 1983, p. 495).

Following Caves (1974), a first wave of cross-sectional studies proceeded to present findings largely in support of the prevalence of positive FDI spillovers. Estimating a variety of production function based empirical models on determinants of value added per worker, several studies on Mexico and Indonesia in particular find positive associations between the industry level of foreign participation and labor productivity of domestic firms (Blomström and Persson, 1983; Kokko, 1994, 1996; Blomström and Wolff, 1994; Sjöholm, 1999; Blomström and Sjöholm, 1999).

A second wave of empirical studies, benefiting from the growing availability of datasets for different host economies containing plant level observations for several years, has produced findings that challenge the original impression of a prevalence of positive FDI spillovers. Instead of the clear tendency of the early studies to find evidence of positive FDI externalities, the evidence produced by these later studies is far more diverse. For instance, Barrios and Strobl (2002) and Girma et al. (2001) find no substantial evidence of FDI effects. Perhaps more importantly, Aitken and Harrison (1999), Djankov and Hoekman (2000) and Konings (2000) present evidence of a negative relationship between industry foreign participation and productivity of domestic firms, suggesting that the presence of FDI can also lead to the materialization of negative externalities.

The evidence of negative FDI externalities has sparked a debate on possible shortcomings of the early cross-sectional evidence of positive FDI effects. The main criticism entails that these studies are unable to control for the possibility that FDI firms gravitate towards high productivity industries. If so, estimates of positive FDI effects are biased upwards, as an estimated positive relation between industry FDI participation and labor productivity incorporates this tendency of foreign-owned firms to locate in these high productivity industries (Rodrik, 1999; Hanson, 2001). In contrast, panel data studies are better able to deal with this issue of causality, by controlling for time-invariant determinants of productivity (Hanson, 2001). The feature that several of the more recent panel data studies present findings of negative FDI spillovers has been interpreted as evidence of the bias that affected the early cross-sectional studies.

Having said this, it appears that this issue is more complex. For one, other panel data studies present evidence of positive FDI spillovers (Haskel et al., 2007; Yudaeva et al, 2003;

Taki, 2005), disputing the idea that only cross-sectional studies are inclined to produce evidence of positive externalities. Second, there is little concrete evidence that all the evidence from cross-sectional studies has indeed been affected by an upward bias caused by FDI locating in high productivity industries. It is not clear at all that FDI will automatically gravitate to high productivity industries, irrespective of the host economy under analysis. Furthermore, the only study that has looked specifically at this issue presents evidence of a downward instead of an upward bias in the estimation of a cross-sectional regression model on FDI spillovers (Jordaan, 2010). Estimating FDI spillovers for a cross-section of Mexican manufacturing industries, the findings indicate that the estimated positive externality effect is much larger when the estimation controls for the feature that foreign-owned firms gravitate towards labor intensive, low productivity, industries. Failing to do so lowers the estimated externality impact of FDI significantly (see Jordaan, 2010). Therefore, it seems to be a too strong criticism to simply discard all cross-sectional evidence of positive FDI spillovers as being biased upwards, especially in cases where FDI is attracted to labor intensive manufacturing industries in a host economy.

A last aspect of the evidence on the prevalence of positive FDI spillovers concerns the distinction between intra- and inter-industry effects. The original estimation strategy entailed estimating FDI spillovers in the same industries in which foreign-owed firms operate. However, there are good reasons to hypothesize that such intra-industry spillovers may be limited. FDI has an incentive to protect its ownership-specific advantages from its competitors. As a result of this, foreign-owned firms will try to minimize any positive externalities materializing among their competitors (Kugler, 2006; Moran, 2005). In contrast, foreign-owned firms may be less inclined to devote many resources to protect technologies disseminating to other industries, at this is less likely to have a negative impact on their competitive advantages. Also, as discussed earlier, FDI may have an active interest in helping to improve their local suppliers. This means that positive externalities are more likely to occur in dissimilar but related industries, in particular in industries that supply inputs to FDI (Kugler, 2006).

Smarzynska (2004) presents findings for Lithuania that support these ideas. Whereas there is no evidence of intra-industry FDI spillovers among Lithuanian competitors of foreign-owned firms, the findings do indicate positive relations between the industry presence of FDI and productivity of domestic firms in input-supplying industries. Similar evidence for other host economies is presented by Blalock and Gertler (2008) for Indonesia, Girma and Wakelin (2007) and Driffield (2004) for the UK, Javorcik et al. (2004) for Romania and Jordaan (2008b) for Mexico. Having said so, again the evidence is of a heterogeneous nature, as other studies fail to produce evidence of inter-industry FDI spillovers (Békés et al., 2006; Crespo et al. 2006) or find evidence that inter-industry spillovers are of a negative nature (e.g. Driffield, 2006; Yudaeva et al., 2003).

In sum, although theoretical notions are clear in predicting universal positive growth and productivity effects from the presence of FDI, the evidence is far less conclusive. Although there are several studies that find positive associations between FDI and productivity of domestic firms, other studies present findings ranging from no effect to significant negative externalities. Previous surveys have pointed out that the difference in findings between cross-sectional and panel data studies is evidence that findings of positive FDI spillovers from cross-sectional studies are flawed. However, other recent panel data studies produce evidence of positive FDI externalities, and there is little concrete evidence of an automatic upward bias in all findings from cross-sectional studies. The distinction between intra- and inter-industry foreign participation represents an advancement of the strategy to identify spillover effects, but as yet has not lowered the large degree of heterogeneity of findings on positive FDI externalities. Finally, it is important to note that the evidence usually does not clarify which channels underlie estimated FDI spillovers. An exception seems to be negative externalities, which are linked to competition effects. One could also argue that findings of positive inter-industry FDI spillovers identify inter-firm linkages as transmission channel, but demonstration effects or labor turnover may also generate these FDI effects.

4. Determinants of FDI Spillovers: Technology Gap and Agglomeration

4.1. Technology Gap, Absorptive Capacity and Spillovers

In a response to the heterogeneous nature of the evidence on FDI spillovers, recent studies are attempting to identify endogenous factors that may facilitate the occurrence (and perhaps also influence the nature) of these externalities. Along similar lines as macro-economic research on FDI growth effects, it is likely that characteristics of host economy firms and industries, as well as characteristics of foreign-owned firms, can affect these externalities. For instance, Haskel et al. (2007) find differences in the level of externalities generated by FDI firms from different home countries (see also Girma and Wakelin, 2007). Another factor that may be important is the level of foreign participation in foreign-owned firms (Sjöholm and Blomström, 1999; Abraham et al., 2007).

The factor that has received most attention in research on determinants of FDI spillovers is the concept of absorptive capacity. This concept originates from the debate on processes of catch up between advanced and lagging countries (Gershenkron, 1962; Abramovitz, 1986). This process of catch up is facilitated by technology flows between these two types of country, whereby the level of absorptive capacity of lagging countries determines the degree to which these countries are able to adopt new technologies (Keller, 1996, 2004). Applying this notion to FDI spillovers, the occurrence of positive externalities will depend on the degree to which host economy firms are able to absorb and use new technologies that are incorporated into FDI.

The central problem with the concept of absorptive capacity arises when trying to identify its effect statistically. The reason for this is that there is no direct measure of the level of absorptive capacity of domestic firms. The majority of research into determinants of FDI spillovers uses the level of technological differences between FDI and domestic firms to capture the level of absorptive capacity of domestic firms. The assumption hereby is that the technology gap is a direct inverse indicator of absorptive capacity; small technological differences are interpreted as an indication that the level of absorptive capacity of domestic firms is relatively high[4].

[4] Other proxies for absorptive capacity that have been used include the level of R&D spending by domestic firms (Kinoshita, 2001), domestic firm plant size (Blyde et al, 2004; Aitken and Harrison, 1999) and export status of domestic firms (Abraham et al., 2007).

Table 1 presents key characteristics of a set of empirical studies that look at the effect of the technology gap on FDI spillovers. The first part of table 1 contains studies that find evidence in line with the original interpretation of the technology gap as direct inverse indicator of absorptive capacity. An early example is Kokko (1994), who estimates FDI spillovers in Mexican manufacturing industries. The findings indicate that there are positive externality effects, except in those industries that are characterized by a combined high presence of FDI and a large technology gap. This is in line with the assumption that large technological differences reflect a low level of absorptive capacity among domestic firms. Haddad and Harrison (1993) find in their study on FDI effects in Morocco that positive FDI spillovers only materialize in low tech industries. This is in line with the interpretation of what the technology gap captures, under the assumption that low tech industries are characterized by smaller technological differences between FDI and domestic firms than high tech industries. Imbriani and Reganati (1997) similarly find for Italy that positive FDI spillovers only materialize in low tech industries. In addition to this, they also find that high tech industries, industries with a presumably large technology gap, are subject to negative externalities. Girma et al. (2001) present a similar finding for the UK. This finding suggests that a low level of absorptive capacity (a large technology gap) reflects a low level of competitive power among domestic firms, resulting in negative competition effects. Finally, Girma (2005) and Taki (2005) find that positive FDI spillovers only materialize when the technology gap is small[5].

Despite these findings of a negative relationship between the technology gap and positive FDI spillovers, a closer examination of the interpretation of the level of technological differences as a direct inverse indicator of absorptive capacity suggests that this interpretation is not without flaws. Looking at the concept of catch-up, the level of absorptive capacity is only one of two key factors that facilitate flows of technology between advanced and lagging countries. In addition to the capacity of lagging countries to absorb technologies, the size of technological differences between the two types of country is positively associated with the level of catch up (Gershenkron, 1962; Nelson and Phelps, 1966; Nelson, 1968; Keller, 1996). In particular, a large technology gap reflects a large scope for lagging countries to learn and advance, suggesting that the catch up effect will be larger than in the case where the technology gap is small.

The importance of sufficiently large technological differences suggests that an alternative hypothesis that a large instead of a small technology gap can facilitate positive FDI externalities is easily posed. For one, a large technology gap indicates that the scope for positive externality effects is large. In fact, one of the few theoretical studies that looks directly at FDI spillover effects argues along these lines (Findlay, 1978; see also Blomström and Wang, 2002). Furthermore, not only is the scope for positive effects large, the large opportunity to improve may spur domestic firms to increase their efforts to adopt new technologies. As Rodrik (1992) argues, the occurrence of externalities depends on efforts by firms to allow these spillover effects to materialize. This suggests that domestic firms will be more inclined to make externality-facilitating investments when the scope to benefit from them is substantial. In a way, this suggests that domestic firms are more likely to engage in

[5] The technology gap between FDI and domestic firms can be measured in various ways. One way is to take the ratio of productivity levels of foreign-owned and domestic firms (e.g. Kokko, 1994; Jordaan, 2005). Another specification is to take the distance of a domestic firm to the efficiency level of best practice firms (e.g. Girma et al., 2001).

absorptive capacity enhancing investments when the technology gap is sufficiently large. In addition to this argument, it may also be the case that large technological differences capture situations where it is less likely that domestic and foreign-owned firms are in direct competition with each other, lowering the chance that domestic firms are affected by negative competition effects.

Table 1. Technology Gap and FDI Spillovers

Author(s)	Country	Measure of absorptive capacity	Effect on FDI spillovers
Kokko (1994)	Mexico	Interaction variable FDI and technology gap	Positive FDI spillovers do not arise in industries with high FDI and large technology gap
Haddad and Harrison (1993)	Morocco	Low tech versus high tech industries	Positive FDI spillovers only in low tech industries
Imbriani and Reganati (1997)	Italy	Technology gap	Positive FDI spillovers in low tech industries, negative FDI spillovers in high tech industries
Girma et al. (2001)	UK	Technology gap	High technology gap lowers positive FDI spillovers
Girma (2005)	UK	Technology gap	Positive FDI spillovers only when technology gap is small
Taki (2005)	Indonesia	Technology gap	Positive FDI spillovers larger when technology gap is small
Blomström and Wolff (1994)	Mexico	Technology gap	Technology gap positive effect on spillovers
Sjöholm (1999)	Indonesia	Technology gap	Technology gap positive effect on spillovers
Zukowska-Gagelmann (2000)	Poland	Interaction between technology gap and FDI	Positive effect of interaction variable on FDI spillovers
Castallani and Zanfei (2003)	Spain, Italy, France	Interaction technology gap and FDI	Positive effect of interaction variable on FDI spillovers
Jordaan (2005)	Mexico	Low tech versus high tech industries; interaction variable FDI and technology gap	Positive FDI spillovers only in high tech industries; positive effect interaction variable on FDI spillovers
Haskel et al. (2007)	UK	Interaction between technology gap and FDI	Positive effect of interaction variable on FDI spillovers
Jordaan (2008b)	Mexico	Interaction productivity gap and FDI	Positive effect of interaction variable on FDI spillovers
Jordaan (2008c)	Mexico	Technology gap	Large technology gap promotes positive FDI spillovers
Jordaan (2011b)	Mexico	Technology gap	Large technology gap increases likelihood of positive technological impact on local suppliers

The findings in the second part of table 1 indicate that there is considerable evidence that large technological differences facilitate positive FDI spillovers, in line with the alternative interpretation of what the technology gap captures. Zukowska-Gagelmann (2005), Castallani and Zanfei (2003), Haskell et al. (2007) and Jordaan (2005, 2008a) all find a positive effect of an interaction variable between the technology gap and industry FDI participation on positive FDI spillovers. Also, Jordaan (2005) estimates FDI spillovers separate for low tech and high tech Mexican industries and finds that positive FDI spillovers only occur in the latter type of industry.

Furthermore, Blomström and Wolff (1994), Sjöholm (1999) and Jordaan (2008b) find a direct positive effect of the technology gap on positive FDI spillovers. Blomström and Wolff (1994) for instance estimate regression models on determinants of productivity growth of Mexican firms and productivity convergence between FDI and Mexican firms. In addition to finding that the industry participation by FDI has a positive effect on both productivity growth and convergence, their estimations also identify a positive association between the level of initial productivity differences between FDI and Mexican firms and productivity growth and convergence. Finally, Jordaan (2011b) presents evidence from a somewhat different setting. Using information from a representative sample of Mexican suppliers of Mexican and foreign-owned producer firms in the north-east of Mexico, this study estimates regression models to identify factors that affect the likelihood that suppliers experience a large positive technological impact from their business dealings with their client firms. The findings indicate that suppliers of those producer firms whose operations are characterized as being substantially more technologically advanced than their suppliers are significantly more likely to experience a large positive technological impact. Again, this suggests that a large technology gap fosters the occurrence of positive spillover effects.

4.2. Agglomeration and FDI Spillovers

4.2.1. Agglomeration and Spillovers

Within the context of trying to improve the empirical identification of FDI spillovers and to generate a better understanding of conditions that foster the materialization of these effects, recent developments in the NEG and regional economics offer important indications that geographical space matters for the creation and dissemination of externalities. In particular, two central notions are that certain types of location of economic activity are linked to the creation of place-based externalities and that geographical distance influences the occurrence of spillovers.

The first notion that the type of location of economic activity can generate spillovers stems from the idea that geographical concentration, or agglomeration, can lead to the generation of agglomeration economies (Eberts and McMillen, 1999; Rosenthal and Strange, 2004). For instance, an agglomeration of economic activity leads to the creation of thick labor markets, generating flexibility and search and match externalities (Gordon and McCann, 2000). In a similar fashion, it allows for the establishment of specialized suppliers of (non-traded) inputs, creating important proximity effects and an increased range of specialized inputs (Duranton and Puga, 2004).

Furthermore, an agglomeration of economic activity may foster the creation of local pools of knowledge and experience (Duranton and Puga, 2004). Here, agglomeration is interpreted not in terms of the scale of economic activity but as a high level of geographical proximity between firms, which can foster the creation and transmission of knowledge spillovers. An empirical application of the idea that proximity can be important is to look at the relation between the level of density of economic activity and regional productivity. In a well-known study, Ciccone and Hall (1996) identify a significant positive effect of density of economic activity on state level productivity in the United States. Ciccone (2002) presents further corroborating findings of such a positive productivity effect of density for regions in the European Union. The importance of proximity may be particularly relevant for knowledge intensive activities, which are closely linked to the creation of regional pools of knowledge and knowledge spillovers (Audretsch and Feldman, 2004; Jaffe and Traitenberg, 2002).

This positive link between agglomeration and regional productivity has important implications for research on FDI spillovers. The channels that underlie agglomeration economies share a great deal of similarity with the channels of FDI spillovers. For both types of externalities, inter-firm linkages, labor markets and knowledge spillovers are the main mechanisms that transmit these effects. Given this large degree of similarity, it is very likely that agglomeration will have positive effects on FDI spillovers. As an agglomeration fosters the development of inter-firm linkages and thick labor markets, it will be easier for FDI spillover effects to materialize when foreign-owned firms are located in such an agglomeration. Similarly, a high degree of geographical proximity between FDI and domestic firms in an agglomeration will promote knowledge spillovers, as the level of formal and informal contacts between the firms is likely to be high. The feature that such geographical knowledge spillovers apply in particular to knowledge and technology intensive activities only serves to underline that it is very likely that geographical proximity will have a positive effect on knowledge spillovers from FDI[6].

Second, an alternative interpretation of the relation between geographical proximity and spillovers is that although geographical distance is likely to have a negative effect on spillovers, this does not mean that these effects do not materialize across geographical space (Henderson, 2007).

In fact, there is ample evidence that such inter-regional effects may play an important role (Audretsch en Feldman, 2004). Anselin et al. (1997) for instance estimate regionalized knowledge production functions for states and metropolitan areas in the United States (see Grilliches, 1979, 1992). Their findings indicate that the regional level of knowledge output (innovations) is positively associated with knowledge inputs in the form of university research in other regions, indicating the presence of inter-regional knowledge spillovers (see also Anselin et al., 2000). Similar evidence of such inter-regional knowledge spillovers is presented for Germany by Bode (2004) and Crescenzi et al. (2007) and Rodriguez-Pose and Crescenzi (2008) for the European Union. At the same time, these studies also find that inter-regional knowledge spillovers are spatially bounded, as they peter out with increasing distances between regions.

The relevance of these findings for studies on FDI spillovers is that it is very likely that FDI externalities may also occur across geographical space. This implies that, in order to ensure that the entire range of FDI spillovers is controlled for, estimations need to incorporate such spatial effects.

[6] The importance of investigating the effect of agglomeration on FDI spillovers is indicated by research on FDI location decisions, of which a majority find that FDI is attracted to agglomerations of economic activity within host economies (see e.g. Head et al., 1995, 1999). See Jordaan (2008a, 2009) for an extensive discussion of the role of agglomeration in FDI location decisions).

4.2.2. Geographical Dimensions of FDI Spillovers

A selection of empirical studies that incorporate an identification of geographical dimensions of FDI spillovers is presented in table 2. The first part of table 2 contains studies that look at the direct effect of agglomeration on FDI spillovers. Overall, these studies all find that agglomeration enhances FDI externalities. Jordaan (2005) for instance estimates determinants of labor productivity of Mexican manufacturing industries separately for industries with a low or a high level of agglomeration within Mexico. The findings confirm the positive effect of agglomeration, as a positive FDI externality effect only materializes in industries with a high agglomeration score. A similar finding that positive FDI spillovers only materialize in agglomerated industries is reported by Driffield and Munday (2001) for the UK and Barrios et al. (2006) for Spain. Related to this, de Propris and Driffield (2006) find in another study on the UK that positive FDI externalities occur in agglomerated industries, whereas non-agglomerated industries are subject to negative externalities, supporting the idea that positive externalities in particular are enhanced by agglomeration. Jordaan (2008b) however presents evidence of a negative effect of an interaction variable between agglomeration and inter-industry foreign participation. This may be caused by an increase in prices of regionally confined inputs following the entrance of FDI, lowering efficiency levels of domestic firms. In contrast, Jordaan (2005) finds a positive effect of an interaction variable between agglomeration and intra-industry foreign participation. Finally, Monastiriotis and Jordaan (2010) present a different type of evidence of the effect of proximity on FDI spillovers in Greece. Their findings indicate that at a broad regional scale, the presence of FDI has a negative effect on productivity of Greek firms. At a more detailed geographical scale, however, there is evidence of positive externalities, suggesting that close proximity between firms fosters the materialization of positive FDI spillovers.

The second part of table 2 presents findings from studies that look at more general spatial dimensions of FDI externalities. Rather than identifying some sort of direct relationship between agglomeration and externalities, these studies address the question whether, in general, there are spatial dimensions to these FDI effects. For instance, in estimating FDI externalities for Venezuela, Aitken and Harrison (1999) add a control variable that captures the level of intra-industry foreign participation in the region of a domestic firm. They do so to test the assumption that, in addition to general industry-wide FDI effects, there may be an additional effect from those FDI firms that are located in the same region of a given domestic firm. Their findings do not support this assumption, as the estimated effect of this regional FDI variable is insignificant. Yudaeva et al. (2003) and Haskel et al. (2007) find a similar insignificant effect for Russia and the UK. In contrast, Karpaty and Lundberg (2004) and Abraham et al. (2007) find that regional foreign participation is significantly and positively associated with productivity of domestic firms in Sweden and China respectively.

In extension of controlling for intra-industry regional foreign participation, related studies use variables capturing separately intra- and inter-industry regional foreign participation, to allow for the presence of spillovers within and between industries. A well-known example of the use of such variables is Blalock and Gertler (2008), who estimate for regional FDI spillovers in Indonesia. Their findings suggest that regional inter-industry foreign participation generates positive spillover effects, whereas intra- industry FDI spillovers are non-existent. Sjöholm (1999), using a different dataset for Indonesia, finds evidence of negative intra-industry and positive inter-industry regional FDI externalities.

Table 2. Geographical Dimensions of FDI Spillovers

Author(s)	Country	Agglomeration	Effect on FDI spillovers
Driffield and Munday (2001)	UK	Distinction between high and low agglomerated industries	Positive FDI spillovers only in agglomerated industries
Jordaan (2005)	Mexico	Distinction between high and low agglomerated industries; Interaction variable FDI and industry agglomeration	Positive FDI spillovers only in agglomerated industries; positive effect of interaction variable on FDI spillovers
De Propris and Driffield (2006)	UK	Distinction between high and low agglomerated industries	Positive FDI spillovers in agglomerated industries, negative externalities in non-agglomerated industries
Barrios et al. (2006)	Spain	Distinction between high and low agglomerated industries	Positive FDI spillovers only in agglomerated industries
Jordaan (2008b)	Mexico	Interaction variable intra- and inter-industry FDI and industry agglomeration	Negative effect of interaction variable inter-industry FDI and agglomeration on FDI spillovers
Monastiriotis and Jordaan (2010)	Greece	Estimation of FDI spillovers at different geographical scales	Positive FDI spillovers only materialize at the very localized level
		Regional FDI participation	
Aitken and Harrison (1999)	Venezuela	Intra-industry intra-regional	Insignificant effect
Yudaeva et al. (2003)	Russia	Intra-industry intra-regional	Insignificant effect
Haskel et al. (2007)	UK	Intra-industry intra-regional	Insignificant effect
Karpaty and Lundberg (2004)	Sweden	Intra-industry intra-regional	Positive effect on FDI spillovers
Abraham et al. (2007)	China	Intra-industry intra-regional	Positive effect on FDI spillovers
Sjöholm (1999)	Indonesia	Intra-industry and inter-industry within region	Intra-industry within region negative effect; inter-industry within region positive effect
Blalock and Gertler (2008)	Indonesia	Intra-industry and inter-industry within region	Intra-industry insignificant effect, inter-industry positive effect
Driffield (2004)	UK	Intra- and inter-industry within region, intra-industry between regions	Intra-industry within region negative effect; intra-industry between regions and inter-industry within region positive effect
Girma (2005)	UK	Intra-industry within region, intra-industry between regions	Intra-industry within and between regions positive effect
Halpern et al. (2007)	Hungary	Intra- and inter-industry within region; intra- and inter-industry between regions	Intra-industry within region and inter-industry between regions positive effect; others insignificant
Girma and Wakelin (2007)	UK	Intra-industry and inter-industry within region; intra-industry between regions	Intra-industry and inter-industry within region positive effect; intra-industry between regions insignificant
Jordaan (2008c)	Mexico	Intra- and inter-industry within region; intra- and inter-industry between regions	Intra- industry within and between regions negative effect; inter-industry within and between regions positive effect
Jordaan and Rodriguez-Oreggia (2010)	Mexico	Total regional FDI and intra-industry within region; total regional FDI and intra-industry between regions	Intra-industry within and between regions negative effect; total regional FDI flows within and between regions positive effect

Finally, several studies broaden the strategy of identifying geographical dimensions of FDI spillovers by including foreign participation variables for regions other than where a domestic firm is located. In this strategy, the assumption is for instance that it is possible that intra-industry foreign participation in a given region may influence productivity of a domestic firm located in another region. Several recent studies on the UK follow this strategy. Driffield (2004) estimates FDI spillovers, distinguishing between intra- and inter-industry foreign participation within regions and intra-industry foreign participation in other regions. The findings indicate that there is a spatial dimension to the FDI effects, as the estimated productivity effect of this inter-regional FDI variable is positive. Girma (2005) similarly finds that this type of foreign participation is positively associated with productivity of UK firms. In a related study that focuses on the electronics industry in the UK, Girma and Wakelin (2007) find an insignificant effect of inter-regional foreign participation, however. Halpern et al. (2007) present evidence for Hungary that inter-regional inter-industry foreign participation may also generate positive spillovers. Finally, Jordaan (2008c) and Jordaan and Rodriguez-Oreggia (2010) present evidence of negative intra-industry and positive inter-industry FDI externalities both within and between regions in Mexico.

Overall, the adoption of the research strategy to include spatial dimensions of FDI spillovers has produced findings that confirm that these dimensions may be important. This indicates that the scope of these FDI effects is much larger than envisaged originally. Having said this, it appears that these studies face several challenges that are not always fully addressed. First, it is important to consider that studies that include regional foreign participation variables only capture part of the relation between geographical proximity and FDI externalities. The studies listed in the first part of table 2 present findings that identify a direct effect of proximity on these spillovers. Studies that include intra-regional FDI variables do seem to be based on the recognition that, in addition to host economy-wide spillovers, there may be additional spillovers between FDI and domestic firms that are confined to regions within the country. This does not necessarily mean that proximity enhances these FDI effects. Rather, it indicates that there are spillovers that appear to be confined at the regional level. As such, these findings should not be interpreted as evidence that proximity enhances spillover effects; instead, they appear to suggest that there is a negative effect of distance on spillovers. Alternatively, it may be the case that foreign-owned firms gravitate towards high productivity regions within a host economy. If this is the case, (part of) the estimated positive association between regional FDI and productivity of domestic firms may reflect this location tendency (see Monastiriotis and Jordaan, 2010).

Second, although the incorporation of regional FDI variables has produced a set of empirical findings that suggests that spatial dimensions are important, at the same time the findings are also characterized by a substantial degree of heterogeneity, in line with the general body of evidence on the prevalence of positive spillover effects. Also, the findings of several of these studies may suffer from an omitted variable bias, as they do not control for all types of intra- and inter-regional FDI participation. Some studies only include intra-regional FDI variables, whereas other studies only control for either intra- or inter-industry inter-regional FDI effects. It may be that a failure to control for all four types of foreign participation influences the estimated effect of the regional FDI variables that are included in the estimation. It could be the case for instance that a region attracts a large number of FDI firms, which subsequently leads to the development of a regional supplier base, containing a second wave of input-supplying FDI. If an estimation only controls for inter-regional intra-industry FDI participation and finds a significant positive effect, it may be that part of this positive effect is actually caused by the positive relation between the high intra-industry presence of FDI and the subsequent development of the regional supplier base, which can generate additional positive spatial spillovers.

Third, the majority of studies that estimate regional FDI spillovers give little consideration to the regional scales at which the foreign participation variables are calculated. Although this may be an issue of data availability and as such perhaps difficult to address, it is important to consider that different regional scales may be subject to different levels, types and also natures of FDI externalities. Sjöholm (1999) for instance estimates FDI spillovers at the district and province level in Indonesia and finds that the nature of the estimated effect of intra-industry regional foreign participation differs between these two regional scales. Another example is Monastiriotis and Jordaan (2010), who use different geographical scales in their estimations of FDI externalities in Greece and also find that the nature of the estimated FDI effect is influenced by this.

Finally, it appears that most of the studies that estimate for the presence of inter-regional FDI effects use ad-hoc interpretations of the relation between geographical space and FDI spillovers. This may be problematic, given the variety of channels that underlie these FDI effects. For instance, it may be the case that the negative effect of distance is stronger for knowledge spillovers than for effects that are transmitted via inter-firm linkages. Furthermore, the effect of distance on the different channels of FDI externalities may also be qualitatively different (Jordaan, 2009). It may be the case that knowledge spillovers seize to exist after a certain distance (e.g. Anselin et al., 1997), whereas externalities that are transmitted via inter-firm linkages may be characterized by a more continuous, gravity-like negative relation with distance. As most studies that look for inter-regional FDI effects estimate regression models with only one specification of the distance decay effect that may affect spatial externalities, findings of an insignificant spatial FDI effect can not be taken as sufficient evidence that spatial spillovers do not occur. Rather, such findings should be interpreted as evidence that there are no spatial externalities under the specific relation between spillovers and distance that is assumed in the estimation of the regression model.

Exceptions to this problem are Jordaan (2008c) and Jordaan and Rodriguez-Oreggia (2010), who test to see whether there may be different relations between inter-regional distances and spatial FDI spillovers. As the findings in these studies clearly indicate, empirical findings can be influenced by the type of specified distance decay effect. Jordaan and Rodriguez-Oreggia (2010) estimate for spatial FDI spillovers between Mexican regions, alternatively using a specification that assumes that spillovers are subject to a spatial cut off point and a specification where spillovers are continuously decreasing with increasing distance. The findings indicate that FDI spillovers only materialize with the first specification of the distance decay effect. Had this study only used the gravity-like specification that spillovers decrease continuously with distance, a specification often used in the studies listed in table 2, it would have erroneously concluded that there are no spatial FDI externalities. In the case of Jordaan (2008c), similar specifications of the distance decay effect are used to estimate for spatial FDI effects. This study finds that whereas negative intra-industry inter-regional FDI externalities are identified with both distance decay specifications, positive inter-industry spatial effects only materialize when using the spatial cut-off point specification. Clearly, as the specification of the relation between externalities and distance can influence the estimated spillover effects from FDI, studies on these spatial dimensions need to allow for this feature.

SUMMARY AND POLICY RECOMMENDATIONS

The large importance of MNEs in the world economy has fostered a growing interest in the identification and analysis of economic effects of FDI in many host economies. In the last two decades, this interest has concentrated largely on externality or productivity effects that may accrue to domestic firms, effects which are thought to represent an important stimulus to processes of economic and technological development. Through channels such as competition effects, inter-firm linkages, labor turnover and demonstration effects, the presence and operations of FDI may lead to the occurrence of technological and/or pecuniary externalities, which affect efficiency or productivity levels of domestic firms.

In contrast to the clear theoretical notion that FDI, interpreted as a bundle of skills, knowledge and technologies, will promote processes of technological and economic development, the rapidly growing body of empirical research on FDI spillovers is characterized by a limited degree of consensus. Although several studies present evidence of positive associations between the presence of foreign-owned firms and productivity of domestic firms, other studies fail to identify such a relationship, questioning the overall prevalence of positive FDI spillovers. Findings that indicate that this relationship may be negative suggest that FDI may also hurt productivity of domestic firms. The recently introduced distinction between intra- and inter-industry FDI participation is welcome, as it enriches the industry scope in which spillover effects can be identified. Having said this, this distinction has so far not lowered the heterogeneous nature of the body of evidence on FDI spillovers. Another feature of the evidence is that, in most cases, it does not clarify which underlying channels are generating and transmitting these FDI externalities.

In response to the heterogeneous nature of the evidence on the prevalence of positive FDI spillovers, several studies try to identify endogenous factors that may facilitate the occurrence (and perhaps also influence the nature) of these spillovers. A majority of this research looks at the importance of the level of absorptive capacity of domestic firms or industries. The main problem with this research is that there is no direct measure of this concept. The most commonly used indicator of absorptive capacity is the level of technological differences between FDI and domestic firms, whereby this technology gap is interpreted as a direct inverse indicator of the level of absorptive capacity of domestic firms.

As the present survey shows, this interpretation of the technology gap can certainly be challenged. Although there are some studies that present corroborating evidence that a small technology gap facilitates positive spillovers, there is also a substantial number of studies that find that large instead of small technological differences enhance positive FDI externalities. An analysis of the use of the concept of absorptive capacity reveals that there is only an imperfect link with the underlying concept of catch-up. Although absorptive capacity is important, the catch up thesis also holds that technological differences need to be sufficiently large in order for meaningful spillovers to materialize. According to the catch up thesis, with a small technology gap lagging countries have little incentive to try to absorb new technologies and the scope for improvement is limited. Applying this importance of sufficiently large technological differences to FDI spillovers, an alternative hypothesis can easily be posed that a large instead of a small technology gap will promote positive FDI externalities. When this gap is large, there will be much scope for domestic firms to improve. Also, a large scope to improve represents important incentives for domestic firms to engage in technology-absorbing investments. In addition to this, one can also argue that large technological differences make it less likely that foreign-owned and domestic firms are in direct competition, lowering the chance of negative competition effects.

Therefore, it seems that the interpretation of the technology gap as direct inverse indicator of absorptive capacity of domestic firms is flawed. Of course, this does not mean that the level of absorptive capacity of domestic firms does not influence the occurrence of FDI effects. Rather, it suggests that alternative indicators of this concept need to be developed. As for the importance of the technology gap, there are several reasons to expect a positive effect of a large technology gap on FDI spillovers. More research is needed to obtain more evidence and a better understanding of this relationship, in particular on why and how large technological differences stimulate domestic firms to make absorptive capacity enhancing investments, allowing positive spillovers to materialize.

The second endogenous factor that the survey analyzes is agglomeration or geographical proximity between firms. In addition, the survey also examines research on more general spatial dimensions of FDI spillovers. Recent notions from the NEG and regional economics suggest strongly that geographical proximity between firms can foster the creation of agglomeration economies. This may be the case in particular for knowledge-intensive activities. One reason why this positive effect of proximity is likely to apply to FDI spillovers is that there is a large degree of similarity between the channels of FDI externalities and mechanisms that generate agglomeration economies. Second, with respect to the creation of knowledge spillovers, the interpretation of FDI as a bundle of skills, knowledge and technologies suggests strongly that foreign-owned firms represent a particularly good source of spillovers in situations where FDI and domestic firms are located in proximity. However, as the survey shows, empirical research on determinants of FDI spillovers has largely overlooked investigating this direct link between agglomeration and FDI externalities. The limited number of studies that do investigate this link find that geographical proximity enhances FDI externalities. Clearly, given the strong similarities between channels that underlie FDI spillovers and agglomeration economies, in combination with these promising initial findings, more empirical research is needed to further establish the nature and degree of the effects of proximity or agglomeration on FDI spillovers.

Research on more general spatial dimensions of FDI externalities is more plentiful. An important contribution of this research is that it shows that the scope of FDI spillovers is much larger than envisaged originally. In particular, in addition to general intra- and inter-industry effects, the evidence indicates that there may be important additional spillover effects resulting from intra- and inter- regional foreign participation. Having said this, the evidence on these regional effects is characterized by a substantial level of heterogeneity, in line with the general evidence on the prevalence of positive FDI spillovers. Also, it appears that most studies that include an assessment of these spatial dimensions suffer from several weaknesses, which seem to be caused by a certain level of ad hoc-ness in the specification of the type(s) of intra- and inter-regional foreign participation and how distance may affect spatial FDI spillovers. Usually, not all types of intra- and inter-regional FDI are controlled for. Also, there is insufficient consideration for the fact that findings on spatial spillovers are partly determined by the type of distance decay effect that is implemented into the estimated regression models. Given that there is a variety of channels that underlie FDI spillovers, channels that may be affected differently by distance, future studies that include estimations of spatial FDI externalities need to incorporate a fuller assessment of the presence of such spatial FDI effects, by testing for the presence of different types of distance decay effect that spatial spillovers may be subject to.

Finally, there are several policy implications that are suggested by the existing body of evidence. First, many governments have adopted policies to increase the level of inward FDI into their economies. Of course, in addition to the buildup of the level of technology and possible technological spillovers, the desire to attract FDI can also be related to other effects, including direct and indirect employment generation and the promotion of exporting activities. Focusing on technological spillovers, it is important to recognize that the evidence indicates that there is no guarantee that FDI will generate positive externalities. The evidence is very mixed and does not suggest that positive effects can be expected automatically. In addition to this, the evidence is also largely inconclusive as to which channels are transmitting these externality effects. As such, there are no prescribed policies that the government of a host economy can implement to facilitate positive FDI effects. Governments will need to assess carefully whether positive spillover effects may materialize, which channels are most likely to underlie these externalities and how they can design policies to facilitate these effects.

Second, the contrasting findings on the effect of the technology gap indicate that it may be difficult to predict which type of FDI is more likely to generate positive spillover effects. The original interpretation of the technology gap suggests that, compared to domestic firms, new FDI firms should be technologically more advanced to only a limited degree. In contrast, the alternative findings that large technological differences promote positive FDI spillovers proposes that new FDI activity needs to be substantially more advanced. As I argue in this survey, I find it more likely to expect that a large technology gap is conducive to the materialization of positive externalities, given the large scope for improvements for domestic firms that it represents. Host economy governments that do decide to attract technologically sophisticated FDI will need to consider implementing additional policies that aid domestic firms in improving their capacity to absorb new technologies, to facilitate the materialization of positive FDI externalities.

Finally, the findings on the spatial dimensions of FDI externalities suggest that, in addition to implementing policies to attract new FDI activity, host economy governments will also need to consider the possibility that the location of foreign-owned firms can influence the occurrence of positive FDI spillovers. In particular, FDI that locates in an agglomeration of economic activity within a host economy is more likely to generate such effects. This suggests that policies that try to attract FDI into lagging regions (for instance to generate employment) may be less effective, as the location of foreign-owned firms in these regions will undoubtedly lower or even prevent the intra-regional generation of positive spillovers. In addition to this, government policies will also need to take into account that FDI spillover effects may occur across geographical space. This means that it is likely that there will be differences between the private and societal returns to regional policy making, as the attraction of FDI into one region may generate positive or negative spillover effects in other regions. Again, this also depends on which channels transmit these effects, as for instance knowledge spillovers and externalities from inter-firm linkages may materialize at different geographical scales. In any case, the likely existence of inter-regional FDI spillovers indicates that national (or at least multi-regional) policymaking and coordination is required that allows for and responds to the materialization of such spatial effects.

REFERENCES

Abraham, F., Konings, J. and Slootmaekers, V. (2007) FDI spillovers in the Chinese manufacturing sector: Evidence of firm heterogeneity. *CEPR Discussion Paper Series*, no. 6573. London: Centre for Economic Performance.

Abramovitz, M. (1986) Catching up, forging ahead and falling behind. *The Journal of Economic History*, vol. 46(2), p. 385-406.

Aitken, B.J. and Harrison, A.E. (1999) Do domestic firms benefit fro direct foreign investment? Evidence from Venezuela. *The American Economic Review*, vol. 89(3), p. 605-618.

Alfaro, L., Chanda, A. and Kalemli-Ozcan, S. (2004) FDI and economic growth: The role of financial markets. *Journal of International Economics*, vol. 64(1), p. 89-112.

Anselin, L., Acs, Z. and Varga, A. (1997) Local geographic spillovers between university research and high technology innovations. *Journal of Urban Economics*, vol. 42(3), p. 422-448.

Anselin, L., Varga, A. and Acs, Z. (2000) Geographic and sectoral characteristics of academic knowledge externalities. *Papers in Regional Science*, vol. 79(4), p. 435-443.

Audretsch, D.B. and Feldman, M.P. (2004) Knowledge spillovers and the geography of innovation, in *Handbook of Urban and Regional Economics*, vol. 4, edited by Henderson, V.J. and Thisse, J.F. Amsterdam: North Holland.

Balasubramanyam, V.N., Salisu, M. and Sapsford, D. (1996) Foreign direct investment and growth in EP and IS countries. *The Economic Journal*, vol. 106(434), p. 92-105.

Barrios, S., and Strobl, E. (2002) Foreign direct investment and productivity spillovers; Evidence from the Spanish experience. *Review of World Economics*, vol. 138(3), p. 459-481.

Barrios, S., Bertinelli, L. and Strobl, E. (2006) Co-agglomeration and spillovers. *Regional Science and Urban Economics*, vol. 36(4), p. 467-481.

Békés, G., Kleinert, J. and Toubal, F. (2006) Spillovers from multinationals to heterogeneous domestic firms: Evidence from Hungary. *Discussion Paper Series*, no. 2006/16, Institute of Economics, Hungarian Academy of Sciences.

Blalock, G. and Gertler, P.J. (2008) Welfare gains from foreign direct investment through technology transfer to local suppliers. *Journal of International Economics*, vol. 74(2), p. 402-421.

Blomström, M. and Persson, H. (1983) Foreign investment and spillover efficiency in an underdeveloped economy: Evidence from the Mexican manufacturing industry. *World Development*, vol. 11(6), p. 93-501.

Blomström, M. and Wolff, E. (1994) Multinational corporations and productivity convergence in Mexico. *NBER Working Paper Series*, no. 3141. Cambridge, MA: National Bureau of Economic Research.

Blomström, M. and Kokko, A. (1998) Multinational corporations and spillovers. *Journal of Economic Surveys*, vol. 12(3), p. 1-31.

Blomström, M. and Sjöholm, F. (1999) Technology transfer and spillovers: Does local participation with multinationals matter? *European Economic Review*, vol. 43(46), p. 915-932.

Blomström, M. and Wang, J-Y. (2002) Foreign investment and technology transfer: A simple model. *European Economic Review*, vol. 36(1), p. 137-155.

Blomström, M., Lipsey, R.E. and Zejan, M. (1994) What explains the growth of developing countries? in Convergence of productivity: Cross-national studies and historical evidence, edited by Baumol, W., Nielsen, R. and Wolff, E. Oxford: Oxford University Press.

Bode, E. (2004) The spatial pattern of localized RandD spillovers: An empirical investigation for Germany. *Journal of Economic Geography*, vol. 4(1), p. 43-64.

Borensztein, E., De Gregorio, J. and Lee, W. (1998) How does foreign direct investment affect economic growth? *Journal of International Economics*, vol. 45(1), p. 115-135.

Blyde, J., Kugler, M., and Stein, E. (2004) Exporting versus outsourcing by MNC subsidiaries: Which determines FDI spillovers? *Discussion Papers in Economics and Econometrics*. Southampton: University of Southampton.

Carkovic, M. and Levin, R. (2005) Does foreign direct investment accelerate economic growth? in *Does foreign direct investment promote economic development?*, edited by Moran, T.H., Graham, E.H. and Blomström, M. Washington, DC: Institute for International Economics.

Castellani, D., and Zanfei, A. (2003) Productivity gaps, inward investments and productivity of European firms. *Economics of Innovation and New Technology*, vol. 12, p. 450-468.

Caves, R.E. (1974) Multinational firms, competition and productivity in host economy markets. *Economia*, vol. 41(162), p. 176-193.

Caves, R.E. (1996) *Multinational enterprises and economic analysis*. Cambridge: Cambridge University Press.

Ciccone, A. (2002) Agglomeration effects in Europe. *European Economic Review*, vol. 46(2), p. p. 213-227.

Ciccone, A. and Hall, R.E. (1996) Productivity and the density of economic activity. *The American Economic Review*, vol. 86(1), p. 54-70.

Crespo, N., Proenca, I. and Fontoura, M. (2007) FDI spillovers at the regional level: Evidence from Portugal. *School of Economics and Management Working Paper Series*, no. 28. Lisbon: Technical University of Lisbon.

Crescenzi, R., Rodriguez-Pose, A., and Storper, M. (2007) The territorial dynamics of innovation: A Europe-United States comparative analysis. *Journal of Economic Geography*, vol. 7(6), p. 673-709.

De Mello, L. (1997) Foreign direct investment in developing countries and growth: A selective survey. *Journal of Development Studies*, vol. 34, p. 1-34.

De Mello, L. (1999) Foreign direct investment-led growth: Evidence from time series and panel data. *Oxford Economic Papers*, vol. 51(1), p. 133-151.

De Propris, L. and Driffield, N. (2006) The importance of clusters for spillovers from foreign direct investment and technology sourcing. *Cambridge Journal of Economics*, vol. 30(2), p. 277-291.

Djankov, S. and Hoekman, B. (2000) Foreign investment and productivity growth in Czech enterprises. *World Bank Economic Review*, vol. 14(1), p. 49-64.

Driffield, N. (2004) Regional policy and spillovers from FDI in the UK. *Annals of Regional Science*, vol. 38(4), p. 579-594.

Driffield, N. (2006) On the search for spillovers from FDI with spatial dependency. *Regional Studies*, vol. 40(1), p. 107-119.

Driffield, N. and Munday, M. (2001) Foreign manufacturing, regional agglomeration and technical efficiency in UK manufacturing industries: A stochastic production frontier approach. *Regional Studies*, vol. 35(5), p. 391-399.

Dunning, J. and Lundan, S.M. (2008) *Multinational enterprises and the global economy*. Cheltenham, UK: Edward Elgar.

Duranton, G. and Puga, D. (2004) Micro-foundations of urban agglomeration economies, in *Handbook of Urban and Regional Economics*, vol. 4, edited by Henderson, V.J. and Thisse, J.F. Amsterdam: North Holland.

Eberts, R.W. and McMillen, D. (1999) Agglomeration economies and public infrastructure, in *Handbook of Urban and Regional Economics*, vol. 3, edited by Cheshire, P. and Mills, E.S. Amsterdam: North Holland.

Gershenkron, A. (1962) *Economic backwardness in historical perspective*. Cambridge, MA: Belknap Press of Harvard University Press.

Girma, S. (2005) Absorptive capacity and productivity spillovers from FDI: a threshold regression analysis. *Oxford Bulletin of Economics and Statistics*, vol. 67(3), p. 281-306.

Girma, S., and Wakelin, K. (2007) Local productivity spillovers from foreign direct investment in the UK industry. *Regional Science and Urban Economics*, vol. 37(3), p. 399-412.

Girma, S., Greenaway, D. and Wakelin, K. (2001) Who benefits from foreign direct investment in the UK? *Scottish Journal of Political Economy*, vol. 48(2), p. 239-248.

Gordon, I.R. and McCann, P. (2000) Industrial clusters: Complexes, agglomeration and/or social networks? *Urban Studies*, vol. 37(3), p. 513-532.

Görg, H. and Greenaway, D. (2004) Much ado about nothing? Do domestic firms really benefit from foreign direct investment? *World Bank Research Observer*, vol. 19(2), p. 723-739.

Grilliches, Z. (1979) Issues in assessing the contribution of RandD to productivity growth. *Bell Journal of Economics*, vol. 10(1), p. 92-116.

Grilliches, Z. (1992) The search for RandD spillovers. *Scandinavian Journal of Economics*, vol. 94, p. 29-47.

Grossman, G. and Helpman, E. (1994) Endogenous innovation in the theory of growth. *Journal of Economic Perspectives*, vol. 8(1), p. 23-44.

Haddad, M. and Harrison, A. (1993) Are there positive spillovers from direct foreign investment? Evidence from panel data for Morocco. *Journal of Development Economics*, vol. 42(1), p. 51-74.

Halpern, L. and Murakozy, B. (2007) Does distance matter in spillovers? *Economics of Transition*, vol. 15, p. 781-805.

Hanson, G. (2001) Should countries promote foreign direct investment? *G-24 discussion paper series*, no. 9. Centre for International Development, Harvard University, Cambridge, M.A.

Haskel, J.E., Pereira, S.C. and Slaughter, M.J. (2007) Does inward foreign direct investment boost the productivity of domestic firms? *The Review of Economics and Statistics*, vol. 89(3), p. 482-496.

Head, K.C., Ries, J.C. and Swenson, D.L. (1995) Agglomeration benefits and location choice: Evidence from Japanese manufacturing investments in the United States. *Journal of International Economics*, vol. 38(3-4), p. 223-247.

Head, K.C., Ries, J.C. and Swenson, D.L. (1999) Attracting foreign manufacturing: investment promotion and agglomeration. *Regional Science and Urban Economics*, vol. 29(2), p. 197-218.

Henderson, V.J. (2001) Urban scale economies. In *Handbook of Urban Studies*, edited by Paddison, R. London: Sage.

Henderson, V.J. (2007) Understanding knowledge spillovers. *Regional Science and Urban Economics*, vol. 37(4), p. 497-508.

Hermes, N. and Lensink, R. (2003) Foreign direct investment, financial development and economic growth. *Journal of Development Studies*, vol. 40(1), 142-163.

Imbriani, C. and Reganiti, F. (1997) Spillovers internazionali di eficienza net settore manufatturiero italiano. *Economia Internazionale*, vol. 50, p. 583-595.

Jaffe, A.B. and Traitenberg, M. (2002) *Patents, citations and innovations: A window on the knowledge economy*. Cambridge, MA: The MIT Press.

Javorcik, B.S. (2008) Can survey evidence shed light on spillovers from foreign direct investment? *World Bank Research Observer*, 23(2), p. 139-159.

Javorcik, B.S., Saggi, K. and Spatareanu, M. (2004) Does it matter where you come from? Vertical spillovers from foreign direct investment and the nationality of investors. *World Bank Policy Research Working Papers*, no. 3118. Washington, DC: World Bank.

Jordaan, J.A. (2005) Determinants of FDI-induced externalities: New empirical evidence for Mexican manufacturing industries. *World Development*, vol. 33(12), p. 2103-2118.

Jordaan, J.A. (2008a) State characteristics and the locational choice of foreign direct investment: Evidence from regional FDI in Mexico 1989-2006. *Growth and Change*, lead article, vol. 39(3), p. 389-413.

Jordaan, J.A. (2008b) Intra- and inter-industry externalities from foreign direct investment in the Mexican manufacturing sector: New evidence from Mexican regions. *World Development*, vol. 36(12), p. 2838-2854.

Jordaan, J.A. (2008c) Regional foreign participation and externalities: new empirical evidence from Mexican regions. *Environment and Planning A*, vol. 40(12), p. 2948-2969.

Jordaan, J.A. (2009) *Foreign direct investment, agglomeration and externalities*. Farnham, Surry, UK: Ashgate Publishing Limited.

Jordaan, J.A. (2010) Cross-sectional estimation of FDI spillovers when FDI is endogenous: OLS and IV estimates for Mexican manufacturing industries. *Applied Economics*, first published on: 01 March 2010 (iFirst).

Jordaan, J.A. and Rodriguez-Oreggia, E. (2010) Regional growth in Mexico under trade liberalization: How important are agglomeration and FDI? *The Annals of Regional Science*, doi:1007/s00168-010-0406-4.

Jordaan, J.A. (2011a) FDI, local sourcing and supportive linkages with domestic suppliers: The case of Monterrey, Mexico. *World Development*, vol. 39(4), p. 620-632.

Jordaan, J.A. (2011b) Local sourcing and technology spillovers to Mexican suppliers: How important are FDI and supplier characteristics? *Forthcoming in Growth and Change*, vol. 42.3.

Karpaty, P. and Lundberg, L. (2007) Foreign direct investment and productivity spillovers in Swedish manufacturing. *Working Paper Series*, no. 2004:2. Swedish Business School, Orebro University.

Keller, W. (1996) Absorptive capacity: On the creation and acquisition of technology in development. *Journal of Development Economics*, vol. 49(1), p. 199-227.

Keller, W. (2004) International technology diffusion. *Journal of Economic Literature*, vol. 42(3), p. 752-782.

Kokko, A. (1994) Technology, market characteristics and spillovers. *Journal of Development Economics*, vol. 43(2), p. 279-293.

Kokko, A. (1996) Productivity spillovers from competition between local firms and foreign affiliates. *Journal of International Development*, vol. 8(4), p. 517-530.

Konings, J. (2000) The effects of foreign direct investment on domestic firms: Evidence from firm level panel data in emerging economies. *William Davidson Institute Working Paper Series*, no. 344. Michigan: William Davidson Institute, University of Michigan.

Kugler, M. (2006) Spillovers from foreign direct investment: within or between industries? *Journal of Development Economics*, vol. 80(2), p. 444-477.

Lipsey, R.E. (2004) Home- and host country effects of foreign direct investment, in *Challenges to globalization*, edited by Baldwin, R.E. and Winters, A.L. Chicago: Chicago University Press.

Lipsey, R.E. and Sjöholm, F. (2004) FDI and wage spillovers in Indonesian manufacturing. *Review of World Economics*, vol. 140(2), p. 287-310.

Monastiriotis, V. and Jordaan, J.A. (2010) Does FDI promote regional development? Evidence from local and regional productivity spillovers in Greece. *Eastern Journal of European Studies*, vol. 1, p. 139-164.

Moran, T.H. (2005) How does FDI affect host economy development? Using industry case studies to make reliable generalizations, in *Does foreign direct investment promote development*? edited by Moran, T.H., Graham, E.M. and Blomström, M. Washington, DC: Institute for International Economics.

Nelson, R.R. (1968) A diffusion model of international productivity differences. *The American Economic Review*, vol. LVIII, p. 1219-1248.

Papandreou, A.A. (1994) *Externality and institutions*. Oxford: Clarendon Press.

Potter, J., Moore, B. and Spires, R. (2002) The wider effects of inward foreign direct investment in manufacturing on UK industry. *Journal of Economic Geography*, vol. 2(2), p. 279-310.

Rodriguez-Pose, A. and Crescenzi, R. (2008) Research and development, spillovers, innovation systems, and the genesis of regional growth in Europe. *Regional Studies*, vol. 42(1), p. 51-67.

Rodrik, D. (1992) Closing the productivity gap: Does trade liberalization really help? in *Trade policy, industrialization and development*: New perspectives. Oxford: Clarendon.

Rodrik, D. (1999) *The new global economy and developing countries: Making openness work*. Washington: John Hopkins University Press for the Overseas Development Council.

Romer, P. (1994) The origins of endogenous growth. *Journal of Economic Perspectives*, vol. 8(1), p. 3-22.

Rosenthal, S. and Strange, W. (2004) Evidence of the nature and sources of agglomeration economies, in *Handbook of Urban and Regional Economics*, vol. 4, edited by Henderson, V.J. and Thisse, J.F. Amsterdam: North Holland.

Scitovsky, T. (1954) Two concepts of external economies. *The Journal of Political Economy*, vol. 62, p. 143-151.

Sjöholm, F. (1999) Productivity growth in Indonesia: The role of regional characteristics and foreign investment. *Economic Development and Cultural Change*, vol., 47(3), p. 559-584.

Smarzynska, B.K. (2004) Does foreign direct investment increase the productivity domestic firms? In search of spillovers through backward linkages. *The American Economic Review*, vol. 94(3), p. 605-627.

Taki, S. (2005) Productivity spillovers and characteristics of multinational plants in Indonesian manufacturing. *Journal of Development Economics*, vol. 76(2), p. 521-542.

UNCTAD (2001) *World investment report 2001: Promoting linkages*. Geneva: United Nations Conference on Trade and Development.

UNCTAD (2005) *World investment report 2005: Transnational corporations and the internationalization of RandD*. Geneva: United Nations Conference on Trade and Development.

Venables, A.J. and Barba Navaretti, G. (2005) *Multinational firms in the world economy*. Oxfordshire, UK: Princeton University Press.

Yudaeva, K, Kozlov, K., Mentieva, N. and Ponomaryova, N. (2003) Does foreign ownership matter? The Russian experience. *Economics of Transition*, vol. 11, p. 383-409.

Zhang, K.H. (2001) Does foreign direct investment promote economic growth? Evidence from East Asia and Latin America. *Contemporary Economic Policy*, vol. 19(2), p. 175-185.

Zukowska-Gagelmann, K. (2000) Productivity spillovers from foreign direct investment in Poland. *Economic Systems*, vol. 24(3), p. 232-256.

In: Foreign Investment
Editor: Torre DeSare and Daniele Caprioglio
ISBN 978-1-61470-358-7

Chapter 2

Globalisation and the Rise of Logistics FDI - The Case of Italy

***Elena Maggi*[*,1] *and Ilaria Mariotti*[2]**

[1]Università degli Studi del Molise, Faculty of Economics, SEGeS, via De Sanctis, Campobasso, Italy
[2]DiAP-Politecnico di Milano, P.zza L. da Vinci, 32 – 20133 Milan, Italy

Abstract

The globalisation of the economy, which has been fostered by the trade barriers reduction and the falling transport, communication and co-ordination costs, has changed the structure of the production processes from being concentrated in few plants to being fragmented in different plants and in different countries and has strongly increased the trade rate. This has fostered a tight increase of exchange flows, affecting the logistics activities, especially transport. Transport, indeed, plays a key role in connecting the different import and export markets and the vertically disaggregated components of production systems, which are widespread in the world. As a consequence, the Foreign Direct Investments (FDI) in logistics have quickly grown: in the last years, the growth rate of FDI in the utilities (energy, gas and water), logistics and communications has more than tripled and outward FDI in the logistics industry equals to 26% of the service total.

The aim of the present chapter is threefold. First, it presents the entity and the characteristics of outward and inward logistics FDI in Italy (section two). This country can be considered an interesting case because it is characterized by a fragmented, small sized transport industry and low value added logistics industry, which has attracted foreign logistics multinational enterprise (MNE) in the integrated logistics. Second, the work investigates in-depth strategies and motivations of the foreign MNE's investment decisions (section three). Specifically, the horizontal, vertical and conglomerate integration strategies are analyzed and the main motivations driving them are discussed. Third, it concerns the main drivers of inward logistics FDI's increase, and generally, the

---

[*] ph. +39 0874 404992; elena.maggi@unimol.it

main factor fostering logistics growth: the manufacturing internationalization, which increases the demand for logistics services in the home country and consequently attracts providers from the other countries (section four).

The data on outward and inward FDI in Italy come from the LogINT database, developed by the Laboratory of Economics, Logistics and Territory (LabELT) of DiAP-Polytechnic of Milan in collaboration with the University of Molise, and covers the period 2000 – 2010.

1. Introduction

The logistics and transportation industry experienced the so-called logistics revolution (Vahrenkamp, 2010) starting in the 1950s. This industry, since that time, showed significant changes, which can be addressed to the following main phenomena: (i) the consumer-oriented economy; (ii) the internet-based information systems; (iii) the fall of transport costs; (iv) the European Traffic Policy; (v) the globalization of the economy.

The consumer-oriented economy (i) is not only addressed to mass consumption but also to mass production and mass distribution of consumer goods (Strasser, 1998). The consumer-oriented economy has, therefore, fostered an increased variety of models in material management, and has increased the complexity of logistics processes in production and trade.

Before the widespread availability of computers and telecommunications, the geographic dispersion of a complex production process was too hard to coordinate (Krugman *et al.*, 1995). The internet-based information systems (ii), developed in the 1990s, have drastically simplified and cheapened the exchange of information; besides, internet-based mail order businesses have strengthened parcel services.

Furthermore, in the last five decades, different technology innovations in freight moving and handling, such as containerization (Levinson, 2006), as well as the liberalisation process developed by the European Union, have contributed to drastically reduce also the transport costs (iii) (van Veen-Groot and Nikamp, 1999; Notteboom, 2007). In particular, over the twentieth century, the costs of goods' moving have declined by over 90% in real terms and this reduction is continuing. Therefore, the average cost of transport a ton a mile has decreased from 18.5 cents in 1890 (in 2001 dollars) to 2.3 cents in 2004 (Glaeser and Kohlhase, 2004).

As concerns the European countries, the Traffic Policy (iv), which has favored the liberalization of truck traffic, has strongly increased the truck fleet and the traffic flows in the European Union (EU). Only in about ten years, from 1990 to 1999, the road traffic within European member states increased by 76% (Vahrenkamp, 2010).

Finally, the globalization of the economy (v) has had a strong impact on logistics. As stated by van Veen-Groot and Nikamp (1999, pp. 331-332): "Globalisation is at present a 'vogue' word that refers to opening up and increasing internationalization of markets, worldwide communications and mobility, changing consumption patterns and lifestyles, key positions of multinational firms in world markets, and shifting of industrial activities all over the world". Globalization has, then, been fostered by the above mentioned phenomena (consumer-oriented economy, the internet-based information systems, the fall of transport costs, the European Traffic Policy), as well as by the fall of goods, services, people and capital barriers, the liberalization of international trade and the adoption of free market principles by a wide range of countries (OECD, 1997). In particular, the structure of the production processes, before concentrated in few plants, became fragmented in different plants and in different countries, at least as long as the costs for logistics and reorganization do not overwhelm the marginal advantage.

A new model of production was spreading: the previously integrated productive activities are segmented and spread over an international network of production sites, which implies the international fragmentation of production (see, among others, Arndt and Kierzhowsky, 2001). As a result, the increasing trade flows do not only include final goods, but also intermediate and unfinished goods being transferred from one country to another in order to be processed (Baldone *et al.*, 2002; 2006).

Within this context, transport and logistics play a key role in connecting the different import and export markets and the vertically disaggregated components of production system, which are widespread in the world (Yieming *et al.*, 2002).

The above described trends have impacted on the Foreign Direct Investments (FDI) in logistics, rising them quickly. In the last years, the growth rate of FDI in the utilities (energy, gas and water), logistics and communications has more than tripled (UNCTAD, 2006) and outward FDI in the logistics industry equals to 26% of the service total.

The FDI is one of the three forms of internationalization which can be chosen by the firms in a globalised era; the others are international trade and cooperation agreements (see, among the others, Ietto-Gillies, 2005). In particular, international trade, consisting of import and export, is the most common form and often the first entry mode adopted by a firm facing the global scenario, because it implies low involvement and risk degree for the internationalized firm.

Cooperation agreement, a more advanced and risky strategy than international trade, is mainly adopted by small and medium size enterprises (SME) because it is of short – medium term and does not require capital investment (non-equity strategy). In fact, it consists in agreements (licensing, franchising, alliances, subcontracting) on the development, distribution, and/or manufacture of final goods to be sold in the foreign market. FDI, instead, on which the present book chapter focuses, represents the most articulated and binding mode to enter the foreign markets, because it requires a significant capital investment through greenfields or mergers and acquisitions and imply a medium-long term obligation. FDI is the main tool adopted by medium and large sized firms, which aim to share the capital of a foreign firm, eventually with one or more partners.

More specifically, the present chapter is dedicated to the analysis of outward and inward FDI in the Italian logistics industry. This industry can be defined as the ensemble of suppliers of single services (transport, storage, handling, etc.) or different integrated services, aiming to manage the flows of materials and goods along the supply chain. This analysis is based on the Log-INT database, which, since 2000, has been developed by the Laboratory of Economy, Logistics and Territory (LabELT) of DiAP-Polytechnic of Milan in collaboration with the University of Molise, and it is the only database available in Italy on the inward and outward FDI in the logistics industry [1].

---

[1] The LogINT database is updated every year and uses different sources: Reprint databank of the Italian FDI (developed by the Department of Management and Engineering of the Politecnico di Milano and sponsored by the Italian Trade Institute – ICE), newspaper and magazines on the logistics industry, direct interviews to logistics MNE, etc.

From the sector point of view, the data are organised according to the European classification of economic activities NACE REV1.1 (2002)[2]. Specifically, the focus of the analysis is on freight logistics firms belonging to the NACE category "I – Transport, warehousing, communications"[3], because they are more impacted by globalisation

The purpose of the present chapter is threefold. First, it aims at presenting the entity and the characteristics of outward and inward logistics FDI in Italy (section two), a country, which can be considered an interesting case because it is characterized by a fragmented, small sized transport industry and low value added logistics industry, which has attracted foreign logistics multinational enterprise (MNE) in the integrated logistics. The second purpose is to investigate in-depth strategies and motivations of the foreign MNE's investment decisions (section three). Specifically, the horizontal, vertical and conglomerate integration strategies are investigated and the main motivations driving them are discussed. The third purpose concerns the main drivers of inward logistics FDI's increase, and generally, the main factor fostering logistics growth: the manufacturing internationalization, which increases the demand for logistics services in the home country and consequently attracts providers from the other countries (section four). Moreover, the third purpose, highlights the importance of the manufacturing internationalization, as strategic component of the economy globalization, in rising the logistics industry FDI, and logistics growth in general.

More precisely, the chapter is structured into five sections. The introduction is followed by the description of outward and inward FDI in Italy. This section presents the number of FDI, sub-sectors and origin and destination areas, and briefly describes the amount of the total outward and inward FDI (in manufacturing as well as in services) in Italy.

Section three is dedicated to the investigation of the strategies and motivations driving logistics inward FDI in Italy in the period 2000-2010. A literature review on the integration strategies (horizontal, vertical and conglomerate), undertaken by foreign MNE, and on the drivers moving these strategies, is presented; besides descriptive statistics follow.

Section four focuses on the impact of manufacturing internationalization on the employment growth in transport and logistics in the home country. A theoretical framework on this issue is presented and particular attention is devoted to one empirical study, carried on by the authors of the present chapter, because the evidence on this topic is rather scanty. This work by Elia *et al.* (2011) investigates the impact of manufacturing internationalization on the transport employment growth at the NUTS2 regions level.

Section five concludes the chapter, drawing feasible policy recommendations and suggesting further research needs.

---

[2] NACE is the acronym ("Nomenclature générale des Activités économiques dans les Communautés Européennes", i.e. Statistical classification of economic activities in the European Communities) used to designate the various statistical classifications of economic activities developed since 1970 in the European Union. It provides the framework for collecting and presenting a large range of statistical data according to economic activity in the fields of economic statistics. NACE is derived from ISIC, in the sense that it is more detailed than ISIC. ISIC and NACE have exactly the same items at the highest levels, where NACE is more detailed at lower levels (for more details see Eurostat, European Commission, 2008). Because of lack of data, we refer to NACE rev 1.1 version, developed by EU in 2002.

[3] In particular, the analysis is based on the following NACE codes: (i) I 60.10 – rail transport; (ii) I 60.24 – freight road transport; (iii) I 60.30 – transport via pipelines; (iv) I 61.10 – sea and coastal transport; (v) I 61.20 – inland water transport; (vi) I 62.10 – scheduled air transport; (vii) I 63.1 – cargo handling and storage; (viii) I 63.21 – other supporting transport activities; (ix) I 63.40 - activities of other transport agencies (forwarders, intermodal transport and logistics integrators); (x) I 64.12 – courier activities.

2. The Rise of Outward and Inward FDI in Italy

As underlined in the previous sections, the globalisation of the economy, together with the consumer oriented economy, the internet-based information systems, the fall of transport costs, the European Traffic Policy, has fostered an increasing demand and, consequently, supply, of logistics activities. Within a country, the demand can be either satisfied locally, by national firms, or by foreign firms, which undertake specific internationalisation strategies. It happens that countries with a fragmented, small sized and low value added logistics sector, like for example Italy, become more and more attractive for foreign investors.

The present section focuses on Italy[4], a European country, which has attracted, in the last decade, an increasing number of foreign logistics FDI, mainly originating from the richest EU countries and concentrated in high value added activities, and shows a relatively limited number of outward FDI.

The first subsection presents the outward logistics FDI in Italy registered in the year 2010, while the second subsection focuses on the logistics inward FDI in the same year. The description of both outward and inward FDI includes details on the investment logistics sub-industry and on the FDI areas of origin and destination. As stated in the introduction, the data on logistics FDI are provided by the LogINT database.

2.1. Outward Logistics FDI in Italy

Italy has been defined a "multinational follower" (Mariotti and Mutinelli, 2009), because of its lower rate of outward direct investments compared to the other industrialized countries. In fact, in 2006 the percentage ratio between the outward FDI and the GDP is about 20% (UNCTAD, 2007), the half of the European Union media and strongly lower than the main ratio of the closest partners (i.e. Germany with a rate of 34.5% and France with 48.3%).

The main cause of this situation is the prevalent small size of Italian firms, which does not allow to have the financial and human resources needed for foreign investments. This competitive gap is higher in the logistics industry than in other sectors: 60% of the logistics firms are single-person companies and 16.2% has two employees (ISTAT, 2007)[5]. According to the REPRINT-ICE database[6], in 2009 the logistics outward FDI are a small percentage (6%) of the total Italian outward FDI (Figure 1), but they account for the 23% of outward FDI in the service sector. As concerns the other industries, Italian outward FDI are concentrated in wholesale (49%), followed by manufacturing industry (28%), services (13%) and construction (5%).

Nevertheless, in the last decades the investments of the Italian logistics firms have grown very quickly. According to Mariotti and Mutinelli (2009), since 2000 to 2006 the number of employees in the foreign affiliates of the logistics Italian MNE increased of 64.3%, while in the same period the investments undertaken by the Italian manufacturing MNE decreased.

4 Italy is a EU country located in south-central Europe. With 60.4 million inhabitants, it is the sixth most populous country in Europe. Its GDP in 2008 amounted to 1,572,243 million euro (Germany: 2,495,800; France: 1,950,085; UK: 1,818,523) (Eurostat data).

5 The Italian firms are small and very small sized: while the average size in the EU is 6.4 workers per firm, in Italy, like in Spain, the average size is 4 workers per firm (ISTAT data, year 2008).

6 For more details see www. ice.gov.it and Mariotti and Mutinelli (2009).

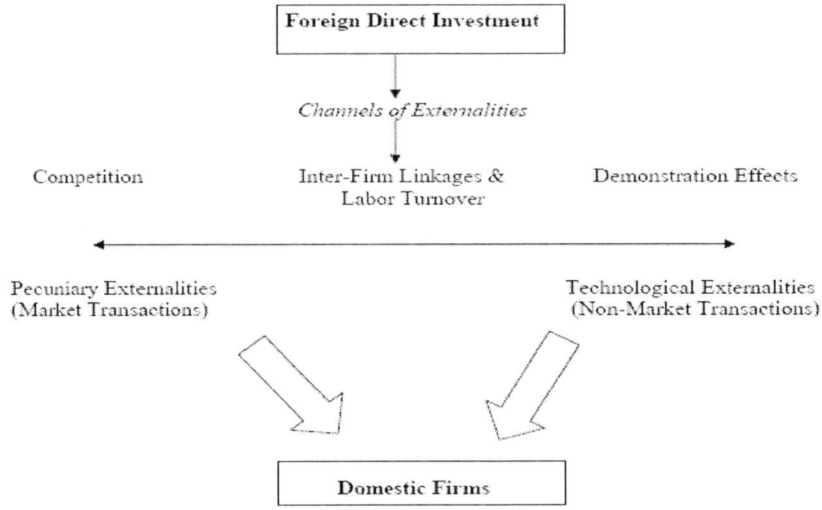

Source: our elaboration on REPRINT-ICE database (2009).

Figure 1. Total Italian outward FDI, by investment industry.

The LogINT database shows that in the Italian logistics industry, at the beginning of 2010, the number of outward FDI (817), is higher than the number of inward FDI (372). Moreover, as it will be stated in the next section, Italy is less attractive to FDI than other countries. The 817 outward FDI have been undertaken by 165 Italian MNE.

Since the logistics industry is very heterogeneous (Carbone and Stone, 2005), a disaggregation of the analysis in different sub-industries needs to be done (Figure 2). The investments mainly concern the forwarding activities (42% - NACE I63.40.1 code), followed by integrated logistics and intermodal transport sector (19% - NACE I63.40.2 code[7]) and by sea transport (21% - NACE I61.10.0 code). Thus, about 70% of the investments belong to the 63 NACE sub-industry ("supporting and auxiliary transport activities of travel agencies"), which comprises higher value-added activities than just transport. The high percentage of investments in the maritime transport can be justified by the important increase of this transport mode, which has occurred in the last decades because of the globalization process and, particularly, the growing trade exchanges between Europe and Asia.

Reflecting a national trend, the larger part of outward FDI comes from the richest areas of Italy (33% from North West and 32% from North East), followed by the Centre (22%) and South and Islands (13%) (Table 1). In particular, Lombardy region, in the North West, which is the region with the highest GDP pro-capite, generates the 20% of the investments; it is, then, followed by Tuscany (18%) and Emilia Romagna (13%), respectively in the Centre and in the North East, where different important industrial districts are located, and by Campania (10%) in the South, in which it is located the headquarter of the Italian most important global players, operating in the sea transport (Grimaldi Group).

[7] Actually, the NACE I63.40.2 code is called "other supporting and auxiliary transport services", but it comprises a large number of firms offering integrated services and intermodal transport which doesn't find alternative location in other specific voices of the NACE REV 1.1 classification.

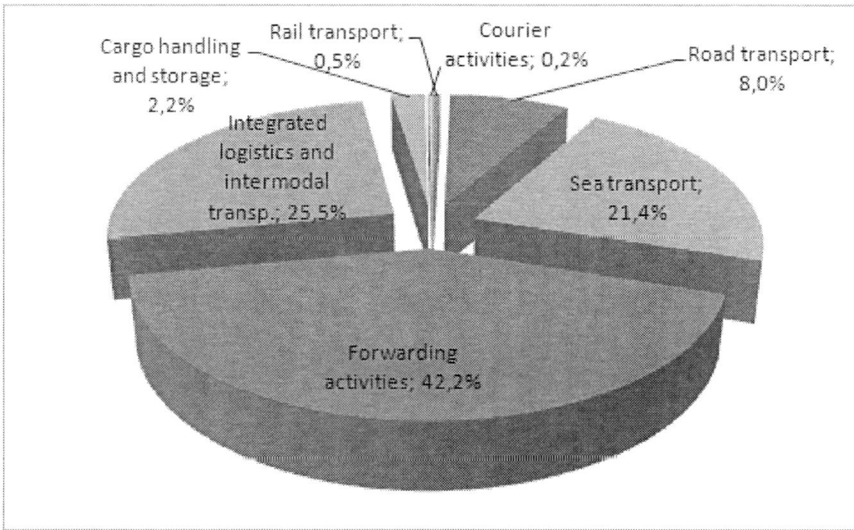

Source: our elaborations on LogINT database, LabELT, 2010.

Figure 2. Italian outward logistics FDI, by investment sub-industry.

Table 1. Areas of origin and destination of the Italian logistics outward investments

Distribution of FDI by destination (100 = areas of destination)

AREAS OF ORIGIN	AREAS OF DESTINATION							
	West Europe	Latin America	Asia	Central East Europe	North America	Africa	Other countries	Total
North West	33.7	38.2	25.3	30.5	28.8	54.0	20.0	33.3
North East	28.3	22.5	40.7	49.6	33.3	12.0	50.0	32.4
Centre	18.9	24.7	33.3	16.8	33.3	10.0	25.0	21.5
South and Islands	19.1	14.6	0.0	3.1	4.5	24.0	5.0	12.7
Total	100.0	100.0	100.0	100.0	100.0	100.0	100.0	100.0

Distribution of FDI by origin (100= areas of origin)

AREAS OF ORIGIN	AREAS OF DESTINATION							
	West Europe	Latin America	Asia	Central East Europe	North America	Africa	Other countries	Total
North West	46.0	12.5	8.5	14.7	7.0	9.9	1.5	100.0
North East	39.6	7.5	14.0	24.5	8.3	2.3	3.8	100.0
Centre	39.5	12.4	17.0	12.4	12.4	2.8	2.8	100.0
South and Islands	68.3	12.5	0.0	3.8	2.9	11.5	1.0	100.0
Total	45.4	10.9	11.0	16.0	8.1	6.1	2.4	100.0

Source: our elaborations on LogINT database, LabELT, 2010.

Similarly to the other industries, the main destination areas of outward logistics FDI are the European countries, especially West Europe (45%), while Central East Europe accounts for the 16% of total FDI. This trend confirms that the logistics industry is strongly demand-driven: the logistics providers follow their customers in the internationalisation processes (market-seeking investments). Specifically, West European countries are the main destination of Italian export, while the Centre-Eastern countries in the '80s and '90s have attracted several manufacturing delocalisation projects (see, among the others, Chiarvesio *et al.*, 2003; Corò *et al.*, 2006; Mariotti and Montagnana, 2008). Asia and Latin America, which are other important areas hosting the Italian industrial delocalisation, both attract 11% of total FDI. North America (8%), Africa (6%) and other countries, particularly Middle East and Oceania, follow.

As concerns the investment countries, Spain, France, United States, UK and Germany are at the first places (Figure 3). Poland and Romania are the main destinations of Central East Europe, China of Asia, Brazil and Panama of Latin America.

The cross table (1), showing the origin and destination areas, confirms that the investments are mainly driven by market-seeking strategies. The logistics providers of the North West macro-area mainly invest in the closest European countries and in Latin America, while the North Eastern logistics MNE in West and Centre-East Europe and Asia. The firms located in the Centre prefer West Europe and Asia. Finally, the South and Islands companies look at West Europe, Latin America and Africa, which are very close to these regions.

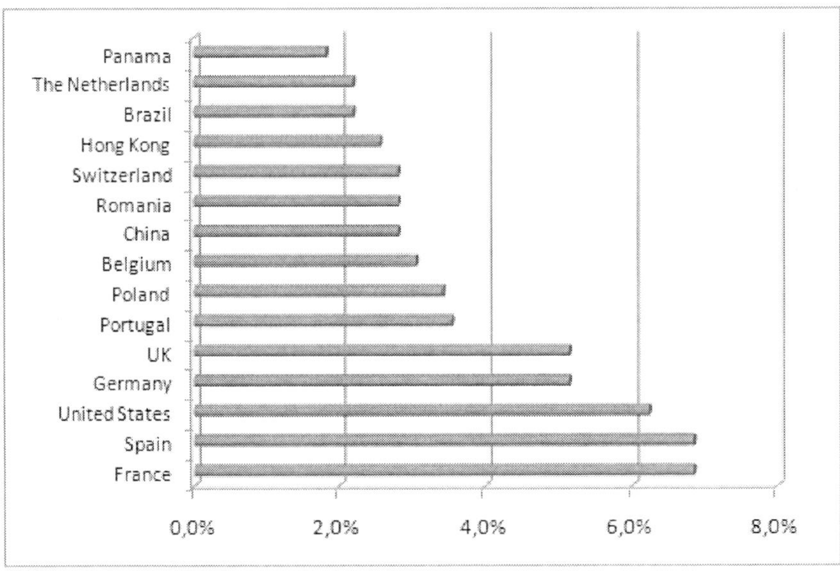

Source: our elaborations on LogINT database, LabELT, 2010.

Figure 3. The first 15 countries of Italian logistics outward FDI.

2.2. Inward Logistics FDI in Italy

Italy shows a poor attractiveness to inward FDI in comparison with the other developed countries. This is mainly due to the lower quality of the localisation factors' supply and of the external economies supply (Mariotti and Mutinelli, 2009). Italy has a limited flow of inward FDI, mainly in the high tech sector and in the advanced services. Several studies (see among the others, Bianchi *et al.*, 2005; Mariotti and Piscitello, 1995; Basile *et al.*, 2005) have stated that the lower attractiveness seems to be associated with some national institutional characteristics, such as the low level of bureaucracy's efficiency and of the ability of the legal system to adequately enforce property rights. In the last decade, the most dynamic sectors of inward FDI have been: (i) utilities (+54%), logistics (+25,2%), and the other professional services (+22,7%). Specifically, services show a higher growth rate than the other sectors in terms of number of firms, employees, turnover and value added.

The recent increase of inward FDI in logistics and professional services is due to new infrastructure and the economy's outsourcing undertaken by the more developed countries. At the same time the increase in inward FDI expresses the higher competitiveness of the foreign logistics providers, in comparison with the Italian firms. As stated by Brouwer and Mariotti (2009), foreign logistics MNE tend to outperform domestic firms in the period 2002-2005, in terms of turnover and productivity. Logistics foreign MNE favor locations in the core area of the country, and have a preference to be active in the higher values added sub-sectors.

In 2009, the Italian industries attracting a significant number of inward FDI are: wholesale (39%), manufacturing (33%), services (25%) (Figure 4). Logistics and transport account for the 23% of inward FDI in the service sector and the 6% of the total FDI (Reprint-ICE database).

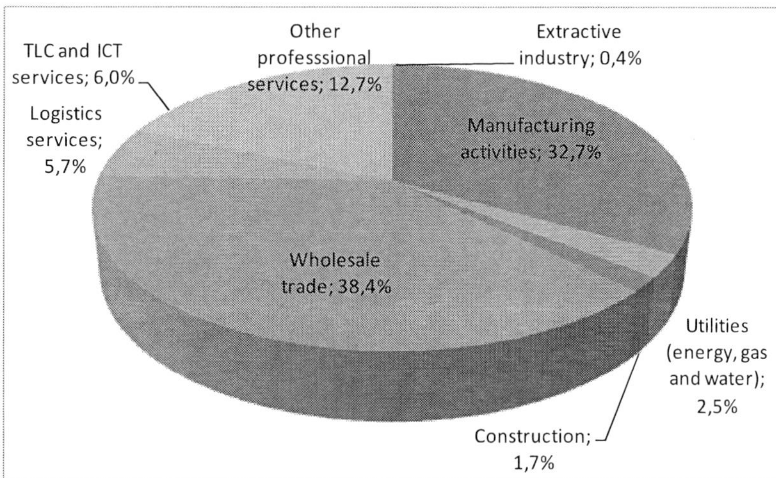

Source: our elaboration on REPRINT-ICE database (2009).

Figure 4. Total inward FDI in Italy, by investment industry.

The structural patterns of the Italian logistics industry and, specifically, the significant pulverization of the firms, attracted international global players, which mainly supply high value added services (integrated logistics, couriers and international forwarding activities). In Italy, the SME predominate the scenario and this structural pattern does not foster the development of know-how, human and financing resources. Besides, SMEs do not develop the specific necessary innovations to offer a multifaceted range of services, able to satisfy the customers' demand. Moreover, the large foreign investing firms, characterized by a logistics network diffused on the territory, are able to supply the increasing demand of the Italian manufacturing firms, which operate in the global market. Foreign MNE, therefore, through an increasing number of Merger and Acquisition and greenfield investments, own significant market shares (see section 3).

The LogINT database accounts, at the beginning of the year 2010, for 372 inward logistics FDI, which have been undertaken by 230 foreign MNE. About 75% of the investments belong to the I63 NACE sub-industry ("supporting and auxiliary transport activities of travel agencies") and I64.12 NACE sector (couriers). In particular, within these FDI, 46% concerns forwarding activities (NACE I63.40.1 code) and integrated logistics and intermodal transport (NACE I63.40.2 code), 22% other supporting activities (NACE I63.2 code, mainly firms managing transport infrastructure), storage (NACE I63.1 code), and, finally, 7% couriers (NACE I64.12 code) (Figure 5). Instead, the investments in transportation gains the remaining 25%: land transport predominates (14%), sea transport (6%), rail transport (4%) and air transport (3%) follow.

As concerns origin and destination areas, the patterns of inward logistics FDI confirm those of the manufacturing industry (Table 2). Italy attracts FDI mainly from western Europe (72.8%), North America (11.3%), Asia (7.3%) and Middle East (3.8%). The MNE investing in Italy mainly belong to industrialized countries like Germany (20%), France (14%), the Netherlands (10%), Switzerland (8%). According to a national trend, the investing foreign MNE originate from the most developed countries.

Foreign FDI are mainly located in the North west (61%), "core area" of the Italian logistics; follow the North east (19%) and the Centre (12%).

South and Islands register the 8% of the total. In particular, Lombardy region, in the North West attracts 43% of the investments and it is followed by Liguria (12%), Emilia Romagna (8%) and Veneto (7%). The central regions of Toscana and Lazio together 11%. Among the southern regions, we find Campania (3%) and Calabria (2%). This trend confirms that the logistics industry is strongly demand driver, i.e. it locates where the manufacturing customers have their local units.

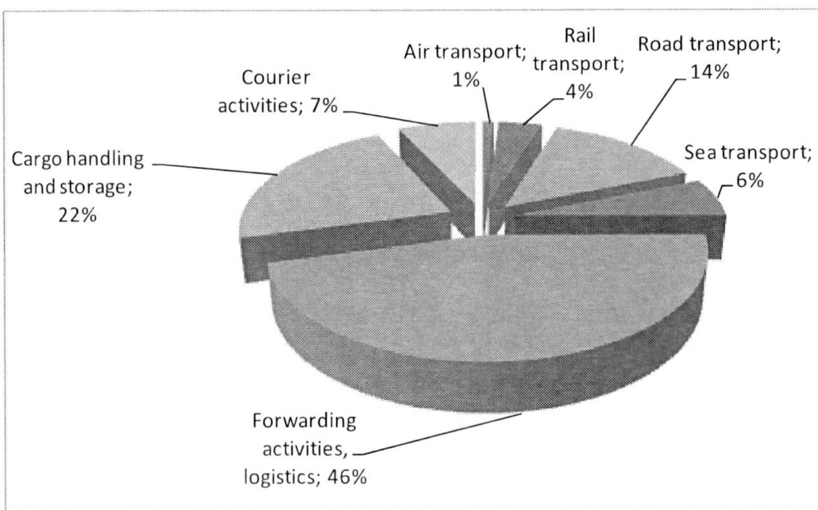

Source: our elaborations on LogINT database, LabELT, 2010.

Figure 5. Inward Logistics FDI in Italy, by investment sub-industry.

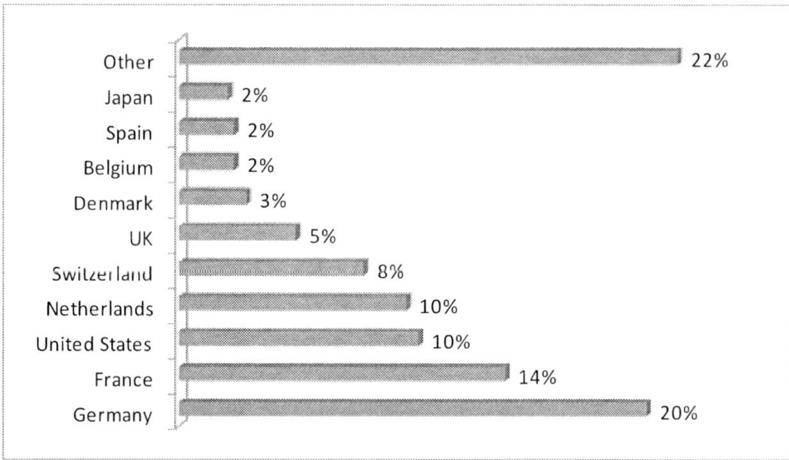

Source: our elaborations on LogINT database, LabELT, 2010.

Figure 6. The first ten countries undertaking FDI in Italy (%).

Table 2. Areas of origin and destination of the Italian logistics inward investments

Distribution of FDI by destination (100 = destination areas)

Areas of origin		Areas of destination			
	Centre	North-east	North-west	South and Islands	Total
Other countries	2,3%	2,8%	2,6%	6,9%	3,0%
Asia	9,1%	5,6%	7,0%	10,3%	7,3%
Centre-eastern Europe	2,3%	2,8%	1,3%	3,4%	1,9%
Western Europe	56,8%	79,2%	74,4%	69,0%	72,8%
Middle East	6,8%	2,8%	3,1%	6,9%	3,8%
North America	22,7%	6,9%	11,5%	3,4%	11,3%
Total	100%	100%	100%	100%	

Distribution of FDIby origin (100= origin areas)

Areas of origin		Areas of destination			
	Centre	North-east	North-west	South and Islands	Total
Other countries	9,1%	18,2%	54,5%	18,2%	100
Asia	14,8%	14,8%	59,3%	11,1%	100
Centre-eastern Europe	14,3%	28,6%	42,9%	14,3%	100
Western Europe	9,2%	21,0%	62,4%	7,4%	100
Middle East	21,4%	14,3%	50,0%	14,3%	100
North America	23,8%	11,9%	61,9%	2,4%	100
Total	11,8%	19,4%	61,0%	7,8%	

Source: our elaborations on LogINT database, LabELT, 2010.

The cross table (2), showing the origin and destination areas, confirms that the 62.4% of the logistics providers from West Europe invest in the North West macro-area. About the

60% of the Asian FDI are located in the North West, which also attract FDI from the Middle East (50%) and the Central Eastern Europe (43%). However, FDI from Central Eastern Europe are also directed towards the North-East macro area, which is geographically closer. This are also exchanges with Central Eastern Europe flows of raw materials, semi-finished products and final goods. The manufacturing SME belonging to the north eastern industrial districts since the beginning of the 1980s have, indeed, undertaken a delocalisation process towards the cheap labour cost countries in the Centre and South of Europe (Mariotti, 2005).

3. Strategies and Motivations of Inward FDI in Italy

3.1. A Literature Review on the FDI Integration Strategies

In literature it is possible to find the following three different strands investigating strategies and motivations driving inward investments[8] (greenfield and merger and acquisition): the business and administration economic literature[9] (Ojala, 1993; Capron, 1999; Chang and Rosenzwei, 2001; Hakkinen *et al.*, 2004), the international economic literature (Buckley and Casson, 1976; Dunning, 1988; Agarwal and Ramaswami, 1992; Barba Navaretti and Venables, 2004; Hjizen *et al.*, 2008) and the transportation economic literature (Shepperd and Seidman, 2001; Fan *et al.*, 2001; Oum *et al.*, 2002; Dörrenbächer, 2003; Carbone and Stone, 2005; Federtrasporto-Nomisma, 2006, 2007, 2008, 2009, 2010; Cruijssen *et al.*, 2007; Van de Voorde and Vanelslander, 2009; Maggi and Mariotti, 2010).

According to this literature, three different strategies can be distinguished. Horizontal integration, when the investment is carried out in the same industry of the parent multinational enterprise (e.g., integration between two shipping companies). Vertical integration when the MNE invests in backward or forward stages of the same industry or in a company offering different services than the MNE (e.g., the integration between a shipping company and a sea terminal operator or a sea transport agency or between a transport and a storage firm). Conglomerate integration when the investment in a logistics activity is carried out by a non-logistics MNE (e.g., a manufacturing or finance MNE). The vertical integration allows the investing firms to diversify their product; in the case of logistics, this business diversification concerns three different aims (Maggi and Mariotti, 2010): (a) the completion of the transport chain, in order to offer door-to-door links to the clients; (b) the integration of different logistics services along the supply chain and the extension of the range of supplied services towards integrated solutions; (c) the supply of auxiliary and complementary activities with respect to the core service. The business diversification is motived by the necessity to satisfy the evolving customer needs and by the search of higher margins by the logistics firms. In particular, the second type of business diversification (b) is typically the strategy adopted by the MNE which aim at becoming integrated logistics service providers (3PLs or 4PLs[10]), by acquiring specialist capabilities.

[8] For a detailed and more extensive description of this issues see Maggi and Mariotti (2010).

[9] The studies belonging to the strategic management literature focus on the acquisition "relatedness", which refers to the degree of correspondence between an acquirer and its target (Haleblian and Finkelstein, 1999).

[10] The Third-Party Logistics (3PLs) and the Fourth-Party Logistics (4PLs) Providers supply process-based than function-based services aimed at the integration and control of a part or even the whole logistics process of

Moreover, these three strategies are promoted by different and often multiple specific drivers, which can be classified as follows in Table 3 (Ojala, 1993; Veugelers, 2002; Hakkinen *et al.*, 2004; Barba Navaretti and Venables, 2004; Hjizen *et al.*, 2006; Cruijssen *et al.*, 2007; Maggi and Mariotti, 2010).

In the last decades, the globalization of the market and the simultaneous liberalization process of different transport services, such as road transport or the postal distribution, have increased the competition in the logistics industry. Thus, new actors coming from the developing countries have been attracted in Europe. The logistics firms have concentrated their efforts in increasing or in defending their market power and in reaching a sufficient size to cope with the high investment in transport and ICT infrastructure efficiently (Carbone and Stone, 2005). More precisely, some companies, often following the process of production delocalization or other forms of internationalization of their clients, have entered in new markets or extended their presence in the traditional markets; other firms have opted for a defensive strategy. The main motivations of this last strategy are: (i) preventing being taken-over; (ii) preventing the target from being taken over by others; (iii) avoiding other merged entities in the industry from becoming too strong (Gorton *et al.*, 1998).

The competitive considerations can drive both the horizontal and the vertical integration; in the first case, the aim is to penetrate new geographical markets and, in the case of logistics, to efficiently extend the transport chain, controlling major traffic flows (Carbone and Stone, 2005). In the second case, the purpose is to penetrate new markets in terms of services and in order to acquire new competencies. According to Heaver (1996), the first type of investments is moved by geographical diversification, while the second one by business diversification.

Table 3. The main drivers and motivations of FDI integration strategies

1) Competitive goals	1a) Increasing market or political power
	1b) Defending market share
2) Efficiency improvement	2a) Research of scale economies
	2b) Research of scope economies
	2c) Reduction of transaction costs
3) Other drivers	3a) Regulation
	3b) Access to technologies and specific capabilities
	3c) High capital return

As concerns efficiency improvement, an acquisition can be motivated by the research of economy of scale and scope or by the transaction costs reduction. The scale and scope economies are very important in all the industries characterized by an high rate of fixed costs, which in the logistics sector mainly concern the structures or infrastructures or the vehicles for transport or warehousing operations. Specifically, reaching scale economies over larger transport or storage volumes, a company can first of all improve the productivity for core activities, for example by optimizing the vehicle capacity utilization, reducing the empty mileage or better using the space in the warehouses. Secondly, it reduces the costs of non-core activities, by organizing safety trainings or using joint fuel facilities. Thirdly, it cuts

their clients (Carbone and Stone, 2005). In particular, the 4PLs are usually non-asset based providers, because they design, plan, co-ordinate and control the supply networks, subcontracting the activities to 3PLs or other specialised transport and logistics providers.

purchasing, marketing and research and development costs (e.g. vehicles, onboard computers, fuel, etc.) (Cruijssen *et al.*, 2007; Van de Voorde and Vanelslander, 2009). Instead, economies of scope arise whenever the total cost of producing two different goods or services jointly is lower than producing each of the goods separately. The business diversification, granted mainly by vertical integration, gives the opportunity to combine complementary skills and often to offer better quality of service at lower costs (e.g. in terms of speed, frequency of deliveries, geographical coverage, reliability of delivery times etc.) (Carbone and Stone, 2005; Cruijssen *et al.*, 2007). Moreover, the economies of scope contribute to improve the operating margins through business process re-engineering and commercial entry into new market segments (Carbone and Stone, 2005). Efficiency improvements can derive also from cutting the transaction costs[11] with the suppliers or distributors along the supply chain, by acquiring them. The transaction costs' reduction results from small number bargaining, enhancing the competitive position or market power of the partners, and meeting the partner's request for organizational knowledge and learning (Kogut, 1988; Goldman and Gorton, 2000).

Finally, the literature identifies other three types of motivations driving the choice of the investment industry: changes of the industry regulation, access to technologies or specific capabilities and capital return from the investment. A change in the regulatory rules of an industry in a country, such as the liberalization of a market previous regulated by a public monopoly, can attract MNE from other countries. Tax savings could result when a loss-making firm merges with a profitable one. Furthermore, the regulated firms might want to diversify into an unregulated market in order to shift profits from the regulated market into the unregulated one (Veugelers, 2002). An acquisition can gives the opportunity to have a quick and cheaper access to new technologies and know-how, rather than to set up 'ex-novo' new activities (greenfield) or do own research and development. As concerns the logistics industry, it is well known that the vast majority of logistics firms are SME, which, by definition, tend to lag behind in implementation of information and communication technology (ICT) systems (Gunasekaran and Ngai, 2004). Cruijssen *et al.* (2007) show that ICT is mainly an issue for horizontal integrations of a medium or high intensity, able to generate sufficient revenues to pay back the ICT investments. Moreover, the acquisition allows the company to have quickly access to specialist capabilities, concerning especially higher value-added services. An increasing number of third-party logistics providers (3PL), in order to answer to the evolving demand of their client, include in their supply activities like contract maintenance and repair, post-manufacturing and reverse logistics, which require a high level of specialization (Plehwe and Bohle, 1998).

The high capital return from the investment is a crucial drivers for conglomerate integrations, especially when they are made by financial and real estate intermediaries, which have the need to invest their money in profitable industries.

Maggi and Mariotti (2010), who focused on both freight and passenger transport, have demonstrated that the competitive drivers are very important both in horizontal and vertical integrations. With concern to the efficiency gains, the scale economies strongly drive the horizontal strategies, while in the vertical ones economies of scope and reductions of transaction costs are more fundamental (Table 4).

[11] There is an extensive literature on transaction costs' reduction due to FDI (see, among the others, Hennart, 1982; Anderson and Gatignon, 1986).

Moreover, referring to other motivations, regulation is an important driver of the investments in the same industry and an high capital return mainly moves the investments of the non-logistics MNE (in particular, financial and real estate intermediaries). Other relevant drivers of the conglomerate strategies made by manufacturing or energy firms, are also the scale economies and the savings in transaction costs.

Table 4. The main drivers of the integration strategies in the logistics industry

Drivers	Integration strategies		
	Horizontal	*Vertical*	*Conglomerate*
Competitive considerations			
1a) Increasing market or political power	***	***	*
1b) Defending market share	***	***	n.t.
Efficiency considerations			
2a) Economies of scale	***	**	**
2b) Economies of scope	*	***	*
2c) Reduction of transaction costs	*	***	**
Other considerations			
3a) Regulation	***	n.t.	n.t.
3b) Access to technologies and specific capabilities	n.t.	n.t.	n.t.
3c) High capital return	*	*	***

Notes: * not relevant; ** relevant; *** extremely relevant; n.t.: not tested.
Source: Maggi and Mariotti (2010).

3.2. The Integration Strategies of the Logistics Foreign Multinational Enterprises in Italy

According to LogINT database, in the period 2000-2010, in Italy the majority of inward FDI, concerning freight transport, is horizontal. This phenomenon reflects a global trend: in 2009 the 70,3% of global logistics investments was made in the same industry of the investing MNE (Federtrasporto-Nomisma, 2009; 2010). In fact, the increment of the market share in the core business allows the companies to easily face the competition and the present global recession period, and simultaneously to improve efficiency, by scale economies.

Specifically, the horizontal integrations (HI) move the 56% of the investments, while conglomerate and vertical integrations (respectively, CI and VI) move the 26% and the 18% of the investments[12], respectively.

Figure 7 shows that the first type of investments (horizontal) is very diversified in different logistics sub-industries, but mainly concerns the NACE I.63 and I.64 codes (73% of the total), specifically, forwarding activities (25%), integrated logistics and intermodal transport (20%), and couriers (12%). The horizontal integration in transport sector mainly regards road (13%), followed by sea (8%) and rail (5%).

As concerns the vertical integrations, the percentage of the NACE I.63 industry is higher than in the other typologies (88%); more precisely, the MNE have mainly invested in forwarders (42%), followed, with a relevant lead, by integrators and intermodal operators (18%), and firms operating in other supporting transport activities (15%).

The conglomerate investments, such as the horizontal ones, are more diversified: the forwarding activities are again the first industry of investment (27%), but in this case the second one is road transport (21%), and the third cargo handling and storage (20%).

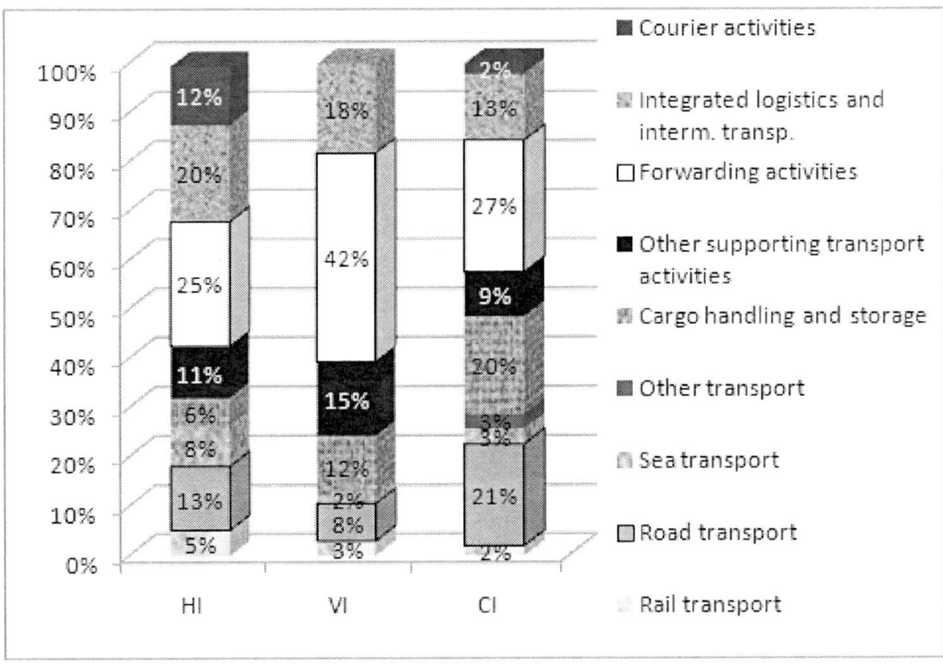

Source: our elaborations on LogINT database, LabELT, 2010.

Figure 7. The integration strategies by investment sub-industry.

The main part (40%) of the conglomerate integration is made by banks or other financial and real estate intermediaries, while the 30% comes from the manufacturing firms (food,

12 The vertical investments have been distinguished by the horizontal ones, using the 6-digit 2002 NACE classification of the economic activities. According to Hijzen *et al.* (2008), the investments which take place within the 4-digit industry have been classified as horizontal FDI, while the investments across 4-digit industries have been classified as vertical. Nevertheless, the investments of the bigger 3PLs or 4PLs providers have been considered as horizontal, because these firms are multiproduct, i.e. they offer a large number of different services both in their country of origin and in the countries of FDI destination.

metal, machinery and electric goods, transport equipment, chemical and pharmaceutical products) and the 22% has been undertaken by the extraction, production and distribution of energy (mainly petroleum) MNE (Figure 8). Trade and construction and other business services follow with the 6% and 2%, respectively.

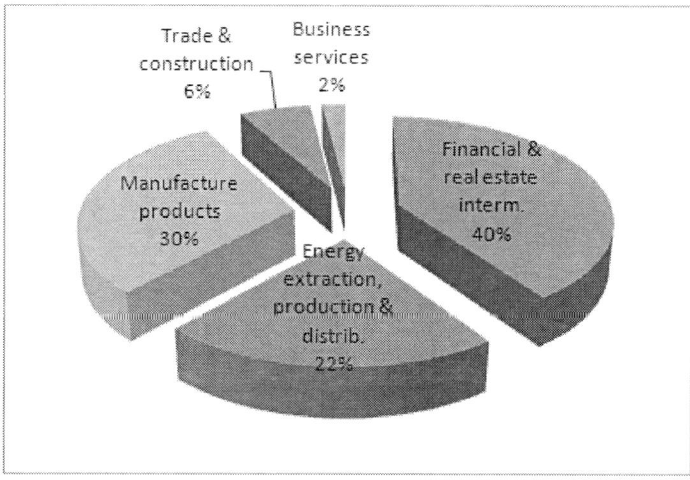

Source: our elaborations on LogINT database, LabELT, 2010.

Figure 8. The distribution of the conglomerate integrations by MNEs' industries.

More than half of the financial operators FDI concerns the higher value added activities of NACE I63.4 (forwarding, integrated logistics and intermodal suppliers), clearly motivated by the search of a high capital return rate. The financial foreign MNE, which have settled in Italy the higher number of investments, are the American Apollo Global Management and the English 3I Group. The first one has acquired the logistics branch of TNT, calling it Ceva Logistics, reaching the 20% of the Italian market in the publishing distribution (Federtrasporto-Nomisma, 2009). The second one has made almost all the investments in Lombardy, acquiring different firms supplying storage, transport and other logistics services.

The investments of the manufacturing MNE are more distributed among the different logistics sub-industries, but again the NACE I63.4 code prevails. These investments are often the result of a spin-off of the industrial firms' internal logistics division and are generally motivated by the search of scale economies, while maintaining the direct control over the logistics function. For example, the Swedish Electrolux controls Electrolux Logistics Italy SpA and other firms, which offer forwarding and handling and storage activities. Two German MNE's in foods (Dr. August Oetker Kg and Theobald Mueller Ag) and the Switzerland Nestlè have made several investments mainly in the NACE 63 industry but also in maritime and freight road transport.

Instead, the FDI of the energy extraction, production and distribution firms are concentrated on road transport and cargo handling and storage. They are driven by the necessity to better control the right management of its products' flows (especially, in terms of security), to reach scale benefits and to reduce transaction costs. The bigger MNE operating in the Italian logistics industry is the Kuwait Petroleum.

The conglomerate integration in the last years is spreading both in Italy and in the global scenario. According to Federtrasporto-Nomisma (2008), the FDI undertaken by financial investors or firms belonging to other industries have grown 12.6% in 2005, 20.6% in 2006, and 23% in 2007.

A cause of the high level of heterogeneity of the logistics sector, it is interesting to make an analysis of the distribution of the different integration strategies among each sub-industry of the acquired firms (Figure 9). The largest part of the investments in the courier sector is of the horizontal type. In fact the liberalization of the postal activities has fostered an increasing concentration process of the couriers in a small number of operators. These are pushed by competitive issues (in particular, defending the market share from the American couriers such as UPS and Federal Express), efficiency considerations and by the aim to develop IT systems and achieve high brand awareness. The two bigger European operators – the Dutch TNT Post Group (TPG) and the German Deutsche Post – have penetrated the Italian market, achieving, respectively, the 14% and the 6% of the first ten global players' total inward FDI (Maggi and Mariotti, 2010). In the Italian couriers sub-industry in the period of analysis, no vertical integrations have been undertaken.

Figure 9 also shows that the NACE I.63 sub-industries present a similar distribution of the three different types of strategies. The horizontal integration prevails, while the percentage of vertical integration is very similar to the percentage of conglomerate integration. The only exception regards the cargo handling and storage, in which the higher number of investments (49%) comes from non-logistics industries (CI).

Referring to transport sectors, the rate of horizontal investments is very high both in maritime and rail transport. This reflects the growing concentration process which recently has characterized the global market, allowing the participating firms to reap benefits of scale, competitive advantages (Shepperd and Seidman, 2001; Fan *et al.*, 2001; Oum *et al.*, 2002) and efficient gains, sharing the high fixed costs among big transport volumes. The percentage of horizontal integrations is instead lower in the other transport modes: in road transport and especially in inland water and pipeline transport the conglomerate investments are consistent.

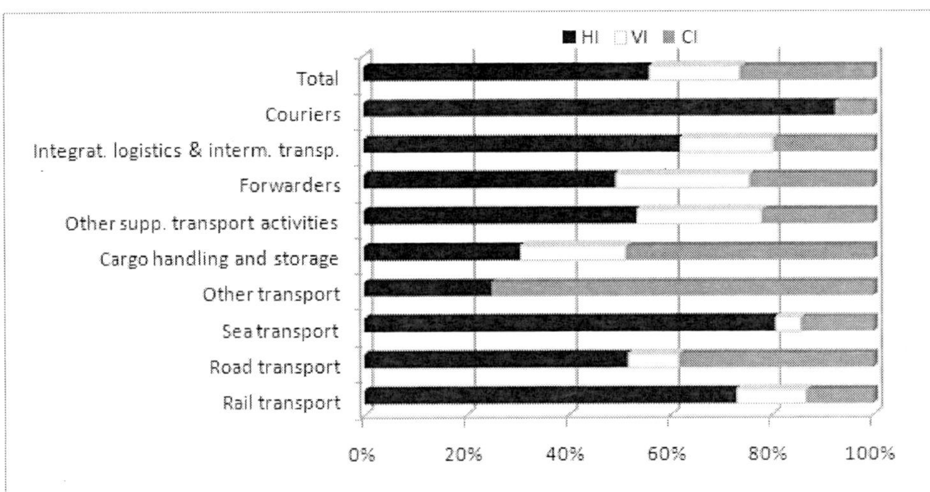

Source: our elaborations on LogINT database, LabELT, 2010.

Figure 9. The distribution of the different types of integration by the acquired industries (data in percentage).

4. The Effects of Manufacturing Internationalisation on Logistics Employment

4.1. Conceptual Framework

The internationalization strategies undertaken by the manufacturing industry highly impact on the logistics activities, as stated in the Introduction. The expansion into large international markets brings about not only more supervision, coordination and control over geographical-dispersed activities, but also the extension of activities and functions that are generally centralized at the headquarters level such as logistics, research and development, marketing, etc. (Blomström *et al.*, 1997). Specifically, the impacts of the different internationalization strategies (trade, cooperation agreements and FDI) on the logistics industry can be summarized as follows (for a detailed review, see Elia *et al.*, 2011).

Firstly (a), an increasing large share of goods and people flows must be managed by transport and other logistics functions. These flows are composed by: (i) the import and export of intermediate and final goods; (ii) the movements of intermediate goods being transferred from one country to another in order to be processed; (iii) the flows of goods and people between the different production and distribution foreign affiliates of the MNEs. Specifically, as concern this last point, when a MNE undertakes a vertical FDI, it tends to transfer to the host country semi-manufactured products, which will be re-imported in the home country. This increaseas the flows of goods. An impact on the logistics services may also be generated by a horizontal FDI because the MNE replace the whole production cycle in a foreign country. They might continue to buy the raw materials or intermediate goods by the same suppliers located in the home countries, thus extending logistics activities. Secondly (b), the need to connect very distant locations and the high number of input and output markets have increased the complexity of the logistics system and have extended the procurement, production and distribution networks leading to a rationalization of the logistics nodes (ECMT, 1996).

These two impacts (a, b) increase the demand for logistics services, causing two additional effects (c, d). The logistics industry is restructuring (c): the logistics firms are becoming larger and are changing their supply, offering an increasing number of "integrated" and high value-added services, able to manage the entire supply chain or a significant part of it (Brewer *et al.*, 2001).

Finally, the labor demand of workers specialized in planning, managing and controlling the logistics activities is increasing (d).

The effects of internationalization on the logistics employment are closely related to the way in which the logistics services are managed. Furthermore, the type of sale and purchase carriage contracts that has been adopted by the manufacturing firms towards foreign customers and suppliers. As well as the relationship of complementarily or substitution among the different internationalization strategies.

As regards the first issue, the effect on employment may occur either within the internationalized manufacturing firm in several ways. When logistics is managed in-sourcing, or within the logistics suppliers, when logistics is outsourced, or both at the manufacturing firm and its logistics suppliers, in case of co-sourcing (joint management of logistics services).

As far as the contracts are concerned, it is expected a higher positive impact on labor demand when a firm adopts the cost, insurance and freight (CIF) sale contract and the free on board (FOB) purchase contract. The CIF sale contract, actually, implies the need to transport the output from the firm's establishment to the customer's production or distributive units, in other words in this case transportation is to the firm's charge. The FOB purchase contract implies that the firm has to manage the handling of the suppliers' raw material, semi-components or manufactured products. In both cases, therefore, it is the manufacturing firm to manage logistics, thus inducing an increase of the logistics services' labor demand. Opposite results can be found when the sale contract is FOB and the purchase contract is CIF.

A final issue that must be taken into account concerns the relationship of complementarily and substitution that might occur among the three internationalization strategies (for a detailed overview see Aitken *et al.*, 1994). Specifically, the literature mainly focuses on the relationship between trade and cooperation agreements or trade and FDIs. Generally, when production segments are moved towards low-wage countries (vertical FDIs or cooperation agreements), an increase of the flows of goods occurs; therefore, the strategies are complementary. When, instead, a FDI is undertaken in an industrialized foreign country (horizontal FDI), in order to reproduce the production cycle of the parent company, it generally substitutes export[13]. In the first case, the effect of internationalization on the logistics' employment is amplified, because of the increasing temporary export and import flows. In the second case, the impact on logistics is negative since the goods that were previously exported are now produced directly in the host country.

4.2. Empirical Evidence

Several theoretical and empirical studies focus on the impact of manufacturing internationalization on the home country (the country from where FDI depart) and on the host country (the country receiving the FDI) (among the others, Dunning and Lundan, 2008; Molnar *et al.*, 2007; Barba Navaretti and Venables, 2004; Castellani *et al.*, 2008). These studies analyze the impact of internationalization on employment, productivity, innovation, etc., and the majority of the works focus on the manufacturing sector. At least to our knowledge, the scanty literature specifically dedicated to the effects of manufacturing internationalization on logistics refers to the home country and analyzes the impact on the logistics labor market. The present section presents the main findings of the literature on the impact on the total labor market at home country level; then a focus is placed to the studies specifically dedicated to the logistics labor market.

In contrast with the general public view, the main findings of the works focusing on the effects of internationalization on the OECD countries show that the impact on aggregate labor market is small and the domestic job losses are slight, although particular skill and occupational groups (especially low skill level) have been affected more strongly (Crinò, 2009; Barry and Walsh, 2008).

[13] More precisely, a part of the literature highlights that, even if the international production replaces exports, the investment may increase the export opportunities of correlated products or the same final products from the country of the investment towards other foreign countries (Cantwell, 1994).

It is possible to identify three different strands of literature analyzing separately the impact of trade, cooperation agreements and FDI on labor demand. As concerns the trade literature, many studies focus on the employment and wage impact on a national scale, generally finding changes in the labor composition (high skilled and low skilled workers). Furthermore, in some circumstances, a decline in the relative demand for low skilled employees, especially in the industries facing import competition (Krugman *et al.*, 1995, Addison *et al.*, 2000) has been highlighted. Nevertheless, recent studies stress that while the effect of increased imports on jobs is generally negative and the impact of increased export is positive, the overall effects of increased trade are positive (Kletzer, 2002). In particular, trade has had no significant effect on the overall unemployment rate of the OECD countries (Hill *et al.*, 2008). Conversely, the few studies on the regional scale highlight that the magnitude of trade's impact on the labor markets remains widely contrasting (Richardson, 1995; Kapstein, 2000). Indeed, the effects of export growth on the employment tend to be mixed, either positive or negative, depending on different regional characteristics and dynamics, such as the regional size, the industrial structure and the trade patterns (Baldwin and Brown, 2004; Leichenko and Silva, 2004; Markusen *et al.*, 1991).

The literature on cooperation agreements stresses the impact on the national employment, mainly focusing on its composition and wage level. For example, a study on two European Countries (Italy and Germany) (Helg and Tajoli, 2005) estimates that, during the 1990s, this strategy has increased the high skilled-to-low skilled labor ratio in Italy, while it has not affected the German demand for high skilled labor. Egger and Egger (2001), by focusing on cooperation agreements between manufacturing industries of EU and non EU-countries during the period 1995–1997, find that they reduce the skill-to-low-skill ratio in EU exporting industries, while have more ambiguous effects in import-competing industries.

The literature on FDI has mainly investigated the effects on the employment at firm level (Castellani *et al.*, 2008 on the Italian case; Head and Ries, 2002 on the Japanese MNE) or at domestic industry level (Slaughter, 2000 on the USA; Falzoni and Grasseni, 2003 on Italy). Conversely, few studies have focused on the effects on both the internationalized firm and its economic environment, adopting the NUTS2 region or the NUTS3 province as scale of analysis (Mariotti *et al.*, 2003; Elia *et al.*, 2009; Federico and Minerva, 2008). Specifically, Mariotti *et al.* (2003) find that in the period 1985-1995 the Italian FDI have significantly affected the labor intensity of the domestic production at a "regional- industry" scale. This is defined as the ensemble of firms operating in the same industrial macro-industry – composed of interdependent sectors belonging to the same *filière* – and localized in the same geographical region. In particular, the impact is negative for investments undertaken in less developed countries and positive for market-seeking investments in advanced countries.

Elia *et al.* (2009), by adopting the same unit of analysis (regional-industry), investigate the impact of outward FDI upon the demand for high and low skilled workers in Italy throughout the period 1996-2002. It results that all outward FDI - regardless of the country of destination - have significant negative effects on the demand for low skilled workers. Outward FDI towards OECD countries instead negatively affect the demand for high skilled workers. Federico and Minerva (2008), who assess the impact of Italy's outward FDI on local employment growth in 1996-2001 for 12 manufacturing industries and 103 administrative provinces, find that net effect of FDI on the employment of the whole local area is positive. Employment growth in local areas investing more abroad appears to be stronger than the industry average, especially in some sectors.

To our knowledge, only Mariotti and Piscitello (2007) devote attention to the effects on the tertiary sector, by investigating the impact of the manufacturing FDI on the labor demand for services between 1996 and 2003 in the industrial districts of Veneto region in the North-East of Italy. The finding is that the more internationally involved an industrial district, the higher the employment growth in the service sector.

The literature concerning the specific impact of manufacturing firms internationalization on the logistics industry is even more scarce. The increasing large share of goods flows, fostered by internationalization, must be managed by transport functions at the level of the manufacturing firm and the transport providers. In the first case, when transport is carried out by the manufacturing firm (insourcing), there is a rise of the labor demand for workers specialized in planning, managing and controlling the transport activities. In the second case, that is when transport is outsourced, the transport operators restructure themselves becoming larger and changing into 3PLs or 4PLs, by modifying their supply from single based services into an increasing number of high value-added services (Brewer *et al.*, 2001).

Only in the second case it is possible to observe an increase of labor demand in the transport industry, which is the object of analysis of the present section. In fact, while the rate of outsourcing of integrated logistics as a whole is very low within the Italian boundaries (13% in 1997 and 16% in 2004 - Commission Européene, 2001), the transportation is outsourced by the majority of the Italian manufacturing firms that go international through one of the three forms identified above, i.e. trade, cooperation agreements and FDI (Confetra, 2002).

To our knowledge, in literature there are only three papers providing some evidences on the impact of internationalization on transport services. The first one (Savona and Schiattarella, 2004) investigates the impact of cooperation agreements, measured by a specific index based on trade data, on different services' labor demand within the Italian NUTS3 provinces over the period 1991-1996. The authors conclude that internationalization towards low wage countries shows a positive significant impact on the more traditional services' employment, such as transport.

The second paper (Maggi *et al.*, 2008) provides evidence on the relationship between FDI and the employment change in the logistics industries, in the Veneto industrial districts between 1996 and 2003. Results show that, although all the internationalized industrial districts exhibit an increase in the logistics labor demand, only in a few of them an internationalization degree above the average is positively correlated to a logistics' employment growth.

Finally, the third paper (Elia *et al.*, 2011), written by the authors, deals with the impact of manufacturing internationalization on the transport industry employment, as it will better explained in the following section.

4.2.1. The Effects of Manufacturing Internationalization on the Italian "Regional Industry"

The work by Elia *et al.* (2011) investigates the effects of manufacturing internationalization (international trade, cooperation agreements and FDI) on the transport industry employment at the regional-industry level in the period 1996-2001. The "regional industry" is defined as the ensemble of firms operating in the same transport sector and localized in the same geographical NUTS2 region (8 transport sub-sectors and 20 regions)

(Table 5). This is the first empirical work, to our knowledge, considering all three internationalization strategies, and testing their specific impact on transport employment through an econometric analysis at the regional scale.

Table 5. Italian NUTS2 regions and the NACE transport sub-sectors

Regions	Transport sub-sectors	NACE Codes
Abruzzo	Land transport; transport via pipelines	60
Basilicata	Transport via railway	60.10.1
Calabria	Auxiliary activities to transport via railway	60.10.2
Campania	Transport by road	60.25.0
Emilia Romagna	Water transport	61
Friuli Venezia Giulia	Sea transport	61.11.0
Lazio	Air transport	62
Liguria	Non-scheduled air transport	62.20.0
Lombardia	Supporting and auxiliary transport activities; activities of travel agencies	63
Marche	Cargo handling – Air transport	63.11.1
Molise	Cargo handling – Water transport	63.11.2
Piemonte	Cargo handling – Land transport	63.11.3
Puglia		
Sardegna		
Sicilia		
Toscana		
Trentino Alto Adige		
Umbria		
Valle d'Aosta		
Veneto		

Source: Elia *et al.* (2011).

The main hypothesis tested by Elia *et al.* (2011) is that manufacturing internationalization, inducing a high increase of goods flows to be moved, implies a reorganization of the supply chain. This leads the manufacturing firm to outsource transport service to special operators, which tend to be closely located. The geographical proximity has, indeed, a strong influence on the selection of the transport suppliers (Hong, 2007).

Data on the transport industry employment come from the Italian Statistical Institute (ISTAT) and refer to the NACE "I – Transport, warehousing, communications" category (Table 4). Data on trade and cooperation agreements come from the Italian Trade dataset (Coeweb) provided by ISTAT, and refer to kilograms by transportation modes. Data concerns the years 1996 and 2001 and are expressed in terms of difference. Finally, data on the Italian outward FDI come from the Reprint dataset. Summarizing, the descriptive statistics underlines that the most internationalized geographical areas, i.e. North-West (Piedmont, Valle d'Aosta, Liguria, Lombardy) and North-East (Emilia Romagna, Veneto, Trentino Alto Adige, Friuli Venezia Giulia), report the highest employment growth (Figure 10), especially as regards transport by road because the majority of the flows are addressed to (or come from) Europe.

However, in order to understand more punctually the relationship between each form of internationalization and the variation of employment in transport industry, Elia *et al.* (2011) carried out a WLS (weighted least square) estimation. Their estimation suggests that the demand for transport workers between 1996 and 2001 within a region is related to: (i) growth rate of the manufacturing production value added, (ii) export and import growth rate, (iii) IPT and OPT growth rate and (iv) the cumulated sum of the manufacturing FDI undertaken in 1994-2000.

The model shows that manufacturing production is not significant for the transport industries' labour demand . This might be due to the fact that most of Italian firms are SME, which mainly produce for local market. As a consequence they are more likely to manage transportation inside (insourcing), since they have to transfer small-medium volumes of freight and have to cover short-medium distances (Confetra, 2002). Besides, the positive impact of FDI and export on the logistics employment occurs mainly because of the increase of goods and people flows, the logistics system's complexity, and the geographical extension of logistics networks. Moreover, the increase in the transport-logistics employment may be found in the characteristics of the internationalized firms, which are larger than domestic uni-national firms (Barba Navaretti and Venables; Castellani and Zanfei, 2006; Brouwer and Mariotti, 2009).

Besides, a negative relationship between import and employment in transport industry occurs; this may be related to the fact that the imports of goods towards Italy are more likely to be managed by foreign suppliers (Confetra, 2002), thus generating a substitution effect. In other words, the increase of import may be partially related to a substitution of national goods with foreign goods. Considering that national goods are mainly transported by national firms while foreign goods are transported by foreign firms, the substitution of national goods with foreign goods is likely to generate a decrease of labour demand in national transport industry and an increase of labour demand in foreign transport industries.

As regards the IPT and OPT components (proxies of the cooperation agreement strategy), the former has a significant positive effect on the labour demand, and the latter shows a negative impact, even if very weak and often not significant. These results can be explained as follows. For the IPT the positive sign reveals that transportation of intermediate and unfinished goods is mainly undertaken by Italian firms, which temporary import raw material and/or semi-components to be processed in Italy and later re-export the processed goods abroad. The opposite is true when the Italian firms send the intermediate goods abroad to be processed, i.e. in case of OPT. Indeed, the negative signs of temporary export and re-import suggest that transportation is still managed by the firms of the country where the intermediate goods are processed. The final impact of OPT is, however, not very significant probably because there is not a substitution effect. Indeed, when firms do not internationalise through OPT, goods are entirely produced by the Italian firms and, hence, transport of intermediate goods abroad are not required. Conversely, when the OPT process starts, the production is fragmented generating a new flow of goods (managed by foreign firms) that did not exist before. Therefore, the final impact on the transport industry employment is not (or not very much) significant. The same consideration holds for the strong positive impact of IPT: after starting IPT, a new flow of goods that did not exist before takes place by generating a labour demand in national transport industry.

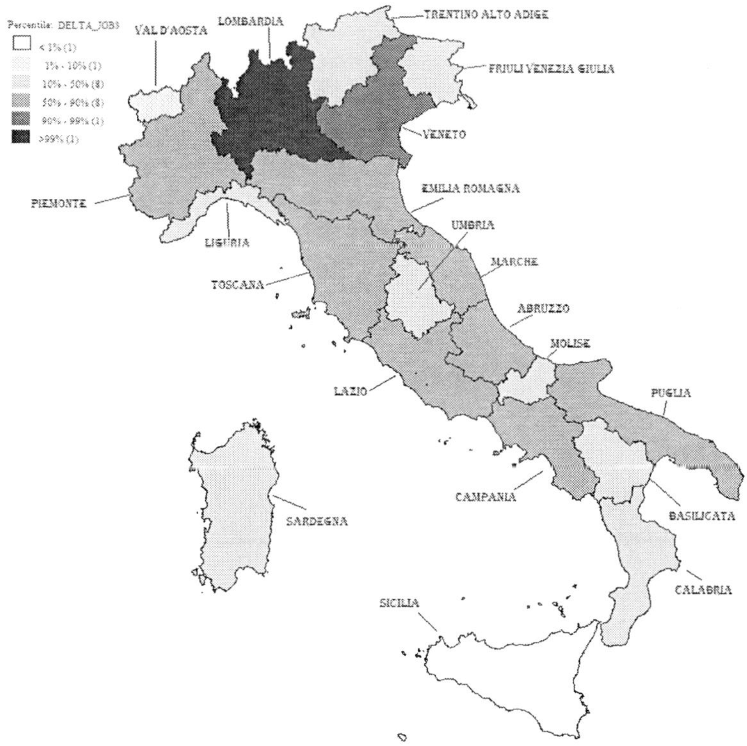

Percentile	Observations	Value of Delta Jobs
<1%	1	N<0
1% - 10%	1	0<=N<200
10% - 50%	8	200<=N<1,600
50 % – 90 %	8	1,600<=N<8,000
90 %- 99 %	1	8,000<=N<15,000
> 99%	1	N>15,000

Source: Elia *et al.* (2011).

Figure 10. Distribution of total employment variation of the transport sub-industries occurred between 1996 and 2001 in Italian regions.

5. Conclusion

The globalization of the economy, together with the consumer oriented economy, the internet-based information systems, the fall of transport costs, the European Traffic Policy, have fostered an increasing demand for logistics activities. Within a country, the demand can be either satisfied locally, by national firms, or by foreign firms, which entry into the country by specific internationalization strategies.

In Italy, the logistics demand growth and a very high fragmentation of the logistics industry, which mainly operates in transport and in other low value added services, have attracted an increasing number of global players, mainly coming from western Europe. These players have acquired high market shares in the logistics activities which are more involved in globalization, i.e. forwarding, couriers and services managed by the 3PL and 4PL. According to the LogINT database, in 2010 the number of inward FDI is 372, which have been undertaken by 230 foreign MNE coming from western Europe (72.8%). The inward FDI result from the horizontal, vertical or conglomerate integration strategies. Specifically, the HI accounts for 56% of the FDI, while VI and CH account for 26% and 18%, respectively. When compared to other industrialized countries, Italy shows a poor attractiveness to inward FDI. This is mainly caused by the lower quality of the supply of localization factors and external economies.

The demand for logistics has also been increased by the internationalization of the Italian manufacturing firms, which have fostered the internationalization of the most innovative Italian logistics operators. These logistics firms started investing in the same foreign areas of their customers choosing the so-called "follow the customer" strategy. In 2010, 165 Italian MNE have undertaken 817 outward FDI mainly towards western Europe (45%) and Central East Europe (16%). Nevertheless, the ratio of Italian outward FDI on GDP is still very low, especially in comparison with other neighboring European countries.

The literature investigating the increasing logistics demand induced by the manufacturing internationalization is rather scanty. The studies mainly focus on the manufacturing industry, while little evidence is provided on logistics. In Italy, only two studies have been carried out on this topic. Specifically, the work by Elia *et al.* (2011) highlights that the transport industry in 1996-200,1 gains jobs in case of export, FDI and IPT while the opposite is true in case of import and OPT.

Since the literature focusing on the issues analyzed in the present chapter (outward and inward FDI in the Italian logistics industry; strategies and motivations driving the location choices of foreign FDI in Italy; the effects of manufacturing internationalization on logistics employment) is rather scanty, the present chapter aims to fill this gap in literature and puts forward the following policy recommendations.

As concerns the low attractiveness of Italy, investments in ICT and transport infrastructural quality and, more in general, investment fostering the localization factors and the external economies supply, are advocated. Moreover, the capitalization system must become more based on the financial organizations and less on the family capitals, falling the entry barriers in the Italian industry.

Referring to the issue: "Italy as a multinational follower" (low rate of outward FDI), policies aiming to encourage the firms to become bigger and to support the Italian companies' internationalization strategies are recommended.

The analysis of the integration strategies, and the related motivations has showed that the investments are more concentrated in the same parent MNE's logistics sub-industry (horizontal integration), even if the conglomerate integrations are quickly growing in the last years. The main motivations behind integration strategies are found in: increasing and defending market, reaching economies of scale and scope and investing the capital in profitable activities. These results allow to highlight that Italy is, thanks to its barycentric position, an interesting market where foreign players may consolidate their market powers, while rising efficiency improvement for their core products. Consequently, Italian manufacturing firms can create an advantage by a more efficient logistics, which is supplied by the foreign logistics providers. This consideration reinforces the positive impact of an high level of attractiveness of inward FDI.

On the other side, the foreign MNE may create a crowding up effect with respect to the Italian small firms, which may be forced to a progressive closing down. As a consequence, policies helping these firms to grow and to innovate can foster the competitiveness and the survival of the Italian logistics industry.

The results of the analysis on the impact of manufacturing internationalization on the transport employment are very interesting in terms of policy implications. Internationalization, at least as concerns export, FDI and IPT, allows an extension of the transport services' demand and, therefore, an increase of the transport providers' potential market. This means that when transport becomes more complex and strategic manufacturing firms tend to outsource the freight movements to specialized suppliers which can reach economies of scale and scope. Therefore, the logistics industry gains in terms of employment and competitiveness. As a consequence, in order to satisfy the growing transport demand, there is a strong need to develop policies able to remove the existing obstacles that limit the development of the transport industry in Italy. We refer to the inefficient and insufficient transport networks and the lack of culture about logistics within the Italian SME.

Investments in transport labor formation, specifically, at the scholar level, may be useful in order to improve the logistics firms competitiveness. Furthermore, policies aiming at increasing the rate of transport outsourcing in Italy, such as the recent edition of the National Plan of Logistics (Ministero delle Infrastrutture e dei Trasporti, 2011) suggests, may be able to better exploit the opportunities offered by the manufacturing internationalization process to the transport labor market.

However, the growth of the road transport produces significant negative externalities affecting the environment. Thus, specific policies aiming, from one side, to reduce those externalities and on the other side, to promote environmentally friendly transport modes and logistics organization, are advocated. For example, in order to gain competitiveness, the reliability of rail and road-rail combined transport should be improved by eliminating the bottlenecks and investing in infrastructure (railways and terminal). Also the maritime transport, which – as shown – is indeed positively affected by internationalization, should be promoted, by improving the efficiency of ports, reducing the duration of the duty controls and the level of bureaucracy.

REFERENCES

Addison, J.T., Douglas, A.F. and Ruhm C.J. (2000). Technology, Trade Sensitivity, and Labor Displacement. *Southern Economic Journal* 66(3): 682-699.

Agarwal, S., and Ramaswami, S. (1992). Choice of foreign entry mode: impact of ownership, location, and interalization factors. *Journal of International Business Studies* 23: 1-27.

Aitken, B., Hanson, G.H., and Harrison, A.E. (1994). Spillovers, foreign direct investment and export behavior. *NBER working paper*, N° 4927.

Anderson, E., and Gatignon, H. (1986). Modes of foreign entry: a transaction cost analysis and proposition. *Journal of International Business Studies* 17: 1-16.

Arndt, S.W., and Kierzhowsky, H. (2001). *Fragmentation. New Production Patterns in the World Economy*. Oxford: Oxford University Press.

Baldone, S., Sdogati, F., and Tajoli, L. (2002). Moving to Central-Eastern Europe: International Fragmentation of Production and Competitiveness of the European Textile and Apparel Industry. In Baldone S., Sdogati F., and Tajoli L. (Eds), *EU Enlargement to the CEEs: Trade Competition, Delocalisation of Production, and Effects on the Economies of the Union*, pp.101-160. Milan: FrancoAngeli.

Baldone, S., Sdogati, F., and Tajoli, L. (2006). On some effects of international fragmentation of production on comparative advantages, trade flows, and the income of countries. *CESPRI working paper*, n.187, Milan.

Baldwin, J.R., and Brown, W. M. (2004). Regional manufacturing employment volatility in Canada: The effects of specialization and trade. *Regional Science* 83: 519-541.

Barry, F. , and Walsh, F. (2008). Gains and losses from sectoral relocation: A review of theory and empirics. *Structural Change and Economic Dynamics,* 19: 4-16.

Barba Navaretti, G., and Venables, A.J. (2004) *Multinational firms in the world economy*. Princeton: Princeton University Press.

Basile, R., Benfratello, L., and Castellani, D. (2005). Attracting Foreign Direct Investments in Europe: are Italian Regions Doomed?, *Development studies working papers*, n. 200. Milan: Centro Studi d'Agliano.

Bianchi, M., Bianco, M., Giacomelli, S., Pacces, A.M. , and Trento, S. (2005). *Proprietà e controllo delle imprese in Italia*. Bologna: Il Mulino.

Blomström, M., Fors, G., and Lipsey, R.E. (1997). Foreign direct investment and employment: home country experience in the United States and Sweden. *The Economic Journal* 445(107): 1787-1797.

Brewer, A.M., Button, K.J., and Hensher, D.A. (2001). (Eds) *Handbook of logistics* and *supply-chain management*. Amsterdam: Pergamon.

Brouwer, A., and Mariotti, I. (2009). Evaluating firms' ownership differences using propensity score estimation and discrete choice modelling. The case of the logistics sector in Italy. *49° Congress of the European Regional Science Association* (ERSA), 25–29 August, Łódź, Poland.

Buckley, P. , and Casson M. (1976). *The Future of the Multinational Enterprise*. New York: Homles and Meier.

Cantwell, J. (1994). The Relationship between International Trade and International Production. In Greenway D. , and Winters L.A. (Eds), *Surveys in International Trade*, 303-328. Oxford: Blackwell.

Capron, L. (1999). The long-term performance of horizontal acquisitions. *Strategic Management Journal* 20: 987-1018.

Carbone, V. , and Stone, M.A. (2005). Growth and relational strategies used by the European logistics service providers: Rationale and outcomes. *Transportation Research Part E* 41: 495-510.

Castellani, D., Mariotti, I., and Piscitello, L. (2008). The impact of outward investments on parent company's employment and skill composition. Evidence from the Italian case. *Structural Change and Economic Dynamics* 19(1): 81-94.

Castellani, D., and Zanfei, A. (2006) *Multinational firms, Innovation and productivity*. USA: Edward Elgar.

Chang, S.J., and Rosenzweig, P.M. (2001). The Choice of Entry Mode in Sequential Foreign Direct Investment. *Strategic Management Journal* 22(8): 747-776.

Chiarvesio, M., Di Maria, E. , and Micelli, S. (2003). Processi di internazionalizzazione e strategie delle imprese distrettuali. *Economia e Società Regionale*, 1.

Commission Européenne (2001). *Impact des NTIC sur la logistique des enterprises commerciales*, Rapport final. Bruxelles: DG Entreprise.

Confetra (2002). *La fattura Italia dei servizi logistici*, Quaderno N° 98/2. Milan: Centro Studi Confetra.

Corò, G., Tattara, G., and Volpe, M. (2006) (Eds.). *Andarsene per continuare a crescere. La delocalizzazione internazionale come strategia competitiva.* Roma: Carocci.

Cruijssen, F., Martine Cools, M. , and Dullaert, W. (2007). Horizontal cooperation in logistics: opportunities and impediments. *Transportation Research – Part E* 43:129–142.

Crinò, R. (2009). Offshoring, multinationals and labour market: a review of the empirical literature. *Journal of Economic Surveys* 23(2): 197–249.

Dörrenbächer, C. (2003). *Corporate reorganisation in the European transport and logistic sector in the 1990s: diversification, internationalisation and integration.* Mnster, Lit.

Dunning, J.H. (1988). *Explaining International Production.* London: Unwin Hyman.

Dunning, J. H. , and Lundan, S. (2008). *Multinational enterprises and the global economy*, 2nd ed. Cheltenham: Edward Elgar.

ECMT (1996). *Polarisation of European logistical areas and new trends in logistics*. Paris: ECMT.

Egger, H., and Egger, P. (2001). Cross-border sourcing and outward processing in EU manufacturing. *The North American Journal of Economics and Finance* 12(3): 243-256.

Elia, S., Mariotti, I., and Piscitello, L. (2009). The impact of outward FDI on the home country's labour demand and skill composition. *International Business Review* 18: 357–372.

Elia S., Maggi E., and Mariotti I. (2011). Does the transport sector gain from manufacturing internationalisation? An empirical investigation on the Italian regions. *European Transport –Trasporti Europei*, forthcoming.

Eurostat and European Commission (2008). *NACE Rev. 2 Statistical classification of economic activities in the European Community*. Luxembourg: Office for Official Publications of the European Communities.

Falzoni, A.M. , and Grasseni, M. (2003). *Outward FDI and skill upgrading in the Italian labor market.* Paper presented at AIEL, 23rd Convegno Nazionale di Economia del Lavoro, Messina, 25–26 September.

Fan, T., Vigeant-Langlois, L., Geissler, C., Bosler, B., and Wilmking, J.(2001). Evolution of global airline strategic alliance and consolidation in the twenty-first century. *Journal of Air Transport Management* 7(6): 349–360.

Federico, S. , and Minerva, G.A. (2008). Outward FDI and Local Employment Growth in Italy. *Review of World Economics* 144(2), 295-324.

Federtrasporto-Nomisma (2006). *Scenari dei trasporti. L'internazionalizzazione del trasporto: la posizione dell'impresa italiana.* Quaderno n. 8, Rome.

Federtrasporto-Nomisma (2007). *Scenari dei trasporti. L'internazionalizzazione del trasporto: la posizione dell'impresa italiana.* Quaderno n. 9, Rome.

Federtrasporto-Nomisma (2008). *Scenari dei trasporti. L'internazionalizzazione del trasporto: la posizione dell'impresa italiana.* Quaderno n. 10, Rome.

Federtrasporto-Nomisma (2009). *Scenari dei trasporti. L'internazionalizzazione del trasporto: la posizione dell'impresa italiana.* Quaderno n. 11, Rome.

Federtrasporto-Nomisma (2010). *Scenari dei trasporti. L'internazionalizzazione del trasporto: la posizione dell'impresa italiana.* Quaderno n. 12, Rome.

Glaeser, E.L. , and Kohlhase, J.E. (2004). Cities, regions and the decline of transport costs. *Papers in Regional Science* 83: 197–228.

Goldman, E., and Gorton, G. (2000). *The Visible Hand, The Invisible Hand and Efficiency.* Working paper 05. Wharton Financial Institution Center.

Gorton, G., Kahl, M. , and Rosen, R. (1998). *Eat or Be Eaten: A Theory of Mergers and Merger Waves.* University of Pennsylvania.

Gunasekaran, A., and Ngai, E. (2004) Information systems in supply chain integration and management. *European Journal of Operational Research*, 159(2): 269–295.

Häkkinen, L., Norrman, A., Himola, O.P. , and Ojala L. (2004). Logistics Integration in Horizontal Mergers and Acquisitions. *The International Journal of Logistics Management*, 15/1: 27-42.

Haleblian, J. , and Finkelstein, S. (1999). The influence of organisational acquisition experience on acquisition performance: a behavioural learning perspective. *Administrative Science Quarterly* 44(1): 29-56.

Head, K., and Ries, J. (2002). Offshore production and skill upgrading by Japanese manufacturing firms. *Journal of International Economics* 1: 81–105.

Heaver, T.D. (1996). *The opportunity and the challenges for shipping lines in international logistics.* World Logistics Conference, London, UK.

Helg, R. , and Tajoli, L. (2005). Patterns of international fragmentation of production and the relative demand for labor. *North American Journal of Economics and Finance* 16: 233-254.

Hennart, J.F. (1982). *The Theory of the Multinational Enterprise*, University of Michigan Press, Ann Arbor, MI.

Hijzen, A., Görg, H. , and Manchin, M. (2008). Cross-Border Mergers and Acquisitions and the Role of Trade Costs. *European Economic Review* 52: 849-866.

Hill, S., Lesher, M. , and Nordås, H.K. (2008). *Trade and Labour Market Adjustments.* OECD Trade Policy Working Papers, No. 64, OECD Publishing.

Ietto-Gillies G. (2005). *Transnational Corporations and International Production, Concepts, Theories and Effects.* Cheltenham: Edward Elgar.

ISTAT (2007). *Statistiche dei trasporti.* Roma: ISTAT.

Kapstein, E.B. (2000). Winners and Losers in the Global Economy. *International Organization* 54(2): 359-384.

Kim, WC. , and Hwang, P. (1992). Global strategy and multinationals' entry mode choice. *Journal of International Business Studies* 23: 29-53.

Kletzer, L.G. (2002). *Imports, Exports, and Jobs. What Does Trade Mean for Employment and Job Loss?.* W.E. Upjohn Institute for Employment Research. Kalamazoo, Michigan.

Kogut, B. (1988). Joint ventures: theoretical and empirical perspectives. *Strategic Management Journal.* 9: 319–332.

Krugman, P., Cooper, R.N. , and Srinivasan, T.N. (1995). *Growing World Trade: Causes and Consequences.* Brookings Papers on Economic Activity, (1), 25th Anniversary Issue, pp. 327-377.

Leichenko, R.M. , and Silva, J. (2004). International Trade, Employment and Earnings: Evidence from US Rural Counties. *Regional Studies* 38(4): 355-374.

Levinson, M.(2006). *The Box: How the Shipping Container Made the World Smaller and the World Economy Bigger.* Princeton University Press.

Maggi, E., Mariotti, I. , and Boscacci, F. (2008). The indirect effects of manufacturing internationalization on logistics. A focus on the industrial districts of Veneto. *International Journal of Logistics Economics and Globalisation* 1(2): 205-224.

Maggi, E., and Mariotti, I. (2010). Logistics FDI in Italy: integration strategies and motivations. *European Transport Research Review* 2: 13–24.

Mariotti, I. , and Montagnana, S. (2008). Italian investments in the agglomeration of Timisoara in Romania: threat or opportunity for the economic development? *Romanian Journal of Regional Science* 2(2): 33-51.

Mariotti, I. (2005). The internationalisation strategies of Italian district SMEs". In Wever E., van Vilsteren G. (Eds), *Borders and economic behaviour in Europe; a geographical approach* (pp. 25-42). Assen, The Netherlands: Royal Van Gorcum.

Mariotti, I. , and Piscitello, L. (2007). The impact of outward FDI on local employment. Evidence from the Italian case. In Arauzo M., Liviano D. and Martín M. (Eds) *Entrepreneurship, Economic Growth and Industrial Location* (pp. 299-320). London: Edward Elgar.

Mariotti, S., Mutinelli, M. , and Piscitello, L. (2003). Home country employment and foreign direct investment: evidence from the Italian case. *Cambridge Journal of Economics* 27, 419-431.

Mariotti, S., and Mutinelli, M. (2009). *Italia multinazionale 2008.* Rubbettino, Soveria Mannelli Catanzaro.

Mariotti S. , and Piscitello L. (1995). Information Costs and Location of FDIs within the Host Country: empirical evidence from Italy. *Journal of International Business Studies*, fourth quarter: 815-841.

Markusen, A.R., Noponen, H., and Driessen, K. (1991). International trade, productivity and US regional job growth: a shift-share interpretation. *International Regional Science Review* 14: 15–39.

Molnar, M., Pain, N., and Taglioni, D. (2007). *The internationalisation of production, international outsourcing and employment in the OECD*, ECO/WKP(2007)21. Paris: OECD.

Ministero delle Infrastrutture e dei Trasporti (2011). *Linee strategiche per l'attuazione del Piano Nazionale della Logistica*, Rome.

Notteboom, T. (2007). Strategic challenges to container ports in a changing market environment. *Devolution, Port Governance and Port Performance Research in Transportation Economics* 17: 29–52.

OECD (1997). *Economic Globalisation and the Environment.* Paris: OECD.

Ojala, L. (1993). Changing logistics patterns and policies in Northern Europe. *The International Journal of Logistics Management* 4(2): 25-40.

Oum, T., Park, J.H., Kim, K. , and Yu, C. (2002). The effect of horizontal alliances on firm productivity and profitability: evidence from the global airline industry. *Journal of Business Research* 854: 1–10.

Plehwe, D., and Bohle, D. (1998). *Uberlegungen zum forschungsfeld transnationale organisation in Europa*. Berlin: WZB-Social Science Research Center.

Richardson, J.D. (1995). Income inequality and trade: how to think, what to conclude. *Journal of Economics Perspectives* 9: 33–55.

Savona, M. , and Schiattarella, R. (2004). International relocation of production and the growth of services: the case of the Made in Italy industries. *Transnational Corporations* 13(2): 57-76.

Slaughter, M.J. (2000). Production transfer within multinational enterprises and American wages. *Journal of International Economics* 2: 449–472.

Shepperd, E., and Seidman, D. (2001). Ocean shipping alliances: the wave of the future. *International Journal of Maritime Economics* 3(4): 351–367.

Strasser, S. (1998). Getting and spending: European and American consumer societies in the twentieth century. Cambridge: Cambridge Univ. Press.

UNCTAD (2006). *World Investment Report 2006 – FDI from Developing and Transition Economies: Implications for Development.* Geneva and New York: United Nations.

UNCTAD (2007). *World Investment Report 2007 – Transnational Corporations, Extractive Industries and Development.* Geneva and New York: United Nations.

Yieming, Z., Han Swee, L. , and Seah Kiat, K. (2002). The Third-Party Logistics Services and Globalization of Manufacturing. *International Planning Studies* 7(1): 89-104.

Van de Voorde, E. , and Vanelslander, T. (2009). Market Power and Vertical and Horizontal Integration in the Maritime Shipping and Port Industry. *Discussion Paper 2009-2*, Joint Transport Research Centre, OECD, International Transport Forum.

Vahrenkamp R. (2010). Driving globalization: the rise of logistics in Europe 1950-2000. *European Transport*, n.45, pp.1-14.

Van Veen-Groot D.B., and Nijkamp P. (1999). Globalisation, transport and the environment: new perspectives for ecological economics. *Ecological Economics* 31, 331-346.

Veugelers, R. (2002). M&A and R&D: A Literature Review. In Idea Consult (eds.) *Mergers and Acquisitions and Science and Technology Policy.* Brussels: Idea Consult.

In: Foreign Investment
Editor: Torre DeSare and Daniele Caprioglio
ISBN 978-1-61470-358-7

Chapter 3

LOCAL SOURCING AND THE TECHNOLOGY IMPACT ON SUPPLIERS: COMPARING FDI AND DOMESTIC PRODUCER FIRMS

Jacob A. Jordaan
Department of Economics and Business Administration,
VU University Amsterdam, The Netherlands

ABSTRACT

This study contributes to the literature on externality impacts that foreign direct investment (FDI) can generate among local suppliers in a host economy. Using unique data from several surveys among firms in the manufacturing sector of Nuevo Leon, Mexico, I present novel qualitative and quantitative evidence on the static and dynamic impact of FDI firms on their Mexican suppliers. Importantly, the data allows me to deal with certain issues and questions that previous research has failed to address satisfactory. In particular, the data makes it possible to compare statistically the operations and impacts of both foreign-owned and domestic producer firms, providing an answer to the question that underlies all research on FDI impacts whether foreign-owned firms actually differ in their impacts from domestic firms. I also use data from an objective sample of actual suppliers in the regional economy to identify the impact of producer firms and to assess whether type of ownership of producer firms matters for this impact.

The main findings can be summarized as follows. First, there are only marginal differences between foreign-owned and Mexican producer firms regarding the level of use of local suppliers. As such, this indicates that type of ownership does not affect the static impact of producer firms. Second, I find several indications that the dynamic impact of foreign-owned firms is significantly larger than the impact of domestic producer firms. FDI firms offer several types of support to their suppliers significantly more frequently. This concerns in particular types of technological support, support that has a direct positive impact on production processes of suppliers. Findings from the survey among local suppliers also indicate that the dynamic impact of foreign-owned firms is larger, as there are significantly more firms among suppliers of FDI firms that indicate to have experienced a large positive impact from their business dealings with their client firms. Related to the finding that FDI firms offer more technological support, the suppliers indicate that it is in particular technological support that is important for generating this large impact. A vast majority of suppliers of FDI firms also indicate that they can use support received from a given client firm to improve their performance to other client firms, indicating the presence of wider positive economic effects from their business dealings with FDI firms.

Third, I conduct a multivariate statistical analysis to identify supplier and business linkage characteristics that influence the likelihood that a supplier experiences a large positive impact. The findings indicate that the level of absorptive capacity of local suppliers facilitates this impact. A large technology gap between a supplier and its client firms, representing a large scope of the potential impact, also fosters the occurrence of a large positive impact of a technological nature. The levels of organizational and technological supportiveness of producer firms are also positively associated with the occurrence of large organizational and technological impacts. Overall, inter-firm linkages characterized by "at arms length" business transactions lower the likelihood that a large impact materializes, suggesting that close relationships between producer firms and suppliers facilitate positive externality effects. Finally, the positive effect of foreign-ownership of producer firms on the creation of large positive impacts among suppliers is maintained in the multivariate analysis. This confirms that the type of ownership of a producer firm clearly matters for the creation of positive dynamic impacts in the regional economy. As such, the findings contain robust indications that FDI firms are a particularly good source of knowledge and technology transfers to their local suppliers, supporting the notion that input-output linkages between FDI firms and domestic firms are a well-suited mechanism for the creation and transmission of positive spillover effects.

1. Introduction

Many governments are engaged in the attraction and facilitation of foreign direct investment (FDI) into their economies. The reason for this is that foreign-owned firms can generate a variety of positive impacts in their host economies, related to capital investments, employment creation and the generation of export revenues (Dunning and Lundan, 2008). In the last two decades, it is increasingly thought that the generation of spillover or externality effects is another central element of the economic impact of FDI. Not only does the entrance of FDI firms foster the build up of the level of technology in a host economy, domestic firms may experience productivity or efficiency improvements when they learn from and adopt new technologies and skills that are incorporated into FDI firms (Jordaan, 2009; Venables and Barba-Navaretti, 2005).

The belief that these technology effects play an increasingly important role in host economies has fostered a rapidly growing research field that is engaged with the empirical identification of these effects. Overall, the findings on these effects are very diverse. Whereas some studies find evidence of positive spillovers, other studies fail to identify these effects or find that the presence of FDI can hurt productivity levels of domestic firms. This large degree of heterogeneity of the findings has fuelled important debates on the occurrence and nature of these FDI externalities and on which domestic firms are most likely to be exposed to them. Recent findings suggest that positive spillovers are more likely to arise between than within industries (Kugler, 2006; Jordaan, 2009). Whereas FDI firms have a clear incentive to minimize any positive spillovers that may accrue to their competitors that operate in similar industries, they are less concerned about spillover effects that materialize in other industries. In particular, the notion is that suppliers of FDI firms may benefit from spillover effects that are transmitted via input-output linkages (Blalock and Gertler, 2008; Smarzynska, 2004; Jordaan, 2008b).

Having said this, the existing evidence on such inter-industry externalities among suppliers is characterized by several limitations. First of all, findings of a positive association between the presence of FDI and productivity of domestic firms in input-supplying industries represents only indirect evidence that input-output linkages are the mechanism via which spillover effects occur. Second, such indirect evidence of productivity effects sheds little light on important questions on how and why these externality effects occur. For instance, what types of inter-firm linkages may be established by foreign-owned firms and what types of activities facilitate the transfer of knowledge and technologies to their suppliers? To find answers to such questions, we need to turn to survey- and case-study based research that looks in detail at the level of use of local suppliers and the linkages that are established. Unfortunately, the evidence from these studies is usually based on small and unrepresentative samples. Also, findings on the technological impact are often circumstantial at best, let alone sufficiently robust to make generalizations. Finally, it is important to recognize that, by design, econometric studies on FDI spillovers are unable to address the central question that underlies all research on FDI effects, whether there are actual differences between the impacts of FDI and domestic firms. As the sole intent of these spillover studies is to identify the effect of foreign-owned firms, it remains unclear whether there are differences between FDI and domestic firms. Especially given the fact that many host economy governments are attracting FDI firms into their economies and try to facilitate the occurrence of positive spillovers, these latter shortcomings of the evidence on inter-industry FDI effects among local suppliers are particularly important.

The purpose of this chapter is to address some of these limitations of empirical research on FDI spillovers among local suppliers in a host economy. To do so, I use unique data that I obtained from several firm level surveys that I carried out in the manufacturing sector of Nuevo Leon, Mexico. I present novel and detailed qualitative and quantitative evidence on the technology impact of FDI firms in this important regional economy of Mexico. Crucially, as the research sample consists of both FDI and Mexican producer firms, I am able to compare statistically the nature and degree to which these two types of firm are integrated into their local economy and to identify differences in technology-disseminating activities to their suppliers. Furthermore, I also use data from a representative survey among local suppliers, which allows me to obtain robust evidence on the level and nature of possible differences between the technology impact of FDI and domestic firms. In extension of this, I use this data also to identify statistically characteristics of suppliers and their business linkages that may facilitate or hinder technological externalities from their business dealings with their client firms.

The chapter is set up as follows. In section two I discuss the concept of FDI spillovers and look at how input-output linkages can be linked to technology dissemination between FDI firms and their suppliers. I also present a brief survey of the existing evidence on the impact of FDI in Mexico. From this, I develop the main research questions for the present study. In section three I discuss the research design of the study and I present the findings from statistical comparisons between FDI and Mexican producer firms regarding their level of use of local suppliers and the degree to which they are engaged in technology-disseminating activities. The main findings of these comparisons are two-fold. First, there are only marginal differences between FDI and Mexican producer firms regarding their static impact. Second, FDI firms generate a larger positive dynamic impact. They are significantly more supportive to their suppliers, in particular concerning types of support that are directly improving production processes of suppliers. Findings from the supplier survey indicate that there are significantly more firms among suppliers of FDI firms that experience large positive impacts, especially regarding technological development.

Section four introduces and presents the main findings from a multivariate analysis that I carry out to identify factors that affect the likelihood that local suppliers experience a large positive impact from their business dealings with their client firms. Next to providing novel evidence on which characteristics of suppliers and their business linkages play a role in the occurrence of positive technological externalities, this part of the analysis also allows me to test in a multivariate setting whether type of ownership of client firms matters for the creation of positive spillovers. The main findings of this section indicate that there is a variety of supplier characteristics that influence the likelihood that suppliers experience a large positive impact, including the technology gap between producer firms and suppliers, the level of absorptive capacity of suppliers and the nature of the business relationships between producer firms and their suppliers. Furthermore, the findings indicate that suppliers of FDI firms are significantly more likely to experience a large positive impact, even when the estimation controls for the feature that foreign-owned firms are more supportive. The confirmation of the positive effect of type of ownership of producer firms in this multivariate setting represents powerful support for the notion that FDI firms are an important source of positive externalities in the regional economy. Finally, section five summarizes and discusses the main policy implications of the empirical findings.

2. FDI, Sourcing and the Impact on Local Suppliers

2.1. Introduction

The presence of FDI in a host economy can generate a positive economic impact in several areas, including capital investment, employment creation and the generation of export revenues. Recently, there is a growing belief that positive spillover or externality effects represent another central element of the impact of FDI. Such externalities arise when the presence and operations of FDI firms affect the level of productivity or efficiency of domestic firms, effects for which the foreign-owned firms are not compensated (Blomström and Kokko, 1998; Jordaan, 2009). These spillover effects can occur for two reasons. First, externalities can arise when a FDI firm acts as a source of knowledge or technologies to domestic firms. For instance, domestic firms may learn about a new piece of technology from the entrance of a new FDI firm. If they are able to absorb this new piece of technology and incorporate it into their production process, a positive spillover has occurred, as the domestic firms do not compensate the foreign-owned firm for this effect. Another example is when an employee substitutes a domestic firm for a foreign-owned firm. The domestic firm will benefit from this, as it can use the skills and knowledge that the employee learned while working for the FDI firm. Second, externalities can arise when the presence of FDI firms forces domestic firms to change their conduct. For instance, the entrance of a foreign-owned firm may lead to increased competition on the host economy market. If domestic firms respond to this increase in competitive pressure by improving their productivity, this increase in productivity represents a form of externalities as it occurs as a result of the presence of the new foreign-owned firm.

As mentioned earlier, the econometric evidence on the general occurrence of positive FDI spillovers is very mixed (Jordaan, 2009). Several studies present evidence that indicates the materialization of positive externalities (e.g. Sjöholm, 1999; Jordaan, 2010; Haskel et al., 2007; Taki, 2005). In contrast, other studies find no evidence of such effects (e.g. Barrios et al., 2002) or find indications that the presence of FDI may hurt productivity levels of domestic firms (e.g. Aitken and Harrison, 1999; Djankov and Hoekman, 2000). In response to this impasse, recent research is trying to develop new identification strategies to obtain improved evidence of these spillover effects. One of these developments concerns making a distinction between FDI externalities that arise within and between industries. The original identification strategy entailed estimating for FDI spillovers in the same industries in which the foreign-owned firms operate (Jordaan, 2009). However, it is likely that these intra-industry spillovers are limited, as FDI firms will try to minimize any positive spillover effects that could benefit their competitors operating in their industries. In contrast, FDI firms are less concerned about spillover effects that disseminate to dissimilar industries (Kugler, 2006). In particular, such inter-industry spillovers appear to affect domestic firms in input-supplying industries, suggesting that input-output linkages between FDI firms and their suppliers act as a transmission channel of positive FDI effects (Blalock and Gertler, 2008; Smarzynska, 2004; Jordaan, 2008b).

2.2. FDI and Local Sourcing: the Static and Dynamic Impact

Looking more closely at the impact that FDI firms may generate among their suppliers in a host economy, the literature reflects that a common distinction is made between static and dynamic impacts (Potter et al., 2002; Jordaan, 2011a) or direct and indirect effects (Dunning and Lundan, 2008). The static impact concerns the level of use of local suppliers. Following the original notion introduced by Hirschman (1958) on the importance of inter-industry linkages as stimulus of economic growth processes, there is a large number of survey- and case study based research that has looked in detail at the level of use of suppliers by FDI firms. Dunning and Lundan (2008) review a selection of these studies and conclude that this level can differ substantially between host economies. Furthermore, the common assumption is that FDI firms use local suppliers to a lower degree than domestic firms (UNCTAD, 2001). This assumption is usually not tested empirically however, as the vast majority of these studies look only at sourcing practices of foreign-owned firms.

Recently, there is a growing interest in the dynamic impact of FDI firms, relating to effects of foreign-owned firms on processes of economic and technological progress. Econometric FDI spillover studies provide evidence that such spillover effects may be important for suppliers in host economies. For instance, Blalock and Gertler (2008) estimate FDI externalities in Indonesia, distinguishing between spillover effects within and between industries. Their estimations identify a significant positive association between the presence of FDI and productivity of Indonesian firms in input-supplying industries, suggesting that input-output linkages are transmitting positive effects. Similar findings of positive productivity effects in input-supplying industries are presented by Smarzynska (2004) for

Lithuania, Girma and Wakelin (2007) and Driffield (2004) for the UK, Smarzynska et al. (2004) for Romania and Jordaan (2008b) for Mexico. At the same time, there is no guarantee that such positive inter-industry externalities occur, as other studies find no evidence of this type of spillover effect (e.g. Békés et al., 2006; Crespo et al., 2006).

The dynamic impact on local suppliers can be explained by using the distinction between the two main sources of externality discussed earlier. The first element of the dynamic impact is that the presence of FDI firms may force domestic firms to become more efficient (Javorcik and Spatareanu, 2005). When a local firm tries to become a supplier of a FDI firm, it is likely that it is confronted with tighter demand schedules and stricter price demands (Blomström and Kokko, 1998). If the local supplier manages to meet these stronger demands, the improvement of the supplier represents a form of positive externalities. A good example of this effect is described by Alfaro and Rodriguez-Claire (2004). From their interviews with several domestic firms in Costa Rica it became clear that the pressure exercised by foreign-owned firms to improve their operations had been an important factor explaining productivity improvements among the Costa Rican firms. Potter et al. (2002) present similar findings from their survey among FDI and domestic firms in the UK.

The second component of the dynamic impact of FDI firms on local suppliers concerns situations where foreign-owned firms act as a source of new knowledge and technologies to their suppliers. Characteristics of input-output markets promote the sharing of knowledge and information (Lall, 1980). There are often limited numbers of buyers and sellers that are in frequent contact. In such cases, it is likely that there will be frequent exchanges of information (UNCTAD, 2001). If so, suppliers will be able to learn a great deal about technologies and skills that are incorporated into their foreign-owned client firms.

Furthermore, FDI firms are often actively trying to improve their suppliers in host economies (Dunning and Lundan, 2008; Blomström and Kokko, 1998). Of course, FDI firms will benefit from this support, as they obtain advantages in the form of better or cheaper inputs in return. However, as it is very difficult in practice for FDI firms to obtain complete compensation for the support that they provide their suppliers with, the common assumption is that supportive linkages generate positive externalities of some degree (UNCTAD, 2001; Jordaan, 2009).

A good example of the existence of such supportive linkages is provided by Potter et al. (2002, 2003) from their survey in the UK. Their findings indicate a variety of types of support that suppliers receive from their foreign-owned client firms, whereby assistance with production processes, quality testing of products and the provision of training programs for employees of suppliers occur most frequent. They also find that in several cases the relationships between FDI firms and their suppliers are characterized by a substantial degree of informal sharing of ideas and personal contacts, facilitating and promoting further exchanges of information.

Javorcik and Spatareanu (2005) present similar evidence of supportive linkages established by FDI firms in the Czech Republic, whereby the training of personnel of suppliers and financial assistance occur most frequently (see also Javorcik, 2008). Related evidence on various types of support from FDI in several developing countries is summarized in UNCTAD (2001).

2.3. The Static and Dynamic Impact of FDI in Mexico

Mexico represents a good host economy to study economic effects of inward FDI. For several decades the country has belonged to a select group of developing countries that receive a majority share of FDI flows towards developing and emerging economies (e.g. UNCTAD, 2005). Levels of inward FDI have grown further following the introduction of policies of economic liberalization and trade promotion in the late 1980s (Jordaan; 2008a; Pacheco-Lopez, 2005; Ramirez, 2003) and of course the creation of the NAFTA trade agreement in the mid 1990s (Cuevas, Messmacher and Werner, 2005). As an indication of the growing importance of FDI in the Mexican economy, the share of the stock of total inward FDI in total GDP has increased from 8% in 1990 to more than 25% in 2003 (Jordaan, 2008a). The Maquiladora industry has grown markedly as well, seeing its share in total manufacturing employment grow from 8% in 1980 to 25% in 2003 (Jordaan, 2009).

There are three types of study that look at issues related to the static and dynamic impact of FDI in the Mexican economy. First, there is a well-established interest in identifying levels of use of Mexican suppliers by FDI firms. The evidence on this static impact is very diverse. On the one hand, there are studies that identify a substantial level of use of local suppliers. For instance, a study in 1990 among 63 of the largest FDI firms found that one out of three firms sourced more than 25% of their inputs from Mexican suppliers (UNCTC, 1992). A more recent survey of similar size among European-owned FDI firms reports a similar percentage (Martinez-Solano and Phelps, 2003). Shaiken (1990) and Ivarsson and Alvstam (2005a, 2005b) also find a considerable use of local suppliers in their case studies of individual FDI firms. On the other hand, other studies report levels of use of Mexican suppliers that are very moderate at best (Buitelaar and Padilla-Perez, 2000; Padilla-Perez, 2008; Paus and Gallagher, 2008; Kenny and Florida, 1994). In the Mexican context, a deciding factor for the level of use of local suppliers is the maquiladora status of FDI firms. Foreign-owned firms that participate in this program receive tax benefits on inputs, imported machinery and re-exported assembled products. As such, they have little incentive to develop linkages with local suppliers (Jordaan, 2009)[1].

The second type of study on the impact of FDI firms concerns econometric FDI spillover studies. Well-known evidence based on the analysis of data from the 1970s is in support of the notion that FDI firms generate positive externalities (Blomström and Persson, 1983; Blomström et al., 2000; Kokko, 1994; Blomström and Wolff, 1994). Evidence for the 1980s is less clear cut; whereas Aitken et al (1996) find no evidence of positive wage spillovers, Aitken et al. (1997) find that the presence of FDI firms increases the likelihood that Mexican firms will be active on export markets[2]. The most recent evidence is based on data from the 1990s and contains strong indications that FDI firms generate externalities (Jordaan, 2005, 2009, 2010; Jordaan and Rodriguez-Oreggia, 2010). Regarding the possible impact of FDI firms on Mexican suppliers, findings presented by Jordaan (2008b, 2008c) are particularly important. Jordaan (2008b) uses regional data for all 32 Mexican states and finds that the

[1] There are indications that current developments in the Maquiladora industry may foster growing levels of use of local suppliers, however. In particular, the scale of economic activity in Mexico's northern states, where the majority of Maquiladora firms are located, has increased rapidly. This increases the scope for new suppliers to develop. Also, new Maquiladora firms are more engaged in actual production rather than assembly style operations. In combination, these developments may foster future increases in the use of local suppliers (see Jordaan, 2011a).

[2] This type of externality is commonly referred to as market access spillovers.

regional level of inter-industry FDI participation is positively associated with productivity of Mexican firms. Jordaan (2008c) uses more disaggregated data for Mexico City and states that share a border with the US. This study finds that positive inter-industry effects occur in particular among Mexican firms that operate in input-supplying industries, suggesting that local sourcing by FDI firms generates positive externalities.

Finally, the third group of studies consists of a limited number of studies on technology dissemination and learning effects that may arise between FDI firms and their suppliers. The earlier referred to study among FDI firms in 1990 found that these firms are active in particular when it comes to providing technical assistance to their suppliers and helping them with improving their quality control procedures (UNCTC, 1992). Carrillo (2004) presents evidence from a case study on the television producing industry in Tijuana that indicates that a limited number of Mexican firms benefit from positive learning effects. Padilla-Perez (2008) presents findings that indicate that FDI firms may offer support in the form of the provision of product specifications and quality control measures. Finally, Ivarsson and Alvstam (2005a, 2005b) present detailed findings from their case study on the Swedish autobus manufacturer Volvo, located in Puebla. They distinguish between support with product technology, production technology and the training of employees of suppliers. Their findings indicate that the foreign-owned firm is mainly involved in providing feedback on product performance and product design.

2.4. Research Questions

Overall, research on linkages between FDI firms and their suppliers in host economies indicates that these linkages may generate important positive effects. This applies in particular to host economies such as Mexico, where the participation of FDI firms in the economy is substantial and will only continue to develop further. At the same time, I belief that the evidence on FDI spillovers, in general and also for Mexico, is affected by certain limitations and shortcomings that I intend to address in the present study.

The empirical setting of the study is the regional economy of Nuevo Leon, located in the northeast of Mexico. The reason for analyzing this regional economy in Mexico is three-fold. First, I believe it to be important to obtain more evidence and a better understanding of the externality effects of FDI in developing country settings. Especially given the fact that most governments of developing countries, including the Mexican government, perceive a growing presence of FDI activity in their economies as a central element of their development strategies, more evidence on the impact of FDI firms is essential. Second, Nuevo Leon has received very little interest in applied economics research on Mexico so far. This is surprising, given the fact that this state constitutes the second most important agglomeration of economic activity after Mexico City (Jordaan, 2009). Also, it has had a substantial level of foreign participation in its manufacturing sector for several decades and is located in proximity to the US market. Finally, by focusing on one regional economy within Mexico, is has proven economically feasible to conduct several firm level surveys among groups of firms in the manufacturing sector and to address issues that are normally omitted from similar survey-based research on FDI effects.

To conduct a study on the impact of FDI via its sourcing practices, the first research question that needs to be addressed relates to the static impact of these firms. In line with previous research, I look at this static impact by investigating the level of use of local suppliers by FDI firms.

However, I belief that, by itself, any finding on the level of use of suppliers by foreign-owned firms will be difficult to interpret. Suppose that the findings of the present study indicate that FDI firms use Mexican suppliers to only a limited degree. This could indicate that foreign-owned firms generate a small static impact. However, is this because these firms are foreign-owned, or are there other reasons that may explain the scale of their static impact? Therefore, in addressing this research question, I intend to compare the level of use of suppliers by foreign-owned firms with the level of use of suppliers by comparable Mexican producer firms, which will help in evaluating the scale of the static impact by the FDI firms.

The second research question concerns the dynamic impact of FDI firms. One strategy to address this question is to estimate regression models to identify the productivity impact of FDI firms on domestic firms in input-supplying industries. The limited existing evidence for Mexico suggests that there are positive productivity effects from FDI firms to these input-supplying industries. Having said this, this evidence is of an indirect nature and does not say anything about whether and how input-output linkages may be linked to the transmission of spillover effects. Also, such a study would, by design, remain silent on the central underlying issue whether FDI firms differ from Mexican firms in the impact that they generate.

The second strategy to address this question is to conduct a targeted survey among firms in Nuevo Leon. The problem with this approach is that it may be difficult to identify actual spillover effects. As a solution to this problem, I adopt the following approach. Instead of trying to identify spillover effects, I look at knowledge transfer activities that are linked to sourcing practices by FDI firms, activities that are very likely to generate positive spillover effects. Again, I will compare FDI and Mexican firms to establish whether foreign-owned firms differ from their Mexican counterparts. Furthermore, I will also look at additional information from a representative survey among actual suppliers of these producer firms to further clarify the impact of these activities and to assess whether the impact differs between the two types of client firm.

The third research question concerns the identification of characteristics of suppliers and their business linkages that influence the dynamic impact that they may experience. Looking at the body of evidence from FDI spillover studies, as well as the findings from survey and case-study based approaches, very little is known on whether and how characteristics of suppliers and their business linkages influence the degree and nature of these spillover effects. Therefore, I intend to use information from the survey among local suppliers to identify statistically characteristics of suppliers and their business linkages that are associated with the technology impact that they experience as a result of their business relationships with their client firms. An additional advantage of this analysis is that it also allows me to test, in a multivariate setting, whether type of ownership of a client firm matters for the technology impact that may be generated via inter-firm linkages between producer firms and their suppliers.

3. Static and Dynamic Impact on Suppliers: Comparing FDI and Mexican Producer Firms

3.1. Introduction

To carry out the study, I applied several firm level surveys among firms in the manufacturing sector of Nuevo Leon, Mexico, in cooperation with the Monterrey branch of the ITESM University. To do so, I compiled a list of FDI and Mexican producer firms that employed at least 150 employees and were active in the car industry, chemical industries or electronics industries. Using information from a variety of sources, including the local branch of INEGI, the local affiliation of the American Chamber of Commerce, the state government and local industry associations, I collected contact details of 180 producer firms in the target industries. In the summer of 2000, I conducted a pilot study by interviewing 30 of these firms. Subsequently, the remaining 150 firms were approached by interviewers to participate in the producer firm survey. Another 52 firms participated, resulting in a total response rate of 46%.

During the same period, I also prepared a survey to be carried out among local suppliers of the producer firms. An important problem with this survey was the construction of a representative and unbiased sample. Asking the producer firms for contact details of a selection of their suppliers would undoubtedly result in a biased sample. To circumvent this problem, I collected contact details of all manufacturing firms in the regional economy that employed less than 150 firms and were registered with a local industry association. This resulted in a list of 1,100 firms, which I treated as the pool of potential suppliers. During the summer of 2000, I organized a telephone survey designed to identify Mexican firms that operated as supplier to the producer firms. After a three month period, all firms had been contacted and 356 had participated. Of this group, 300 firms indicated that they operated as supplier to the large producer firms. In the autumn of 2000, I carried out a pilot study by interviewing 20 of these suppliers. In the spring and summer of 2001, the other suppliers were approached by interviewers to participate in the supplier survey. In the end, 100 out of 300 firms participated, representing a response rate of 33%.

3.2. Comparing FDI and Mexican Producer Firms

The first component of the impact of FDI firms concerns the level of use of suppliers. Table 1 presents the findings on this from the producer survey, whereby the key characteristics of the static impact are compared between foreign-owned and Mexican producer firms. What is striking is that the comparison between FDI and Mexican producer firms shows that they do not differ significantly in most of the characteristics of their static impact. For instance, both types of firm are similar in terms of the relative importance of material inputs in total production costs, as well as the level of in-house production of inputs. The use of local suppliers of material inputs is substantial for both types of producer firm, averaging well over 25% of total material input costs. It is somewhat higher among Mexican producer firms, but the difference with FDI firms is insignificant. Therefore, there does not seem to be a difference in the static impact that both types of firms generate. Both types of producer firm are also similar in the level of local purchasing of both routine and sophisticated inputs. The only difference concerns the use of local production services, as Mexican producer firms purchase on average more of these services from local suppliers[3]. Finally, FDI and Mexican producer firms also sell a similar share of their products to firms in the regional economy, suggesting that the scope of the impact from this forward linkage is also the same. FDI firms do sell a larger share of their products on the international (US) market.

Next to the static impact, the producer survey contains several findings on the dynamic impact that FDI and Mexican producer firms generate in the regional economy. Table 2 presents indicators on this that relate to product development, innovation, the sourcing of machinery and cooperation with local suppliers.

Table 1. Characteristics of the Static Impact of FDI and Mexican Producer Firms

Local linkages	Mean	FDI	Mexican firms	Equality of means test (*)
Material inputs as % of total production costs	61.2	61.37	60.87	0.11
% of material inputs produced in-house	15.80	15.80	15.59	0.08
% of material inputs bought in Nuevo Leon	27.54	22.10	32.10	1.60
% of routine material inputs bought in Nuevo Leon	38.83	36.64	43.60	0.56
% of sophisticated material inputs bought in Nuevo Leon	11.37	9.26	15.10	0.78
% of production services purchased in Nuevo Leon	8.86	6.61	12.1	2.30 (b)
% of sales in Nuevo Leon	19.93	17.4	23.5	1.37
% of sales in US	39.01	49.0	24.5	2.97 (a)

Source: Producer Survey.

(*) this column reports the absolute value t statistic. (a) and (b) indicate significance levels of 1 and 5 %.

Material input variables are measured as % of total material input costs, production services are measured as % of total production costs, sales variables are measured as % of total sales.

Looking at the findings, there is mixed evidence of a large dynamic impact. A large majority of firms is involved in the development and introduction of new products. Also, many FDI and Mexican producer firms have an official policy to use preferred suppliers in Nuevo Leon. Producer firms establish long lasting and stable business relationships with these suppliers, which enhances the chance that information and technology is transmitted.

[3] Local production services are normally not included in surveys on FDI local sourcing. Production services refer to cases where intermediate inputs leave the factory of a producer firm to receive some form of treatment by a local supplier, after which they are returned to the producer firm to be reintegrated into the production process. Production services include activities such as metal plating and stamping, plastic molding, surface conversion and coating, assembly activities and product finishing activities.

Table 2. Product Development, Innovation, Machinery and Cooperation with Local Suppliers

	FDI	Mexican
Has firm introduced new product in last three years?	75	84
Does firm have official preferred suppliers in Nuevo Leon?	52	45
Does firm cooperate with local suppliers to develop new inputs?	57	64
Does firm cooperate with local suppliers to develop new product?	6	3
Does firm obtain machinery and equipment in Mexico?	6	7

Source: Producer Survey.

Table 2 reports % of firms that responded yes to the questions listed in the first column. Differences between FDI and Mexican producer firms were tested with the Kendal Tau-b statistic. For all five questions, there are no significant differences.

Furthermore, there is a tendency to cooperate with local suppliers in the development of new inputs, which may generate learning effects among these suppliers. However, there is no meaningful cooperation between suppliers and the producer firms when it comes to developing new products[4]. Another interesting feature is that the vast majority of the producer firms obtain their machinery and equipment on international markets, rather than from within Mexico. Finally, again the findings show that there are no significant differences between FDI and Mexican producer firms.

As discussed in the previous section, a major feature of input-output linkages is that they can be associated with a variety of technology-disseminating activities. For this reason, an important part of the producer survey addressed these activities. I distinguished between two main types of support. Technological support concerns support that is directly linked to improving the production processes of suppliers. This includes the provision of blue prints, product designs and specifications, the provision of machinery, the provision or lending of special tools, assistance with technical production and quality control and the training of personnel of suppliers. Organizational support includes assistance with the start up of new suppliers, assistance with general business and organizational development, financial assistance (grants, loans, accelerated payments) and assistance with sourcing. The main findings on the frequencies of these various types of support are presented in table 3.

The findings are interesting in two respects. First of all, it appears that FDI firms in Nuevo Leon are engaged in a variety of types of support to a very substantial degree. For instance, almost 85% of the foreign-owned firms indicate that they offer assistance with technical production and quality control measures to their suppliers. Another type of support that occurs very frequently is the sharing of blue prints, product designs and specifications, with more than 70% of the foreign-owned firms indicating to provide this type of support. Other types of support occur less regularly, but the overall impression is that most types of support are a common feature characterizing the linkages between FDI firms and their suppliers.

Second, there are significant differences in the level of supportiveness between FDI firms and Mexican producer firms. Of course, the findings for the Mexican producer firms indicate

[4] Table 2 presents the findings on cooperation with local suppliers. The producer survey findings indicate that there is also very little cooperation among producer firms regarding product development. Instead, most producer firms develop new products primarily in their own research and development departments.

that they are also engaged in the provision of several types of support. As such, this is an important finding in itself, as existing research on FDI effects does not consider the possibility that domestic producer firms may also be a source of new technologies to local suppliers. However, FDI firms are significantly more supportive for several types of support. More precisely, it is technological support where FDI firms show to be more involved in with their suppliers. Following the assumption that technological support is directly linked to improving the production processes of the suppliers, the finding that foreign-owned firms are significantly more involved in this type of support suggests strongly that FDI firms are a good source of positive technological externalities to the local suppliers in the regional economy[5].

Table 3. Support offered by Producer Firms to Local Suppliers of Material Inputs

Type of support	FDI	Mexican firms
Technological Support		
Product designs, blue prints and specifications	71.8 (a)	14.8
Provision of machinery	25.6 (a)	3.7
Provision of special tools	59.0 (a)	11.1
Assistance with technical production and quality control	84.6 (c)	66.7
Training personnel of suppliers	59.0 (a)	22.0
Organizational Support		
Assistance with start up new suppliers	61.5	59.3
General business development	35.9	25.9
Grants/loans/accelerated payments	33.3 (b)	11.1
Assistance with sourcing	48.7	33.3

Source: Producer Survey.

Table 3 reports % of firms that indicate that they provide a particular type of support frequently to local suppliers of material inputs. (a), (b) and (c) indicate significance levels of 1, 5 and 10%, based on Kendal Tau-b statistic.

The supplier survey provides additional information on the impact of input-output linkages between the producer firms and their suppliers and on whether this impact differs between the two types of producer firm. The main findings are presented in table 4, which shows the responses given by local suppliers of FDI firms and suppliers of Mexican producer firms. Again, the findings are interesting in several respects. Looking at the responses given by suppliers of FDI firms, it is clear that inter-firm linkages generate a substantial positive impact. Almost 45% of the suppliers of FDI firms indicate that their production processes have improved to a great extent as a result of being a supplier to FDI firms. Looking at the types of support, it is in particular technological support that the suppliers indicate as being important. In extension of this, over 90% of these suppliers indicate that the support that they

[5] Table 3 presents indicators of the occurrence of support to suppliers of material inputs. The findings from the producer survey on support offered to local providers of production services present a similar picture: there is a variety of types of support that occur frequently and foreign-owned firms are significantly more involved in the provision of technological support in particular.

receive from a given client firm can be used to improve their performance for other client firms, indicating that the positive impact of the support has clear wider economic effects[6].

Table 4. Impact of Producer Firms on Local Suppliers

	Suppliers of FDI firms	Suppliers of Mexican firms
Production process has improved to a great extent as a result of being supplier to producer firms	44.4 (a)	11.1
Support from client firms is very important for technological improvement	53.7 (a)	11.4
Support from client firms is very important for organizational improvement	33.3	26.7
Support offered by one client firm can easily be used to improve performance for other client firms	90.7 (a)	60.0

Source: Supplier survey.
Table 4 reports % of suppliers that responded yes to the statements listed in column 1.
(a) indicates significance level of 1%; Kendall's tau-b statistic.

Furthermore, a comparison of the responses given by suppliers of FDI firms and Mexican producer firms reveals important differences. There are significantly more firms among suppliers of FDI firms that indicate that their production processes have greatly improved, indicating that the positive impact of foreign-owned firms occurs significantly more frequently. This also applies to the wider effects of the support provided by producer firms, as there are significantly more suppliers of FDI firms that indicate that they benefit from such effects. Having said this, a majority of suppliers of Mexican producer firms also indicate to experience these wider economic effects. Again, this confirms the impression that domestic firms are also a good source of positive externalities. Finally, the responses of the supplier firms indicate that it is in particular technological support that is important for the improvements that suppliers of FDI firms experience. This is in line with the findings presented in table 3 that indicate that FDI firms are significantly more supportive in particular when it comes to providing forms of technological support. As the findings from the supplier survey indicate, it is exactly the impact of this technological support where there are significant differences between suppliers of foreign-owned and Mexican firms.

In sum, the findings from the producer and supplier survey contain several indications on both the static and dynamic impact of the producer firms on their local suppliers. The variety of findings on the static impact indicates that there is only a marginal difference between FDI and Mexican producer firms. Both types of firm are similar in the share of inputs in total production costs and source a similar level of material inputs from local suppliers. The only difference is that Mexican producer firms appear to use more local providers of production services.

Overall therefore, it appears that FDI and Mexican firms are very similar in their operations. This feature makes it even more important that the producer survey identifies significant differences between the level and nature of supportiveness of the two types of

[6] This is in support of the assumption that support offered by a FDI firm generates positive externalities, even when considering that the foreign-owned firm receives advantages in return.

producer firm towards their suppliers. Comparing the variety of types of support that producer firms are offering their suppliers, it is clear that FDI firms are significantly more supportive for several types of support. In particular, foreign-owned firms are more supportive when it comes to providing support of a technological nature, support that directly affects production processes of their suppliers. Given that there is a great deal of similarity between FDI and Mexican producer firms, this finding suggests strongly that type of ownership of a producer firm affects its supportiveness, whereby FDI firms clearly generate important positive technological effects more frequently. This is also confirmed by the findings from the supplier survey that indicate that there are significantly more firms among suppliers of FDI firms that experience a large positive impact. Technological support is particularly important, and the support that is provided by a given foreign-owned firm can be used by suppliers to improve their performance to other firms. As such, the overall impression of these findings is that FDI firms generate a larger positive technological impact, a positive impact that is evidently closely related to the high level of technological supportiveness of foreign-owned producer firms.

4. Determinants of the Dynamic Impact

The findings in the previous section contain clear indications that FDI firms are generating a larger positive dynamic impact among their suppliers in Nuevo Leon. However, we need to interpret the evidence with some caution, as it consists of dichotomous comparisons between FDI and Mexican producer firms and suppliers of both types of firm. The feature that there is a great deal of similarity between the two types of producer firm in terms of their static impact does heighten the robustness of the finding that they differ in the dynamic impact that they create. Having said this, it may be the case that there are other features that also play a role. In particular, the analysis so far has remained silent on whether and how characteristics of suppliers and their business linkages influence whether or not they experience a large positive impact from their business dealings with their client firms.

4.1. Developing the Regression Model

To identify firm characteristics that influence whether suppliers experience a large positive impact from their business dealings with their client firms, I set up the following regression model:

$$\text{IMPACT}(i) = \beta 0 + \beta\ \text{FDI}\ (i) + \beta X(i) + \beta\ \text{INDUSTRY}(i) + \varepsilon(i) \quad (1)$$

The variable IMPACT is a binary variable taking the value of 1 if supplier firm (i) indicates to have experienced a large positive impact from their business dealings with producer firms in Nuevo Leon. The variable FDI captures whether a supplier has foreign-owned or Mexican client firms. The vector X contains several characteristics of the supplier firms and their business linkages that I hypothesize to influence whether a supplier experiences a large positive impact. The variable INDUSTRY contains dummy variables for the car, chemical and electronics industries and ε is the error term of the estimation.

X contains two main factors. The appendix presents a full list of the variables with definitions. In line with econometric research on FDI spillovers, the first main factor that I include concerns the capacity of suppliers to absorb skills and technologies from producer firms. However, I use a set of variables that represent an improved measurement of this absorptive capacity. The majority of research on the impact of absorptive capacity on FDI spillovers tries to identify this impact by estimating the effect of the technology gap on these FDI effects. As argued elsewhere in this book (Jordaan, 2011b; see also Jordaan, 2009), this interpretation of the technology gap as direct inverse indicator of the level of absorptive capacity of domestic firms is flawed. In the present study, I include the level of technological differences between the producer and supplier firms to capture the scope of positive effects that may arise. Therefore, I expect a positive effect of the technology gap on the impact that suppliers experience (see Jordaan, 2005; 2008b; Blomström and Wolff, 1994). As for the capacity of the suppliers to absorb this impact, I include several variables. I use the size of the supplier firm and the level of experience that a supplier has with being a supplier firm to producer firms in Nuevo Leon. I expect a positive effect of both these variables. Furthermore, I use two indicators of the level of sophistication of production processes of a supplier and the degree to which a supplier experiences difficulties with its quality control systems. I measure both variables on a Likert scale of 1 to 4, with 1 representing a high level of sophistication and a low degree of problems with quality control systems and procedures. Given this measurement scale, I expect a negative effect of these two variables on the impact that suppliers experience.

The second main factor concerns the type of business relationships that are established between a supplier and its client firms. I include a dichotomous variable to capture the type of contract, with 1 representing contracts that are characterized as "at arms' length" relationships and 0 representing relationships that involve frequent contacts and coordination between a supplier and its client firms. With this measurement scale, I expect a negative effect of this variable, as arms' length relationships are less likely to be associated with the dissemination of knowledge and information (see UNCTAD, 2001). I also include a variable that captures the level of dependence of a supplier firm on a limited number of client firms. This variable may have a positive or negative effect. A negative effect could occur if a high level of dependency weakens the bargaining position of the supplier (UNCTAD, 2001). However, it may also be the case that there is a positive effect, as suppliers may find it easier to concentrate their efforts to benefit from inter-firm linkages on a limited number of client firms. The third element that I include is the level of technological and organizational supportiveness of a supplier firm's client firms.

Given that the dependent variable is of a binary nature, a standard OLS estimation of the regression model is inappropriate, as it would violate central assumptions of the linear regression model including linearity, homoscedasticity and normality of the errors (Wooldridge, 2003). Therefore, I estimate regression models that relate to the odds of a supplier experiencing a large positive impact, whereby these odds are defined as the ratio of the probability that a supplier experiences a large positive impact (π) and the probability that a supplier does not experience this impact ($1-\pi$). Taking the natural log of this ratio gives the logit, which can be taken to be a linear function of the explanatory variables:

$$\mathrm{Ln}(\pi/1\text{-}\pi) = \beta 0 + \beta \text{ FDI} + \beta X + \beta \text{ INDUSTRY} + \varepsilon \quad (2)$$

I can estimate this regression model with maximum likelihood techniques, which produces the linear effect of the explanatory variables on the logit. With this information I can then calculate the odds ratios, which reflect whether the explanatory variables have a positive or negative effect on the likelihood that a supplier experiences a large positive impact.

4.2. Empirical Findings

The main empirical findings from estimating several specifications of regression model (2) are presented in table 5. The first column with findings confirms that both the technology gap and the level of absorptive capacity of a supplier affect the likelihood that it experiences a large positive impact on its operations. The odds ratio of the technology gap is larger than one, indicating that a supplier with client firms that are substantially more technologically advanced is significantly more likely to experience a large positive impact. The odds ratios of the variables that capture problems with quality control processes and the level of sophistication of a supplier's production process are both smaller than one, indicating that suppliers with a relative low level of absorptive capacity are less likely to experience a large positive impact.

In the next column I add the characteristics of the linkages between a supplier and its client firms to the regression model. Interestingly, it appears to be organizational rather than technological support that enhances the likelihood that a large positive impact materializes among suppliers. The type of contract is also important; the odds ratio being smaller than one indicates that suppliers that deal with their client firms via linkages that are characterized by at arms length market transactions are less likely to experience a positive impact, suggesting that some level of mutual contact and information exchange is important for this impact. A large dependence on a limited number of client firms does not appear to be important.

Finally, the third column presents the findings from adding type of ownership of a supplier's client firms to the regression model. All five variables that are linked to the technology gap and the absorptive capacity of a supplier are significantly associated with the likelihood that a large impact occurs. Again, it is mainly organizational support that appears to be important for this impact. As for the effect of type of ownership, the odds ratio of the FDI variable is larger than one, indicating that suppliers with FDI client firms are significantly more likely to experience a large positive impact, ceteris paribus. This finding is in line with the results presented in section three. The present findings shows that the positive externality impact of FDI producer firms is robustly confirmed in a multivariate setting.

Table 5. Determinants of a large positive impact among local suppliers; logistic regressions; odds ratios

	Large positive impact			Large technological impact				Large organizational impact	
	All suppliers			All suppliers		No production services	No material inputs	All suppliers	
Size	1.16 (1.19)	1.29 (19.87) a	1.26 (3.74) a	1.19 (3.97) a	1.16 (2.62) a	1.25 (1.00)	1.38 (2.04) b	1.16 (0.77)	1.12 (0.63)
Experience	1.08 (0.14)	1.16 (0.51)	1.94 (1.92) b	1.17 (0.96)	1.26 (1.06)	2.22 (2.63) a	4.38 (2.58) a	5.15 (4.58) a	5.82 (4.19) a
Quality Control	0.30 (3.03) a	0.30 (3.96) a	0.26 (3.11) a	0.86 (0.47)	0.52 (2.94) a	0.29 (2.24) b	0.23 (1.18)	2.67 (2.67) a	2.72 (2.71) a
Sophistication	0.34 (8.35) a	0.36 (4.10) a	0.36 (10.18) a	1.21 (0.57)	1.29 (0.65)	0.41 (2.59) a	0.63 (7.71) a	0.79 (0.39)	0.85 (0.31)
Technology Gap	5.10 (2.17)b	5.57 (2.59) a	4.26 (3.74) a	4.02 (14.94) a	3.65 (10.16) a	7.44 (3.85) a	2.74 (1.33)	1.01 (0.10)	0.94 (0.07)
Technological Support		1.05 (1.38)	0.95 (0.72)	1.38 (4.17) a	1.37 (4.73) a	1.30 (10.25) a	0.68 (1.04)	0.99 (0.37)	0.97 (0.58)
Organizational Support		1.38 (3.54) a	1.20 (2.70) a	1.12 (2.33) a	1.07 (1.10)	1.02 (0.49)	1.51 (2.88)a	1.22 (2.75) a	1.20 (2.31) b
Contract		0.39 (1.78) c	0.31 (1.75) c	0.65 (3.15) a	0.66 (3.91)	0.31 (1.93) b	0.27 (0.88)	1.52 (3.61) a	1.50 (3.82) a
Dependent		-0.32 (1.40)	0.66 (1.46)	1.95 (2.63) a	2.03 (2.57) a	0.57 (1.00)	0.86 (0.33)	1.37 (1.62) a	1.40 (1.98) b
FDI client			9.13 (4.34) a		1.67 (2.74) a	7.98 (6.52) a	11.75 (2.50) a		1.68 (2.13) b
Log likelihood	-52.48	-49.25	-42.77	-57.99	-57.41	-29.66	-29.13	-53.29	-52.69
Chi square	11.20	18.09	31.03	17.98	19.13	26.87	18.78	11.12	11.60
Significance model	0.09	0.03	0.00	0.03	0.02	0.00	0.03	0.10	0.08
Observations	100	100	100	100	100	67	69	100	100

Table 5 reports the odds ratios on the effect of the explanatory variables on the likelihood that a supplier experiences a large positive impact. The odds ratios are calculated as exp(β) of the estimated β coefficients from regressions of the logit on the control variables. Absolute t-values in brackets, robust to heteroscedasticity. All estimations include dummies to control for industry effects. a, b and c indicate significance levels of 1, 5 and 10%.

The second set of findings concerns determinants of a supplier firm experiencing a large technological impact. There are important similarities and differences with the findings on the overall impact. Again, a large technology gap facilitates the occurrence of a large impact and several of the absorptive capacity variables also have significant odds ratios. Suppliers that use business linkages with at arms length characteristics are less likely to experience a large technological impact.

The significant odds ratio of the variable that captures whether or not a supplier is dependent on a limited number of client firms indicates that a supplier with a few main client firms is more likely to experience a large technological impact. This can be explained by the feature that to maximize the beneficial impact of their business linkages, such suppliers can concentrate their efforts on only a few client firms. For the technological impact, it is the overall level of technological support that has a positive effect. Again, type of ownership has an odds ratio larger than one, indicating that a supplier with foreign-owned client firms is significantly more likely to experience a large technological impact. Recalling the findings from section three, foreign-owned firms are significantly more supportive when it comes to providing support of a technological nature. The present findings from the multivariate analysis indicate that, even when controlling for the fact that FDI firms offer more support related to technological improvement, suppliers of FDI firms are still more likely to experience a large technological impact.

The next two columns show the findings from estimating the regression model on two sub-samples of suppliers, one consisting of all suppliers except providers of production services and the other containing all suppliers except suppliers of material inputs. There are several important differences between the findings for these two sub-samples. First, the positive effect of the level of technological differences only materializes among those suppliers that do not provide production services. This suggests that the positive effect of a large scope for suppliers to learn from their business dealings with their client firms only applies to those suppliers that are involved in the production of material inputs. When it comes to suppliers that offer treatment services for intermediate inputs, this effect appears to be unimportant. An explanation for this could be that producer firms are familiar and knowledgeable about the production of inputs, which facilitates the materialization of positive impacts among their suppliers. In contrast, production services may concern types of activity that producer firms have less experience with. Second, the provision of technological support is important in facilitating a large impact only among suppliers of material inputs. In contrast, when it concerns providers of production services, it is mainly organizational support that is important. Again, this can be explained by producer firms having more experience in matters concerning the production of inputs, facilitating technological support. A lesser degree of familiarity with production services may result in producer firms opting to offer types of organizational support to providers of these services. By and large, the estimated effect of the other control variables is similar. This also applies to type of ownership of client firms: for both suppliers of material inputs and production services, FDI client firms are significantly more likely to generate a large technological impact among their suppliers.

Finally, the last two columns present the findings on determinants of a positive impact of an organizational nature. One difference with the other findings is that the technology gap is not important for this type of impact. In combination with the insignificance of the technology gap for a technological impact among providers of production services, this suggests that the technology gap promotes a positive impact especially when there are direct links, or similarities, between the production processes of suppliers that produce material inputs and their client firms. Unsurprisingly, for a large impact of an organizational nature it is the level of organizational support that a supplier receives from its client firms that is important. Interestingly, the findings also indicate that firms that deal with their client firms via at arms length business linkages are more likely to experience a large organizational impact. This may be explained by client firms preferring to provide technological support to suppliers with whom they have closer relationships. Suppliers that do not have such relationships receive organizational support, support that may require less detailed knowledge about the operations of supplier firms. As is the case with the findings from the other estimations, suppliers of FDI firms are significantly more likely to experience a large positive impact.

Summary and Policy Recommendations

Many host economy governments perceive the attraction of inward FDI as an important element of their development strategies. The reason for this is that the presence and operations of FDI can be linked to a variety of positive impacts. In the last two decades, it is in particular the externality impact that foreign-owned firms may generate that is receiving increased interest. Recent research suggests that these externality effects may be more likely to materialize in industries other than the industries in which foreign-owned firms operate. In particular, current research on the externality impact of FDI is attempting to identify these spillover effects among domestic firms that operate in input-supplying industries.

The purpose of this study is to contribute to the literature on the technology impact of FDI on their suppliers. Using unique firm level data from several surveys among firms in the manufacturing sector of Nuevo Leon, Mexico, the study attempts to present novel qualitative and quantitative findings on the impact of FDI firms on local suppliers. In doing so, the study addresses some limitations or shortcomings that challenge existing research on these inter-industry FDI effects. In particular, the dataset contains both foreign-owned and Mexican producer firms, which makes it possible to address the central question that underlies all research on the impact of FDI, whether there are actual differences between foreign-owned and comparable domestic firms. Furthermore, I also use data from a representative survey among actual local suppliers to obtain objective indicators of the impact of producer firms on their suppliers and to further assess whether and how foreign-owned and domestic producer firms may differ.

The main findings of the empirical study are three-fold. First, there are only marginal differences between FDI and Mexican producer firms regarding the static impact that they generate. The sample average use of local suppliers is more than 25% of total material input costs, which appears to be substantial. Mexican firms do report a higher average, but there is no significant difference with FDI firms. As such, the findings in the present study refute the commonly held assumption that FDI firms tend to use fewer local suppliers than domestic firms. Of course, this finding only applies to the regional economy of Nuevo Leon, but the fact that the comparison between FDI and domestic producer firms shows no significant difference between the static impacts of these two types of firm indicates that research on the use of local suppliers should test empirically whether foreign-owned firms actually differ from domestic firms.

Second, the findings indicate that the positive dynamic impact of FDI firms is significantly larger. Findings on the level and nature of supportive linkages indicate that foreign-owned firms are statistically different from their Mexican-owned counterparts. FDI firms offer several types of support more frequently than Mexican firms. This difference applies in particular to types of technological support, support that is directly linked to improving the production processes of suppliers. Findings from the supplier survey lend further support to the impression that FDI firms generate a larger dynamic impact. There are significantly more firms among suppliers of FDI firms that indicate to have experienced a large positive impact as a result of their business relationships with their client firms. Furthermore, suppliers relate this difference in impact in particular to technological support that they receive from their foreign-owned client firms. In addition, there is evidence of wider positive effects, as a vast majority of suppliers of FDI firms indicate that they can use the support received from one client firm to improve their performance to other client firms.

Third, the multivariate statistical analysis of factors that may influence the occurrence of a large positive impact among local suppliers identifies several characteristics of suppliers and their business linkages that affect the likelihood that this impact occurs. In particular, the level of absorptive capacity of a supplier and the existence of a sufficiently large technology gap between a supplier and its client firms both foster a positive impact. The type of business linkage between a supplier and its client firms also affects this impact. Depending on whether the analysis considers a large technological or organizational impact, the level of technological or organizational supportiveness of producer firms is also important. Having said this, the effects of these factors may differ somewhat between different types of supplier. In particular, the technology gap and technological supportiveness are important for facilitating a large technological impact among suppliers of material inputs, whereas this is not the case for suppliers of local production services. Finally, the importance of type of ownership is confirmed in all the estimations: suppliers of FDI firms are significantly more likely to experience a large positive impact, irrespective of whether the analysis focuses on a large technological or organizational impact or distinguishes between different types of supplier. The powerfulness of this finding is also indicated by the feature that, even when the multivariate analysis controls for the fact that FDI firms offer significantly more support, the results persist to indicate that suppliers of FDI firms are significantly more likely to experience a large positive impact. Overall, this represents strong and robust support for the main finding of the study that, compared to domestic producer firms, foreign-owned firms generate a larger dynamic impact among local suppliers in Nuevo Leon.

Finally, the empirical findings carry several important policy implications. First of all, the finding that domestic and foreign-owned firms source a similar level of local inputs suggests that special policies that try to increase the level of local integration of FDI firms may not always be required. The literature on the impact of FDI contains a lengthy debate on the need for such policies, based on the assumption that foreign-owned firms tend to use less local suppliers. The findings in the present study indicate that the need for such policies needs to be verified empirically. Of course, governments may consider designing all kinds of policies on local economic development, including promoting the development of a competitive and well-used local supplier base. Whether the findings for Nuevo Leon apply to other regions in Mexico and other developing country settings is a matter of empirical verification. In the present case, policies to enhance the use of local suppliers should be aimed at the general population of producer firms, rather than targeting foreign-owned producer firms to enhance their use of Mexican suppliers.

Second, the finding that FDI firms are very supportive to their local suppliers suggests that governments may design policies that aim to work with foreign-owned firms to further facilitate their supportive linkages with domestic firms. For instance, a government may work with FDI firms to try to solve possible problems that these firms experience when trying to offer support to local suppliers. Also, a government may consider policies that help local suppliers to benefit even more from the support that they receive. Having said this, the fact that the findings of the present study indicate that domestic producer firms are also offering a variety of support indicates that policies of local economic and technological development may not have to be confined to working exclusively with foreign-owned producer firms. As domestic producer firms may also generate a positive impact on their suppliers, they need to be considered as a potential source of technological and organizational improvement in a host economy. In any case, the findings are promising as they suggest that it is in the area of the dynamic impact of producer firms where there is a real scope for governments to design facilitating policies to further improve the externality impact that these firms create among local suppliers.

Finally, the multivariate analysis identifies a variety of characteristics of suppliers and input-output linkages that have beneficial or detrimental effects on the impacts that producer firms generate among their suppliers. As such, this again suggests that there are clear opportunities for a government to try to enhance the local impact of producer firms. For instance, the finding that the nature of the business relationships between suppliers and their client firms affects the impact that suppliers experience suggests that a government could facilitate this impact by promoting business linkages between firms that involve exchanges of information and mutual coordination between buying and selling parties.

Also, the multivariate analysis identifies the level of absorptive capacity of suppliers to be important for the materialization of technological externalities. This suggests that a government can work with local suppliers to improve the capacity of these firms to learn from their client firms and better absorb positive externalities. The positive effect of a large technology gap on the likelihood that a large technological impact materializes implies that the local government should take into account that such large impacts are facilitated by the existence of sufficiently large technological differences between producer firms and suppliers. In combination, this implies that it is important for government policies to try to promote impacts between those producer firms and suppliers where the potential for these impacts is large. In other word, such policies should not be targeted towards suppliers that are technologically sufficiently advanced. Although the level of absorptive capacity of such suppliers may be relatively higher, the scope for these firms to benefit from positive externalities will be minimal. A host economy government will be more successful when it focuses its efforts on trying to improve the level of absorptive capacity of those suppliers that are in a position where there is a large scope to improve, indicated by sufficiently large technological differences with their client firms. Again, these efforts may not have to be confined to linkages between foreign-owned firms and local suppliers, as domestic firms may also be an important source of positive externalities to their suppliers. Having said this, it remains the case that the findings of the present study clearly indicate that FDI firms in

Nuevo Leon are generating a significantly larger positive dynamic impact, acting as a particularly good source of positive externality effects to their local suppliers.

APPENDIX. EXPLANATORY VARIABLES SECTION 4

Variable	Description	Measurement
Size	Size of supplier firm	(ln) nr employees 2000
Experience	Experience of supplier with supplying to producer firms in the region	(ln) nr years supplying in region
Quality control	Frequency of problems with quality control processes	Scale of 1-4; 1=no problems, 4 = frequent problems
Sophistication	Level of sophistication production processes supplier	Scale of 1-4; 1 = sophisticated production processes, 4 = standard production processes
Technology gap	Level of technological differences between supplier and client firms	Scale of 1-4; 1= no technology gap, 4= large technology gap
Technological support	Level of technological support that supplier receives from client firms	Does supplier receive support frequently; ∑ product design, machinery, special tools, quality control, training of employees
Organizational support	Level of organizational support that supplier receives from client firms	Does supplier receive support frequently; ∑ business organization, finances, sourcing inputs, assistance with exporting, diversification of products
Contract	Type of contract between supplier and client firms	1 = purchasing orders; 0=direct contacts between firms, coordination and sharing of information
Dependent	Degree to which supplier is dependent on a few client firms	1 = large dependence on 1-2 clients; 0 = more client firms
FDI	Type of ownership client firms	1 = FDI, 0 = Mexican

All variables are calculated with information from the supplier survey.

REFERENCES

Aitken, B.J., Harrison, A.E. and Lipsey, R.E. 1996. Wages and foreign ownership: A comparative study of Mexico, Venezuela and the United States. *Journal of International Economics* vol. 40(3): 345-371.

Aitken, B.J. and Harrison, A.E. 1997. Do domestic firms benefit from direct foreign investment? Evidence from Venezuela. *American Economic Review* vol. 89(3): 605-618.

Aitken, B.J. and Harrison, A.E. (1999) Do domestic firms benefit fro direct foreign investment? Evidence from Venezuela. *The American Economic Review*, vol. 89(3), p. 605-618.

Alfaro, L. and Rodriguez-Claire, A. 2004. Multinationals and linkages: An empirical investigation. *Economia* (Spring 2004).

Barrios, S., and Strobl, E. (2002) Foreign direct investment and productivity spillovers; Evidence from the Spanish experience. *Review of World Economics*, vol. 138(3), p. 459-481.

Békés, G., Kleinert, J. and Toubal, F. (2006) Spillovers from multinationals to heterogeneous domestic firms: Evidence from Hungary. *Discussion Paper Series*, no. 2006/16, Institute of Economics, Hungarian Academy of Sciences.

Blalock, G. and Gertler, P.J. (2008) Welfare gains from foreign direct investment through technology transfer to local suppliers. *Journal of International Economics*, vol. 74(2), p. 402-421.

Blomström, M. and Persson, H. 1983. Foreign investment and spillover efficiency in an underdeveloped economy: Evidence from the Mexican manufacturing industry. *World Development* vol. 11(6): 493-501.

Blomström, M. and Wolff, E. (1994) Multinational corporations and productivity convergence in Mexico. In: Baumol, W., Nelson, R. and Wolff, E. (eds.) *Convergence of productivity: Cross-national studies and historical evidence*. Oxford: Oxford University Press.

Blomström, M. and Kokko, A. (1998) Multinational corporations and spillovers. *Journal of Economic Surveys*, vol. 12(3), p. 1-31.

Blomström, M., Kokko, A. and Zejan, M. 2000. *Foreign direct investment: Firm and host economy strategies*. Basingstoke: MacMillan.

Buitelaar, R.M. and Padilla Perez, R. 2000. Maquila, economic reform and corporate strategies. *World Development* vol. 28(9): 1627-1642.

Carrillo, J. 2004. Foreign direct investment and local linkages: The case of the Mexican television industry in Tijuana. *Research in the Sociology of Work* vol. 13: 99-124.

Crespo, N., Proenca, I. and Fontoura, M. (2007) FDI spillovers at the regional level: Evidence from Portugal. *School of Economics and Management Working Paper Series*, no. 28. Lisbon: Technical University of Lisbon.

Cuevas, A., Messmacher, M. and Werner, A. 2005. Foreign direct investment in Mexico since the approval of NATA. *World Bank Economic Review* vol. 19(3): 473-488.

Djankov, S. and Hoekman, B. (2000) Foreign investment and productivity growth in Czech enterprises. *World Bank Economic Review*, vol. 14(1), p. 49-64.

Driffield, N. (2004) Regional policy and spillovers from FDI in the UK. *Annals of Regional Science*, vol. 38(4), p. 579-594.

Dunning, J. and Lundan, S.M. (2008) *Multinational enterprises and the global economy*. Cheltenham, UK: Edward Elgar.

Girma, S. and Wakelin, K. 2007. Local productivity spillovers from foreign direct investment in the UK electronics industry. *Regional Science and Urban Economics* vol. 37(3): 399-412.

Haskel, J.E., Pereira, S.C. and Slaughter, M.J. (2007) Does inward foreign direct investment boost the productivity of domestic firms? *The Review of Economics and Statistics,* vol. 89(3), p. 482-496.

Hirschman, A.O. 1958. *The strategy of economic development*. New Haven, CT: Yale University Press.

Ivarsson, I. and Alvstam, C.G. 2005-a. Technology transfers from TNCs to local suppliers in developing countries: A study of AB Volvo's truck and bus plants in Brazil, China, India and Mexico. *World Development* vol. 33(8): p. 1325-1344.

Ivarsson, I. and Alvstam, C.G. 2005-b. The effect of spatial proximity on technology transfers from TNCs to local suppliers in developing countries: The case of AB Volvo in Asia and Latin America. *Economic Geography* vol. 81(1): 83-111.

Javorcik, B.S. (2008) Can survey evidence shed light on spillovers from foreign direct investment? *World Bank Research Observer*, 23(2), p. 139-159.

Javorcik, B.S. and Spatareanu, M. 2005. Disentangling FDI spillover effects: What do firm perceptions tell us? In: Moran, T.H., Graham, E.M. and Blomström, M. (eds.) *Does foreign direct investment promote development?* Washington, DC: Institute for International Economics.

Jordaan, J.A. (2005) Determinants of FDI-induced externalities: New empirical evidence for Mexican manufacturing industries. *World Development*, vol. 33(12), p. 2103-2118.

Jordaan, J.A. (2008a) State characteristics and the locational choice of foreign direct investment: Evidence from regional FDI in Mexico 1989-2006. *Growth and Change*, lead article, vol. 39(3), p. 389-413.

Jordaan, J.A. (2008b) Intra- and inter-industry externalities from foreign direct investment in the Mexican manufacturing sector: New evidence from Mexican regions. *World Development*, vol. 36(12), p. 2838-2854.

Jordaan, J.A. (2008c) Regional foreign participation and externalities: new empirical evidence from Mexican regions. *Environment and Planning A*, vol. 40(12), p. 2948-2969.

Jordaan, J.A. (2009) *Foreign direct investment, agglomeration and externalities*. Farnham, Surry, UK: Ashgate Publishing Limited.

Jordaan, J.A. (2010) Cross-sectional estimation of FDI spillovers when FDI is endogenous: OLS and IV estimates for Mexican manufacturing industries. *Applied Economics*, first published on: 01 March 2010 (iFirst).

Jordaan, J.A. and Rodriguez-Oreggia, E. (2010) Regional growth in Mexico under trade liberalization: How important are agglomeration and FDI? *The Annals of Regional Science*, doi: 1007/s00168-010-0406-4.

Jordaan, J.A. (2011a) FDI, local sourcing and supportive linkages with domestic suppliers: The case of Monterrey, Mexico. *World Development*, vol. 39(4), p. 620-632.

Jordaan, J.A. (2011b) Technology gap, agglomeration and FDI spillovers: A survey of the literature. In: Desare, T. and Caprioglio, D. (2011) *Foreign Investment: Types, Methods and Impacts*. Nova Science Publishers, Inc.

Kenney, M. and Florida, R. (1994). Japanese Maquiladoras: Production organization and global commodity chains. *World Development* vol. 22(1): 27-44.

Kokko, A. (1994). Technology, market characteristics and spillovers. *Journal of Development Economics* vol. 43(2): 279-293.

Kugler, M. (2006) Spillovers from foreign direct investment: within or between industries? *Journal of Development Economics*, vol. 80(2), p. 444-477.

Lall, S. 1980. Vertical interfirm linkages in LDCs: An empirical study. *Oxford Bulletin of Economics and Statistics* vol. 42: 203-226.

Martinez-Solano, L.E. and Phelps, N.A. 2003. The technological activities of EU MNEs in Mexico. *International Planning Studies* vol. 8(1): 53-75.

Pacheco-Lopez, P. 2005. Foreign direct investment, exports and imports in Mexico. *World Economy* vol. 28(8): 1157-1172.

Padilla Perez, R. 2008. A regional approach to study technology transfers through foreign direct investment: the electronics industry in two Mexican regions. *Research Policy* vol. 37(5): 849-860.

Paus, E. and Gallagher, K.P. 2008. Missing links: Foreign investment and industrial development in Costa Rica ad Mexico. *Studies in Comparative International Development* vol. 43(1): 53-80.

Potter, J., Moore, B. and Spires, R. (2002) The wider effects of inward foreign direct investment in manufacturing on UK industry. *Journal of Economic Geography*, vol. 2(2), p. 279-310.

Potter, J., Moore, B. and Spires, R. 2003. Foreign manufacturing investment in the United Kingdom and the upgrading of supplier practices. *Regional Studies* vol. 37(1): 41-60.

Ramirez, M.D. 2003. Mexico under NAFTA: A critical assessment. *The Quarterly Review of Economics and Finance* vol. 43(5): 863-892.

Shaiken, H. 1990. *Mexico in the global economy: High technology and work organization in export industries*. San Diego, CA: Centre for US-Mexican Studies, UCDS.

Sjöholm, F. (1999) Productivity growth in Indonesia: The role of regional characteristics and foreign investment. *Economic Development and Cultural Change*, vol., 47(3), p. 559-584.

Smarzynska, B.K. (2004) Does foreign direct investment increase the productivity of domestic firms? In search of spillovers through backward linkages. *The American Economic Review*, vol. 94(3), p. 605-627.

Taki, S. (2005) Productivity spillovers and characteristics of multinational plants in Indonesian manufacturing. *Journal of Development Economics*, vol. 76(2), p. 521-542.

UNCTAD (2001). *World investment report 2001: Promoting linkages*. Geneva: United Nations Conference on Trade and Development.

UNCTAD (2005). *World investment report 2005: Transnational corporations and the internationalization of RandD*. Geneva: United Nations Conference on Tariffs and Trade.

UNCTC (1992). Foreign direct investment and industrial restructuring in Mexico. *UNCTC Current Studies Series A*, no. 18. New York: United Nations.

Venables, A.J. and Barba Navaretti, G. (2005) *Multinational firms in the world economy*. Oxfordshire, UK: Princeton University Press.

In: Foreign Investment
Editor: Torre DeSare and Daniele Caprioglio

ISBN 978-1-61470-358-7

Chapter 4

FOREIGN DIRECT INVESTMENT, POLITICAL RISK AND CORPORATE SOCIAL RESPONSIBILITY. OPPORTUNITIES FOR A PROACTIVE RISK-MANAGING STRATEGY

Alfredo Jiménez Palmero[1]* and Juan José Durán Herrera[2]

[1]Departament of Business Administration and Management. University of Burgos, Spain

[2]International Center Carlos V. Autonomous University of Madrid, Spain

ABSTRACT

The conventional view of political risk held by the management of multinational enterprises considers it an exogenous factor. However, recent studies have pointed out that political risk may also provide firms with an opportunity to obtain competitive advantages over their competitors in certain locations. MNEs operating in countries with poor institutional development, high corruption levels or whose governments exercise a high degree of discretionary power may already have or may develop political competitive advantages, in order to manage the political risk and mitigate the market failure of those environments (Henisz, 2003; Hillman and Hitt, 1999; Holburn, 2001; McWilliams, Fleet, and Cory, 2002). Those with better political capabilities will be better positioned to take advantage of the market through the proactive use of political risk.

This study reviews the theoretical background behind this particular strategy, which influences both the decision to set up a subsidiary in a given country and the magnitude of Foreign Direct Investment flows. It also offers further evidence on the use of this strategy by Spanish MNEs, as a positive relationship has been identified in recent literature between the degree of internationalization and the level of political risk, measured by several variables including political constraints or corruption indices (García-Canal and Guillén, 2008; Jiménez, 2010, Jiménez *et al.* in press).

Political risk may therefore be considered not only as a threat but also as an opportunity that plays a key role as a determinant of a firm's internationalization strategy.

* E-mail: ajimenez@ubu.es

However, its implications in relation to Corporate Social Responsibility should not be overlooked, as MNEs that resort to corrupt practices sacrifice their social legitimacy and run the risk of losing influence and effectiveness due to the negative impact on their status within the world community (Ghosal and Moran, 2005).

Keywords: Foreign Direct Investment, Political Risk, Multinational Enterprise, Social Corporate Responsibility, Corruption, Political Discretionality.

1. INTRODUCTION

Institutional issues have been highlighted as one of the most relevant lines of research in international business (Dunning and Lundan, 2008; Griffith *et al.* 2008), to such an extent that some authors have even coined the term 'institution-based approach' (Peng *et al.* 2008). These factors have come to play such a determining role in the location of productive activities, that even in spite of globalization, Multinational Enterprises (MNEs) react in selective and very different ways to the opportunities that offered by the global economy (Henisz and Delios, 2001).

In this context, the importance of political risk is worth noting as a key factor in Foreign Direct Investment (FDI), both in the investment decision and the subsequent management of activities carried out by the relevant subsidiary companies. Country risk encompasses so-called political risk (probability of expropriations, unexpected governmental control, regulatory changes, etc.) and sovereign risk (associated with the risk assumed by international lenders due to incompliance with the contractual terms of the debt incurred by the government).

Two levels may be distinguished for this type of risk: macro-level risk that is assumed by all foreign investors due to their exposure to the country in question and micro-level risk, due to the differences between investors in their sensitivity to the country risk by sector (for example, hydrocarbons, banking, automobile components, etc.) or country of origin.

Likewise, firms from the same sector of activity may be assuming more favourable risk differentials in the same country, which inherently assumes that this class of risk may be managed through the development of skills related, for instance, to risk assessment, negotiation with host governments or even of a linguistic nature (López-Duarte and Vidal-Suárez, 2010).

In other words, firms may develop political capabilities, related to negotiation and action, in such a way that allows them to effectively manage country risk and face up to market failings that may be present in poorly developed institutional environments and with high discretional power of the government (Wan, 2005). In fact, some recent studies have pointed to the possibility that certain MNEs, particularly American and Spanish ones, may obtain competitive advantages through the political capabilities that they might have developed (Holburn, 2001; Henisz 2003; Jiménez, 2010; Jiménez, in press), thanks to which they could be seen to benefit in negotiations with governments, especially where there are high levels of political discretionality and corruption (García-Canal and Guillén 2008, Jiménez *et al.* in press).

In concrete, corruption has been revealed as an especially important factor in the configuration and explicitation of country risk and is identified as an influential element in FDI and therefore in MNEs. Therefore, corruption has been turned into a topic of international interest (UN Global Compact, OECD), and for firms themselves through their Corporate Social Responsibility (CRS) and governance programmes.

Thus, the "Global Reporting Initiative" (GRI), is of great influence on firms, not only Spanish but from all around the globe, in the preparation of CRS reports. Its section on corruption requests information on the percentage and total number of business units analyzed for risks related to corruption (SO2), the percentage of employees trained in the organization's anti-corruption policies and procedures (SO3) and actions taken in response to incidents of corruption (SO4), all of which are classified as 'core' indicators.

As an illustrative example, we may mention that in the majority of codes of conduct and reports on social responsibility drawn up by some of the principal Spanish MNEs (BBVA, Santander, Telefónica, Iberdrola, Inditex, etc.), reference is also made to the fight against corruption, despite the results obtained in the studies cited earlier. Nevertheless, we should not forget that these are voluntary codes and are hardly subject to external evaluation (Jiménez and Durán, 2009).

The internationalization process of Spanish firms, especially since the 1990s, may be considered relatively successful insofar as it has allowed some MNEs to grow to a large enough size and to gain enough of a market share to become relevant competitors and even leaders in various markets. This is all due to an important effort by investors, appropriate strategic planning, decisive support to technological improvements and enhancement of quality and excellence. However, the role that institutional variables have also played should not be forgotten.

Therefore, the objective of this study is, on the one hand, to review the scientific literature that analyzes the effect of discretionary powers in host government policy and the level of corruption in the host country on the internationalization strategy of MNEs. It will lend special attention to the use of these variables by Spanish MNEs as opportunities for the creation of competitive advantages instead of considering them as a threat. On the other hand, however, it also wishes to make a critical reflection on the drawbacks that may arise for the MNE of a behaviour that the public might understand as verging on the irresponsible and that can occasion serious damage to the company's public image.

The rest of the article is organized in the following way: in the second section, the relation between the institutional environment, opportunistic behaviour and the internationalization strategy is analyzed. Special attention is lent to the most widely used measures to analyze the effect of the discretionary power of host government and the corruption levels in the country, their advantages and drawbacks and any attempts to improve on the situation.

In the third section, a bibliographic review is conducted of the scientific literature and its results when analyzing those variables in an international context. In the fourth section, arguments are advanced on the advantages that this type of variable represents in the internationalization strategy of Spanish MNEs. This is given as an example of the opportunities that they entail for those MNEs that develop satisfactory political capabilities, but without forgetting the potential dangers or threats, derived especially from the consequences in their Corporate Social Responsibility (CRS) strategy. Finally, the main conclusions drawn from the study are presented.

2. Institutional Environment, Opportunistic Behaviour and Internationalization Strategies

Acknowledging that markets operate in a political, administrative, legal and social context, recent scientific research under the name of "New Institutional Economics" has expressed interest in analyzing the organization of public sector institutions and their interaction with economic activity in the private sector (North, 1990; Holburn, 2001). Thus, although up until now the Theory of Transaction Costs (Williamson, 1975, 1985) has lent greater attention to opportunistic behaviour in the marketplace (defined as the *ex-post* redistribution of economic rents between the two contracting parties through the exploitation of points that are not specified in the written contract), other participants are increasingly included in the analysis of the environment of the organizations, in particular the threat of opportunism in the public sector (Henisz, 1998; Zelner, 1999).

The conventional view in the scientific literature has associated a negative relation between the magnitude of inward FDI flows or the probability of setting up a subsidiary with different variables related to political risk in the host country, by considering that in those places the threat of nationalistic behaviour (discrimination of foreigners relative to nationals) or opportunistic behaviour by the public sector was greater.

Defined in a wide sense, political risk is the probability that the state will employ its monopoly for legal coercion to overturn the agreements reached with the MNEs, so as to influence the redistribution of rents between the public and private sectors (Holburn, 2001). It is such a complex phenomena that the attempts to measure it with only one variable have run into severe criticism, as they do not account for the different aspects by which it is constituted (Kobrin, 1982; De la Torre and Neckar, 1988). In this sense, it is advisable to complement the analysis with various measures in an attempt to provide a complete image of the various elements that influence the global institutional quality of the host country (Slangen and Tulder, 2009). The evolution of the literature on two fundamental aspects will be reviewed in this section: the level of political discretionality and corruption.

2.1. Political Risk and Political Discretionality

A survey carried out by the U.S. Conference Board confirmed the heightened interest of firms in the analysis of political risk since the early 70s (Blank *et al.* 1980). However, it also underlined that these efforts were limited to proposing recommendations on the quality of the investment climate in an intuitive and not in a systematic way in North-American (Root 1968) and in French firms (Marois 1981), preferring methods based on random observations made by trusted executives (Rummel and Heenan 1978).

Measures improved as the years passed by, although Henisz and Zelner (1999) were critical of those generally used up until today because they were either based on macro accounting measures or on ratings drawn from investors' perceptions. This entailed several of problems: in the first place, as pointed out by Kobrin (1982), the measures are by nature retrospective instead of prospective; secondly, macroeconomic measures are subject to the possibility of manipulation; and in third place, the perceptions are to a certain extent tautological – all they reveal is that investors prefer not to invest there where perceived risk is high, without tackling the fundamental source of the risk. The investigation should therefore include other types of objective measures: the structure of the political system, the credibility of governments to adjust to the policies which they have chosen or the possibility that pressure groups lobby for changes that are contrary to the interests of the MNE. In short, the measures to be used should be those that examine past tendencies and risk perceptions, but do not focus on their direct extrapolation, but on their interpretation in the context of the political and regulatory structures of the nation (Henisz and Zelner 1999).

The link between political institutions and economic results started with the study of the differences between democracies and autocracies (North, 1990; Olson, 1965, 1982, 1993, Wittman, 1989). However, this comparison ignores the study of mechanisms that may be established to prevent policies from being directed at particular interest groups in each country, by means of restrictions on the discretionality of leaders in democracies as well as in autocracies (Henisz 2004).

The first studies that analyzed the credibility of institutions instead of comparing democracies with autocracies were grounded in subjective indices based on the opinions of experts or business leaders in the country (Borner *et al.* 1995; Knack and Keefer, 1995; Brunetti and Weder, 1997), which in the opinion of Henisz (2004) entails various limitations. In the first place, the lack of historic information on individual opinions can lead to a problem of endogeneity. In second place, such indices do not manage to explain the relation between institutions and economic results. Instead, they are based on the relationship, which is not necessarily known, between the investors or expert opinion and those same institutions. Finally, the correlation between those indices and the true nature of the institutions becomes hazy when a greater need arises as, for instance, during speculative bubbles in which investors are unaware of the dangers of a change in the policy of the country.

Subsequently, further efforts to measure the institutional environment have been based on the use of indices such as the "Gastil Index of Democracy" (www.freedomhouse.org) which attempts to quantify the degree of democracy or civil liberties in the country. However, it has an important failing in that such measures may not be correlated with the degree of commitment to private property rights (Knack and Keefer 1995). Other indices such as those on political instability that take assassinations or murders into account have better results, but are weakened if more autocratic regimes are included in the sample. Finally, the indices that make up the "International Country Risk Guide" (ICRG)[1] try to quantify the risk faced by the MNE. This question is broader than the mere analysis of the commitment shown by the authorities.

In the opinion of Henisz (2000), these indices are based on subjective measures that on occasions bear no relation to political institutions, and for which data from recent years is all that is available, which reduces their potential and limits sample selection. Moreover, identifying the most satisfactory way of combining the different measures that they use, as well as those of the relevant political institutions in each case is a complicated affair. In conclusion, the author points to four limitations in the measures found in the empirical literature: many of them have no relation with the ability of the government to deliver a credible commitment not to interfere in private property rights, they are also subjective measures, solely available for a limited period of time or for certain countries and finally, they are frequently used outside of a theoretical framework. Therefore, basing his work on

[1] This index is prepared as an arithmetic mean of three other indices: economic, financial and political.

spatial modelling techniques of positive political theory, the author sought to develop a structural and comparable model of the degree of restriction of a government, in order to modify a certain policy according to the number of independent veto points in the political system and the distribution of political preferences between and among the different powers. For Henisz, the policies adopted are a function of the country's political structure, and the author assumes that the possibility of changes entail uncertainty and lower levels of investment and growth.

Thus, authors such as Henisz (1998) and Beck *et al.* (2001) propose the use of objective measures (although it has been argued that measures are never neutral and they involve some degree of cultural or political bias) of institutional credibility, assuming that those countries with more veto points in their political systems will turn out to be more stable (and finding support in the preliminary evidence presented in works such as those by Hallerberg and Basinger, 1998 or Treisman, 2000 which show higher levels of stability for various macroeconomic measures in those countries with a larger number of veto points). Other authors, such as Tsebelis (1995), also share this opinion and argue that the potential for change in the policies of a nation decreases as the number of veto points, the lack of congruency (differences in the positions between the different powers) and cohesion (similarities in the positions of the units that make up each of the powers) increase; and in turn abundant academic literature contends that investors would prefer to invest in those countries whose policies are easier to predict as they perceive it as involving less risk (Bennet and Green, 1972; Green and Cunningham, 1975; Root and Ahmed, 1978; Loree and Guisinger, 1995; Gastanaga *et al.* 1998; Wei, 2000a; Fine, 2003; Huang *et al.* 2003; Vial, 2003), although there are also factors that diminish this effect such as the previous experiences in the host country (Henisz and Delios, 2001) and in other countries with high levels of risk (Delios and Henisz, 2003).

The Political Constraint (POLCONV) index of Henisz (developed in his work of 1998) has the objective of analyzing the degree of discretion that a government may exercise as a function of the existence and role played by other possible powers established in the host country. It starts by identifying the number of independent veto points in the political system of a country, (the executive branch and the two legislative chambers, the judicial branch, and sub-federal or sub-regional institutions). For the author, the ability of governments to convince third parties of their commitment not to interfere in private property rights is fundamental to secure FDI, which is necessary for economic growth, as otherwise, if the investment is retracted or postponed, the economy may be damaged, capital flight is encouraged and the development of the black market is increased (Henisz 2000).

This index therefore takes into account the number of independent powers with a veto capacity within a country (which can be executive, legislative distinguishing between one or two chambers, judicial, and sub-federal, regional or autonomous), modifying the scores obtained in accordance with the possible alignments that might arise between the different powers, in such a way that it corresponds to the actual constraints to which the government is subjected. Additional modifications are also necessary to that score when some political powers are neither totally aligned nor totally opposed, in such a way that their composition is relevant, in order to determine the degree of political constraint. The heterogeneity in this composition, modifies the costs of changing a specific policy for the aligned or opposing powers is measured through the degree of "fractionalization" of the chamber, calculated as the probability of randomly selecting two members that belong to different parties. Henisz concluded that each additional veto point in the index adds a positive but decreasing effect on the total level of constraints, and that similarities in the preferences of the parties within an opposing power positively correlates with the constraints on changes in the policies.

Some criticism has been directed at the POLCONV index because it generates noise due to the inclusion of excessive amounts of information in a single index, unlike for example corruption indices. Furthermore, criticism was even taken up by Henisz himself (2004), relating to the absence of data on the level of "fractionalization" in the opposition and the majority power, for which reason "fractionalization" of the chamber as a whole should be used, and on lack of evidence as to whether the judicial branch and sub-federal powers may be considered completely independent veto points or whether, on the contrary, they depend on other powers. However, and despite such criticism, it is true that the index has been used in works published in highly prestigious journals, as the econometric evidence, the greater significativity and the lesser importance of the limitations set out in the POLCONV index mean it is preferable to other alternatives such as the CHECKS2a index developed by Beck *et al.* (2001). Despite taking the complex relation between the veto points, the preferences of parties and heterogeneity into account, the latter index also assumes a linear relation between the adjusted number of veto points and the degree of political constraint and that the number of veto points increases linearly in parliamentary systems with each new political party that joins the coalition holding power, without taking account of its relative size. On the contrary, Henisz's POLCONV index (1998) shows marginal decreasing performances by adding new veto points, and moreover in a non-arbitrary way that is derived from a spatial model. It also analyzes the impact of a new party on the coalition through the degree of "fractionalization" of the chamber. Finally, this index uses the same methodology for parliamentary and presidential systems, although it takes into account that the former are usually characterized by alignment between the executive and legislative branch and that they usually have more fragmented chambers, in such a way that the differences between the two systems come from the spatial model in use and not from an ad-hoc construction.

2.2. Political Risk and Corruption

Corruption occurs when laws, regulations and rules are, in an illegitimate and illicit way, "bought" or "put in place", and the same applies to the way in which they are interpreted and applied for the benefit of private interests. It is stated explicitly in terms of administrative decisions and awards of tenders for public works, the payment of subsidies, the provision of services and other advantages such as legal decisions, etc.

Data gathered by Transparency International (TI) has played a prominent role in the empirical analysis of the effect of corruption on FDI. This organization defines itself as a coalition that seeks to put and end to the devastating effect of corruption on men, women and children, with the specific mission of working towards a world free from corruption. Created in 1993, it seeks to increase awareness of corruption, reduce apathy towards corruption and its tolerance, at the same time as designing and implementing practical actions to combat it.

TI has chapters in 90 countries, from which it reports on and combats corruption in relation to governments, communication media and relevant actors in the world of business and civil society, at all times from a politically independent perspective, although working jointly on occasions with other organizations. Corruption for TI is defined as "*the abuse of entrusted power for private gain. It hurts everyone whose life, livelihood or happiness depends on the integrity of people in a position of authority."* Negative global consequences ensue, trapping millions of people in poverty and provoking social, economic and political problems. Its pernicious effects are especially remarkable in those people in serious economic difficulties, by obliging them to spend part of their income on bribes, but it also distorts both national and international commerce, constitutes a threat to the security and the sustainability of natural resources, fosters gender-based discrimination and is an attack on democratic values.

Motivated by the concerns arising from the persistent existence of corruption and its pernicious effects, TI has also developed a series of measures to assist with corruption-related research and to raise awareness of its extension and relevance in the world[2]. Thus, the "Global Corruption Barometer" is a survey on the attitudes and experience of society with regard to corruption and the "Bribe Payments Index" evaluates the corrupt practices in the host country, in other words, the probability that MNEs from developed countries will make use of bribes when operating abroad. In its attempt to combat this, TI has developed a series of recommendations contained in its "National Integrity System Approach" (NIS), which consists of key institutions, laws and practices that contribute to promoting integrity and transparency in society. TI has also published a guide, known as the "Anti-Corruption Handbook (ACH): National Integrity System in practice", in order to put the fundamental reforms into practice that are needed to develop and apply anti-corruption measures in accordance with the NIS, which has become a worldwide reference.

But undoubteldy the most well-known and widely used measure has been the "Corruption Perception Index". Updated annually since 1995, it analyzes the level of perceived corruption in 180 countries in accordance with expert opinion and surveys. This index has been one of the most widely used to measure corruption levels in the countries included in it. Recently, though, it has been the target of criticism and proposals for its improvement such as for example Kaufman *et al.* (1999), who proposed the WBI's "Control of Corruption" index which includes a greater number of sources and countries, although the requirements to estimate the scores are, on occasions, less demanding.

However, both indices are criticized by Knack (2006), who considers them "obscure" to a certain extent, as some sources are not publicly available and others require prior payment, comparisons over time must be made with caution as their content varies, some sources suffer from excessive interdependence and he is not in agreement with the weight assigned to each source. In fact, the author considers that despite the fact that these indices have managed to raise global awareness of the pernicious effects, they are, by definition, subject to conceptual imprecision and inconsistency by using diverse aggregated sources. In his opinion, other measures such as the "Business Environment and Enterprise Performance Survey" (BEEPS), which he himself employs, are more satisfactory, because they centre on corruption between firms and host government officials, instead of trying to provide a broader but imprecise overall view.

Nevertheless, the fact that on occasions the problems of corruption do not stem from host government officials as well as the number of counties that are not in the survey, means that in the meantime the imperfect measures offered by TI are still regularly used in the majority of scientific studies, until new and improved measures arrive that allow researchers not to

[2] Available on the website www.transparency.org.

make sacrifices in the scope of the research either with regard to the countries that make up the sample or the type of corruption under analysis.

The available evidence centred on corruption has mainly been directed at the analysis of the economic and social consequences of the phenomena. Thus, Dreher *et al.* (2007) consider corruption as endemic, perverse and a significant contributory factor to low economic growth that dampens investment and increases inequalities. They obtain results that show how corruption is converted into a loss of GDP growth, especially worrying in Africa and Asia, and less so, although still in a significative way, in Europe. Besides, Gupta *et al.* (1998) point out in their work that corruption entails important negative implications in the distribution of wealth in a country, such that measures that minimize corruption will also reduce poverty and inequalities. Finally, Tanzi (1995) warns that individuals that are well connected in society are those that benefit most from corruption, and are normally those with the greatest wealth.

There are also works with a normative approach. For instance, Cuervo-Cazurra (2008) identifies and analyzes the conditions under which national and international coordination at a legislative level can reduce the attractions of FDI in countries characterized by high corruption rates. The author underlines the fact that in the absence of mechanisms for coordination, legislations become ineffective as MNEs from home countries, in which measures are in place against investments in regions with high-corruption rates, will be obliged in any case to continue investing, forced to react to the strategy of their competitors who are not subjected to these constraints.

3. Efects of Political Risk on Direct Foreign Investment. Review of the Literature

Despite the abundant research that points to the importance of the institutional context for the market structure in the host country (Nee 1992; Granovetter 1995; Fisman and Khana 1998; Khanna and Palepu, 1998 and 1999; Khanna 2000) and some seminal studies that have examined the ability of the firm to plug into institutional idiosyncrasies (Root 1968; Vernon 1971 and 1978; Behrman *et al.* 1975); the international literature on relations with institutional idiosyncrasies was still relatively underdeveloped at the start of the 21st century in comparison with the literature on market or economic variables (Henisz 2003; Boddewyn, 2003). Numerous recent lines of research attempting to cover that gap in the scientific literature have focused on the analysis of various aspects, associated with formal institutions (corruption, employment regulation, political rights and civil liberties, property rights, taxation policy) as well as informal ones (related to cultural and psychological aspects), introducing an institution-based approach of increasing importance that complements the traditional resource-based and industrial-based approaches and OLI paradigm (Dunning and Lundan, 2008; Peng *et al.* 2008, Cantwell et al. 2010).

The relevance of the discretional power of host government, as well as the level of corruption in the host country are particularly noteworthy in the literature on political risk, together with recent studies on the impact of terrorism (Branzei and Abdelnour, 2010; Czinkota *et al.* 2010) and some new analyses based on market measures (Click and Weiner, 2010). The increased risk faced by MNEs that invest in those countries may be pointed out, although for those MNEs from countries with similar institutional environments, normally developing countries, this gives them a competitive advantage over MNEs from more developed countries when channelling FDI to less-developed countries (Cuervo-Cazurra and Genc, 2008).

Thus, Henisz and Zelner, in their works of 2001 and 2002, use the POLCONV index to demonstrate that in the telecommunications and telecommunications and electricity sectors, respectively, the political discretionality of governments undermines the credibility of the commitments they have acquired. This in turn leads to reductions in FDI, especially in sectors with large sunken costs, which means that they may not easily be redeployed and large quasi-rents are therefore associated with them (Goldberg, 1976; Spiller, 1993).

Henisz and Zelner (2002) explain that even if expected income declines as a consequence of price reductions, firms will remain in the market, fundamentally in regulated sectors, in which given their high-fixed costs, their operating costs only represent a small part of total costs. This creates incentives for politicians to benefit from the occasion by behaving in opportunistic ways and to modify the conditions or even go so far as to order expropriations for political reasons. The combination of the economic opportunity to expropriate a steady source of rents, together with the political benefits of doing so, imply greater difficulties in maintaining the stability of the "rules of the game" and in not making discretional alterations to previously settled agreements. This is due to the fact that these are high consumption services helps the consumers appreciate the improvements obtained through these measures and at least in the short term, increases support for the government that can even use the foreign MNEs as "scapegoats", trying to get public opinion to blame them for the economic woes of the country.

Moreover, the authors consider that, together with the possibility of pressure groups lobbying for change that would run contrary to the interests of the MNE, the structure of the political system and the credibility of its political leaders should be analyzed, in order to satisfactorily evaluate the political risk faced by the MNE. They argue that in the case of a government subject to higher political constraints, MNEs will be more insensitive to the possibility of lobbying by pressure groups, as there would be a much lower probability of the policy actually changing. However, if governmental constraints are weak, a great deal of attention should be paid to the possibility that influential lobbies will achieve change that is harmful to the interests of the MNE. This happens, with greater frequency, when the consumer base is an industrial one, as this type of consumer has greater weight than individuals or small firms.

The authors, however, also point out that greater powers of political discretion exercised by host government can represent a source of competitive advantage, in which case larger FDI flows may be expected. In effect, if the other pressure groups have little weight, it is the MNE which may try to force through policy changes that would benefit it, so that there is an incentive for the MNEs to invest there. On the contrary, when the other pressure groups have power, the MNEs behave as may be expected, preferring political systems with constraints that guarantee stability, and they move away from those countries in which such constraints are not on offer. For their part, Henisz and Mansfield (2006) analyzed the influence of macroeconomic conditions -involving pressure group lobbies in support of protectionist measures- on the probability of changes in economic and commercial policies, especially in the case of the unemployment rate. The authors found evidence that such pressures are given greater consideration in those countries with fewer political constraints.

Henisz (2003), when studying the electricity sector, pointed out that in these types of regulated sectors, the predictions of Buckley and Casson (1976), on the internationalization of activities rooted in competitive advantages arising from technology or marketing capabilities, might not be acceptable if the ability to negotiate with host-country institutions is not included as a possible source of advantage. These sectors in which the investment pattern differs from what is foreseen are characterized by:

- The central role that the government plays as a provider or supervisor, arising from the strong social values that create tensions with private ownership.
- The need for foreign capital, which obliges the host government to open up the sector to public participation.
- Institutional idiosyncrasies, which hinder international credit institutions and investors from being able to cover their exposure to risk with financial instruments.

The author argues that the joint presence of these three characteristics allow MNEs to generate rents, thanks to the management of relations with the government, or in a general way with the institutional idiosyncrasies of the host country.

Moreover, this possibility of obtaining competitive advantages through the management of political risk as an opportunity and not as a threat is highly influenced by the previous international experience of the MNE. Delios and Henisz (2003) contend that experience provides greater benefits to firms embarking on international expansion when gained sequentially, through successive steps that maximize the opportunities for learning about specific dimensions of the environments in which they are found. At the same time, experience minimizes the degree of uncertainty that affects the firm in its international expansion, as it acquires knowledge and skills applicable to environments in which new investments are made in accordance with its absorption capacities (Cohen and Levinthal 1990). In their study, relating to the international expansion of Japanese firms over the two decades of the 1980s and 1990s, Delios and Henisz found evidence that the firms with the greatest degree of experience in countries with a high political risk have less sensitivity towards political risk. Moreover, those firms with experience in a certain culture are better prepared to place new FDI in countries from the same cultural block. Finally, they argue that if the MNE has carried out investments in production plants rather than distribution plants, which implies that they have experience in opening channels of communication with hostauthorities, contracting employees, negotiating over taxes or permits needed for international commerce or the repatriation of dividends, then it will be better prepared to understand the political process of the nation to which it is directing its new investment. This prior experience of the MNE can even come to alleviate the negative effect that a high risk policy in the host country can have on the total FDI that it receives, in such a way that despite the high level of uncertainty that exists, the levels of inward FDI are greater than those that might be expected.

In addition and also producing controversial results, academic literature has studied the effects of corruption on firms. For instance, Djankov *et al.* (2002) claim that in corrupt countries, firms need to comply with a larger number of requirements to begin their activity, because in this way governments officials can extract higher rents through bribes to speed up the administrative processes. Smarzynska and Wei (2002) confirm that when the higher the level of corruption in the country, the higher the costs for the MNE. They also suggest that having a local partner can reduce them but, in exchange, it increases the risk of technology and knowledge leaks. They therefore point out how firms with well-known brands, good reputation and technological capabilities are more reticent to set up joint ventures and more likely to exercise complete control over their investment (their subsidiary). As additional evidence of this traditional negative view of corruption for the firm, the previously cited article by Knack (2006) shows how greater levels of corruption are associated with a lower probability of the MNE carrying out a FDI, results in line with those obtained by Brouthers *et al.* (2008).

Recently, Hakkala *et al.* (2008) have underlined that the effects of corruption are functions of the motivation of the FDI. In concrete, the effect is negative for those investments made for the purpose of selling goods in the country and to take control of a market quota, but positive for those that are looking for lower costs and that export from the home country. Moreover, their results showed that a greater level of corruption reduces the probability that a firm will invest in a certain country and lose its position with regard to domestic firms, with a deeper knowledge of the prevailing "rules of the game" in the territory. In the opinion of the authors, this can mean that those benefiting from corruption and local firms that wish to avoid international competitors over which they do not consider that they have competitive advantages might, openly or secretly, oppose anti-corruption measures that are beneficial for the country as they ease market tensions and promote efficiency.

The influence of corruption on the FDI and on the MNEs can come up in different ways. Thus, it may be argued that when corruption is predictable (it may be anticipated), its negative effect on FDI is lower than when it is less predictable. A firm that uses corruption as a means of facilitating the development of its activity in a country, can improve (more or less transitorily) competitive advantages in that country with respect to competitors that make no use of that possibility or do so less efficiently. Corruption is, therefore, a determining factor in the business and the investment climate, affecting FDI (Wei, 2000; Habib and Zurawicki, 2002); the entry strategy (Rodriguez *et al.* 2005) and the behaviour of the MNE (Luo, 2006). In this sense, it may be concluded that firms from countries with a high degree of corruption invest relatively more in countries that also reflect a high level of corruption (Cuervo-Carruza, 2006).

4. The Proactive Strategy of Spanish Multinationals with Regard to Political Risk

As pointed out earlier, the conventional view of the scientific literature has associated a negative relation between the size of inward flows of FDI or the probability of implantation of a subsidiary with a range of variables related to political risk in the host countries. It considers that in those places the threat of opportunistic behaviour within the public sector was greater. Various works have shown empirical evidence of this negative relation for the level of political discretionality (Henisz and Zelner 2001 and 2002), and corruption (Wei, 2000a, 2000b; Habib and Zurawicki, 2002; Lambsdorff, 2003; Cuervo-Cazurra, 2006, 2008).

However, some papers have shown evidence of the proactive use of political risk by Spanish MNEs in their internationalization strategies in different regions of the world (García-Canal and Guillén, 2008; Jiménez, 2010; Jiménez, *in press*), as well as by MNEs from North America (Holburn, 2001) or MNEs from developing countries investing in least developed countries (Cuervo-Cazurra and Genc, 2008).

The internationalization of the Spanish firm, which began in the 1970s and experienced an spectacular growth in the 1990s by taking advantage of various liberalization and privatization processes in Latin America, is well documented in the literature. For instance, it has been underlined the importance of technological advantages of a sectorial nature (Molero, 1999), the specificity of resources (Pla, 1999), the use of international alliances (García-Canal *et al.* 2002), the strategic relevance of a territory as leverage in the process of expansion into other geographical zones or areas (Durán, 2005) or the impact of language diversity on the entry mode (López-Duarte and Vidal-Suárez, 2010). However, with regard to the use of political capabilities to manage political risk, it may be affirmed that Spanish MNEs have not stuck with the conventional view of political risk that is seen only as a threat. Instead, they have sought to use it and convert it into an opportunity in accordance with their own resources and, principally, with the capabilities that they have developed, in order to achieve competitive advantages useful for their internationalization processes.

Thus, García-Canal and Guillén (2008) demonstrate that in the case of Spanish MNEs from regulated sectors a bias exists towards countries with a certain discretionality shown by hostgovernments. Despite their aversion towards macro-economic uncertainty, these MNEs invest in these types of locations as they can take advantage of their negotiating skills to win advantageous entry conditions, better than the possible potential damage that might occur were the rules of the game that affect that FDI to change. The authors consider that this is due to the Spanish MNEs being accustomed to negotiation and maintaining relations with the government and regulators in the home country. They are able to make good use of this previous experience in the countries within their internationalization process.

Taking into account the criticism on the attempts to measure political risk with a single variable, Jiménez *et al.* (in press) continued the research line of García-Canal and Guillén (2008), but introducing the level of political constraints, perceived corruption and the level of economic freedom and the protection of property rights into the model. The results show that some greater levels of political constraints increase the probability of investment in Europe and North America, in line with the results of Galan *et al.* (2007); whereas lesser corruption increases that probability in Asia and once again in Europe. However, in the case of Latin America, it is the higher levels of corruption and not the political constraints that favour Spanish FDI (see Annex 1 which offers a summary of the results).

Moreover, Jiménez (2010), using a sample of 166 large Spanish MNEs from various sectors, analyzed the relation between political risk and the extent of the internationalization strategy. The results show that, as well as other variables such as size, solvency and product diversification, the variables of political risk are very significant (see Annex 2). It is true that, in accordance with the Uppsala model (Johanson and Vahlne, 1977 and 1990; Johanson and Wiedersheim-Paul, 1975; Welch and Luostarinen, 1988), those companies with a wider international expansion are those that invest in more risky locations and that the aggregate flows of FDI are of a gradual nature with respect to their location. However, at an individual level, and especially those created more recently, MNEs try to gain competitive advantages in those markets where their resources and capabilities are of greater use, which leads them to invest in countries with very different levels of political risk, where they can make the most of their negotiating skills. By investing in a portfolio of countries with great diversity in their levels of political risk, MNEs gain such advantages as the acquisition of *know-how,* access to managerial talent, new competitive skills and the achievement of better international diversification that can protect against regional fluctuations in both offer and demand (Jiménez, 2010). It should be highlighted that the proactive use of political risk is not exclusive to Spanish MNEs. Together with the quoted studies on American MNEs by Holburn (2001) or on FDI from MNEs in developing countries towards very underdeveloped countries (Cuervo-Cazurra and Genc, 2008), Jiménez (in press) analyzes the FDI flows from three countries in the South of Europe (Spain, Italy, and France) towards the new members of the European Union incorporated in 2005 and some economies from North Africa. The panel results during the period 1999-2006, in addition to an export orientation and the positive effect of good economic perspectives, a high level of human capital and satisfactory infrastructural development, also reflect that these MNEs head for the locations that are characterized by greater levels of political risk, especially of perceived corruption (see Annex 3). This does not mean that MNEs from these countries do not positively value low levels of political risk when choosing the region of the world to locate their investment.

MNEs are averse to risk when selecting the region, but once they have decided to invest in a region characterized by high levels of political risk in general, they will select a specific location where they can maximize the advantages that may be forthcoming from their political capabilities. In any case, it should be emphasized that these results do not necessarily imply that MNEs make active use of ethically reprehensible strategies such as corruption, but they might be the consequence of the fact that MNEs positively value the possibility of resorting to such strategies on the basis of need, in the face of threats of expropriation or unilateral modifications of the agreements reached with governments. Nevertheless, in accordance with the 2008 "Bribe Payers Index", prepared by Transparency International, Spain found itself in group 2, together with the United States, France and Singapore, countries with a greater propensity to use corruption than others from the European environment found in group 1, such as Belgium, Germany, the Netherlands, Switzerland or the United Kingdom. From among all the European countries under study, only Italy, in group 3, and Russia in group 4, both have a greater propensity than the Spanish to make use of corruption. In any case, this trust in governments from countries with high levels of political risk, especially corruption, is not free from drawbacks, especially at a time like the present, in which the concept of CSR is assuming ever greater importance in society. Thus, it is as well needed to underline that MNEs should not forget that by using certain techniques, especially corruption, they might sacrifice their social legitimacy and run the risk of losing influence and effectiveness due to the negative impact on their "*status*" in the international community (Ghosal and Moran 2005). Moreover, the greater levels of political risk, especially corruption, imply worse perspectives for future economic growth in the host country, which may also be very harmful to the interests of the MNE.

CONCLUSION

Political risk constitutes a variable with an undeniable impact on the decisions of MNEs regarding the location FDI. It is, nevertheless, a complex phenomenon, due to its own nature and to the different aspects that it encompasses. Its measurement is complicated and controversial, given its qualitative nature. The extensive literature revised in this work seeks to show the important effect that political discretionality and the level of corruption in the host country has on FDI. The majority of studies have considered both phenomena as risks associated with the destination of FDI and only recently has the possibility been considered that such a risk can be in reality an opportunity, at least in the short term, when considered as an internal and manageable variable for the firm instead of an exogenous one.

This is possible because MNEs can develop capabilities of a political nature that allow them to obtain competitive advantages against their competitors through negotiation with political powers in the host country (Holburn, 2001; Wan, 2005; García-Canal and Guillén, 2008) or through corrupt practices (Jiménez, 2010; Jiménez, *in press*). These capabilities, however, are especially difficult to measure because of their highly tacit component. Thus, the literature has only been able to show evidence of the proactive use of political risk thanks to these capabilities, but is unable to delve more deeply into their origin, development and exploitation beyond a merely theoretical perspective. However, it is worth asking whether this strategy may be advisable in the long term and the prudent answer is no. Gupta *et al.* (1998) point out that some consider that corruption improves efficiency, as it allows those who are more prepared to pay to achieve what they need. However, permanent distortions that allow some groups to benefit more than others are ignored. Moreover, there is no reason why those that are more prepared to pay should be held as the beneficiaries of governmental programmes. In addition, this approach involves problems that relate to the distribution of rents and poverty, and economic growth (Dreher *et al.* 2007) and constitute the principal obstacle to achieving economic and social development (World Bank, 2001). The worse macroeconomic perspectives for these types of countries should not be forgotten by Spanish firms in their long-term planning. In addition, the growing awareness within society and firms of CRS, and the ever more important role of society as one of the firms' principal "stakeholders" might mean that non-compliance with the expected CSR requirements could turn out to be negatively and significantly affected. In fact, firms that sacrifice social legitimacy, by applying practices that relate to corruption run the risk of losing influence and effectiveness as a consequence of the negative impact on their status in the world community (Ghosal and Moran 2005). It is true that on occasions it is not necessary to be superior to competitors in all areas to achieve success (Erramilli *et al.* 1997) and that possessing the appropriate resources and capabilities in each environment will allow a firm to operate in various external markets without necessarily being the most powerful global competitor (Wan, 2005). In this sense, Spanish MNEs have known how to position themselves there where their negotiating capabilities have been useful, but should not forget the possible positive relation between the social responsibility of the firm and financial profitability found by Waddock and Grave (1997) or Mahon and McGovan (1998). On the other hand, other authors argue that no correlation exists, such as Aupperle *et al.* (1985) or McWilliams and Siegel (2001). Besides, social responsibility is increasingly understood as a strategy of the firm linked to its mission, vision and values, and that by putting it into practice in a satisfactory way as a "social strategy", it can generate competitive advantages in the long term that help in the creation of value (Husted and Allen, 2000). The active management of political risk by Spanish MNEs as an opportunity instead of a threat is an unmistakeable symptom of the professional approach of their management teams towards the internationalization strategy, aware of the relevance of using all the resources and abilities efficiently to achieve success and to ensure the survival of the firm. However, abusive political use of the negotiating capabilities that they have developed, with the aim of gaining advantageous competitive positions through negotiation with governments with excessive powers of discretionality or thanks to the corruptibility that they find in the host countries, might be interpreted as a negligent attitude towards compliance with responsible behaviour that society expects today from all firms, the negative consequences of which should not be underestimated. As future lines of research in this field of investigation, it is worth highlighting the challenge involved in achieving an empirical measurement of these political capabilities, which would permit intra- and inter-sectorial comparative studies both at a national and at an international level. Moreover, these political capabilities appear to lose value with the passage of time (García-Canal and Guillén, 2008), such that it would be of interest to compare whether this characteristic strategy of the Spanish MNEs is profitable in the short and long term. Finally, the referenced studies have centred on the case of large companies, but whether small and medium-sized MNEs share this strategy has yet to be analyzed.

Annex 1. Logistic Regressions of the determinants of FDI by geographic region. Source: adaptation from Jiménez *et al.* (2008)

	Europe	*Latin Amer.*	*North Amer.*	*Asia*
1. Food Ind.				
2. Construction				
3. Regulated Sector		.6182*		-1.0351*
		(.2598)		(.41442)
4. Financial		1.4685***		
		(.3515)		
5. Other sectors	-.70904***	1.3602***		-.87020**
	(.20099)	(.19799)		(.28826)
6. Employees		.3049*		
		(.1277)		
7. ROE				
8. Sales Growth				
9. Solvency		.0115*		
		(.0046)		
10. FDI/GDP	.0426**	-.0293	.14954*	.1007**
	(.0184)	(.01867)	(.0735)	(.0301)
11. GDP Growth	-.3919***	.1911***	.5125*	.3739***
	(.0303)	(.0268)	(.2010)	(.0401)
12. Population	-1.3728***	-.3875**	4.3092***	1.3071***
	(.1411)	(.1158)	(.6750)	(.1635)
13. Index of economic freedoms	-1.7529***	2.6899***	3.2482***	
	(.1423)	(.1871)	(.8019)	
14. Corruption Index	.6862***	-1.6037***		.2422**
	(.0635)	(.0993)		(.0856)
15. POLCONV Index	.3404***		3.8446***	-.3498***
	(.0409)		(.6161)	(.0413)
16. Number of foreign countries in which the MNE operates		-.02411***		.0207***
		(.0043)		(.0042)

* $p < 0.10$; ** $p < 0.05$; *** $p < 0.01$

Standard error between brackets.

Annex 2. Binomial Regression of the internationalization scope of Spanish MNEs. Source: Adapted from Jiménez (2010)

VARIABLES	All MNEs	MNEs 6 o + countries	MNEs -6 countries
RELATED DIVERSIFICATION	.0606394 (.1214588)	-.1067046 (.131643)	-.0779455 (.2192114)
UNRELATED DIVERSIFICATION	.2512023 (.1766675)	.0490005 (.1847853)	-.0018333 (.3498968)
MANUFACTURERS	-.0662715 (.1463041)	-.037212 (.1571783)	.048676 (.266202)
FOOD INDUSTRY	-.2334848 (.2042772)	-.0001396 (.251165)	.0263211 (.2719587)
CONSTRUCTION	-.0257188 (.2271894)	-.139788 (.2366364)	.4136949 (.4153016)
REGULATED SECTORS	.0998837 (.2515646)	-.1041117 (.2541457)	.4153016 (.510106)
FINANCIAL	-.0102892 (.278747)	.3974911 (.314073)	-.1139751 (.5765283)
AVERAGE - INDEX OF ECONOMIC FREEDOM	-.0582908 (.0921442)	-.1029813 (.1000447)	-.0837397 (.1543246)
VARIANCE – INDEX OF ECONOMIC FREEDOM	.2195244* (.1284289)	.1177398 (.1324984)	.2924538 (.1845853)
AVERAGE - CORRUPTION INDEX	-.0858199 (.0595903)	-.284758*** (.1058534)	-.0495323 (.0621873)
VARIANCE - CORRUPTION INDEX	.3460202*** (.0348047)	.2713834*** (.0465981)	.178586*** (.0534808)
AVERAGE – POLCONV INDEX	.0719552 (.0934825)	.1614522 (.1892196)	.0038283 (.0972934)
VARIANCE - POLCONV INDEX	.0669221** (.0277337)	.026855 (.0456749)	.0222259 (.0298065)
AGE (LOG)	-.0331316 (.1931581)	-.59674*** (.2123497)	.3597339 (.3253405)
STOCK MARKET	-.1323725 (.132346)	-.0910293 (.1446069)	.1545473 (.2183)
ASSETS (LOG)	-.0564966 (.1314836)	.0524798 (.1423197)	.0679713 (.2402216)
EMPLOYEES (LOG)	.4450738*** (.156092)	.3130502* (.1652868)	-.0611333 (.291737)
ROE	-8.85e-06 (.0002678)	-.0001649 (.0039062)	.0000888 (.0002384)
SALES GROWTH	-.0000342 (.0022354)	-.0034053 (.0028376)	.0009022 (.0026534)
SOLVENCY	.0031323 (.0033431)	.0077687 ** (.0032826)	.0017886 (.0063141)
CONSTANT	-.2063863 (.9440196)	2.031679 (1.366301)	.267085 (1.570047)
NUM. OBSERVATIONS	166	96	70
LOG LIKELIHOOD	-469.94127	-319.3846	-102.04712

Standard error between parenthesis * $p < 0.10$; ** $p < 0.05$; *** $p < 0.01$.

Annex 3. Dynamic Panel Estimation of flows of Spanish, French and Italian FDI in Eastern Europe and North Africa Source: Adapted from Jiménez (in press)

Two-step results	Model 1
	Number of groups: 42
VARIABLES	
1. Δ FDI RECEIVED LAST YEAR	-.0495363** (.0201206)
2. Δ UNEMPLOYMENT	-5.650629 (8.016718)
3. Δ ENROLMENT IN SECONDARY EDUCATION (%)	15.25624** (7.608557)
4. Δ URBAN POPULATION	-.1071958 (4.041277)
5. Δ ELECTRICITY LOSSES	-7.926122 (6.787112)
6. Δ GDP GROWTH IN HOST COUNTRY	25.21672*** (6.740312)
7. Δ FIXED CAPITAL FORMATION (% OF GDP)	21.16896** (9.095827)
8. Δ GDP GROWTH COUNTRY OF ORIGIN	-23.43183 (20.35731)
9. Δ CORRUPTION INDEX	-21.09358*** (3.392054)
10. Δ POLCONV INDEX	-47.30001*** (8.932868)
11. Δ INDEX OF ECONOMIC FREEDOMS	-26.87632*** (5.28111)
12. Δ FDI/GDP	-13.1611*** (3.34974)
13. Δ PER CAPITA GDP	-.0169492** (.0075378)
Sargan test of over-identifying restrictions:	chi2(254) = 27.85 Prob > chi2 = 1
Arellano-Bond test that average autocovariance in residuals of order 1 is 0:	z = -1.64 Pr > z = 0.1009
Arellano-Bond test that average autocovariance in residuals of order 2 is 0:	z = -1.15 Pr > z = 0.2521
	Wald chi2(18) 155408.04

The results of the temporal *dummies* are not included in the table.
Standard error between parenthesis.
* $p < 0.10$; ** $p < 0.05$; *** $p < 0.01$.

References

Aupperle, K. Carroll, A. and Hatfield, J. (1985) "An empirical examination of the relationship between corporate social responsibility and profitability". *Academy of Management Journal*. Vol. 28, Is. 2, pp. 446-463.

Beck, T. Clarke, G. Groff, A. Keefer, P. and Walsh, P. (2001) "New tools in comparative political economy: the database of political institutions". *World Bank Economy Review*. Vol. 15, No. 1, pp. 165-176.

Behrman, J.N. Boddewyn, J.J and Kapoor, A. (1975) "*International Business-Government communications*". Lexington Books: Lexington, MA Berenbeim.

Bennet, P. D. and Green, R. T. (1972). "Political Instability as a Determinant of Direct Foreign Investment in Marketing". *Journal of Marketing Research*, 19(May): 182-86.

Blank, S. (1980) "*Assessing the political environment: an emerging function in international companies*". New York. The Conference Board.

Borner, S. Brunetti, A. and Weder, B. (1995) "*Political credibility and economic development*". St. Martin´s Press, New York.

Branzei, O. and Abdelnour, S. (2010) "Another day, another dollar: Enterprise resilience under terrorismo in developing countries". *Journal of International Business Studies*. Vol. 41, pp. 804-825.

Brouthers, L.E., Gao, Y. and McNicol, J.P. (2008) "Corruption and market attractiveness influences on different types of FDI". *Strategic Management Journal*. Vol. 29. pp. 673-680.

Brunetti, A. and Weder, B. (1997) "*Investment and institutional uncertainty: a comparative study of different uncertainty measures*". International Finance Corporation Technical Paper.

Buckley, P. and Casson, M. (1976) "*The future of the multinacional enterprise*". London: MacMillan.

Cantwell, J. Dunning, J.H. and Lundan, S. (2010) "An evolutionary approach to understanding international business activity: The co-evolution of MNEs and the institutional environment". *Journal of International Business Studies*, Vol. 41, Iss. 4, pp. 567-586.

Click, R.W. and Weiner, R.J. (2010) "Resource nationalism meets the market: Political risl and the value of petroleum reserves". *Journal of International Business Studies*. Vol. 41, pp. 783-803.

Cohen, W. M. and Levinthal D.A. (1990) "Absorptive capacity: a new perspectiva on learning and innovation". *Administrative Science Quarterly*, Vol. 35, pp. 128-153.

Cuervo-Cazurra, A. (2006), "Who Cares about Corruption?". *Journal of International Business Studies*. Vol. 37, Iss. 6, pp. 803-822.

Cuervo-Cazurra, A. (2008), "The Effectiveness of Laws against Bribery Abroad". *Journal of International Business Studies*. Vol 39, Iss. 6, pp. 957-979.

Cuervo-Cazurra, A. and Genc, M. (2008) "Transforming disadvantages into advantages: developing-country MNEs in the least developed countries". *Journal of International Business Studies*. Vol. 39, pp. 957-979.

Czynkota, M.R. Knight, G. Liesch, P. and Steen, J. (2010) "Terrorism and international business: A research agenda". *Journal of International Business Studies*. Vol. 41, pp. 826-843.

De la Torre, J. and Neckar, D.H. (1988) "Forecasting political risk for international operations". *International Journal of Forecasting*. Vol. 4 pp. 221-241.

Delios, A. and Henisz, W.J. (2003) "Political hazards, experience and sequential entry strategies: the international expansion of Japanese firms 1980-1998". *Strategic Management Journal*. Vol. 24, Iss. 11 pp.1153.

Djankov, S. La Porta, R. López-de-Silanes, F. and Shleifer, A. (2002) "The regulation of entry". *Quarterly Journal of Economics*. CXVII, Iss. 1, pp. 1-37.

Dreher, A. Kotsogiannis, C. and McCorriston, S. (2007) "Corruption around the world: evidence from a structural model". *Journal of Comparative Economics*. Vol. 35, Iss. 3, pp. 443-466.

Dunning, J.H. and Lundan, S. (2008) *Multinational Enterprises and the Global Economy*. ,Cheltenham: Edward Elgar.

Durán, J.J. (2008), "La geografía de la empresa multinacional española". *Boletín de Estudios Económicos*. LXIII (193), pp. 17-44.

Durán, J.J., De la Fuente, J.M. and Jiménez, A. (2008) "Political risk as a determinant of investment of Spanish Multinational firms in Europe. Is there a East-West Structure?" Working Paper presented at the 34th EIBA Conference in Tallin, Estonia.

Fine, A. (2003). "Dealing Away Risk in Foreign Infrastructure Investment". *Journal of Structured and Project Finance*. Vol. 9, Iss. 2, pp. 53-64.

Fisman, R. and Khanna, T. (1998) "*Facilitating development: the role of business groups*". Working Paper, 98 (76) Harvard Business School.

Galan, J.I. Gonzalez_Benito, J. and Zúñiga-Vicente, J.A. (2007) "Factors determining the location decision of Spanish MNE: an analysis based on the investment development path". *Journal of International Business*. Vol. 38. pp. 975-997.

García-Canal, E. López, C. Rialp, J and Valdés, A. (2002) "Accelerating International expansion through global alliances: a typology of cooperative strategies". *Journal of World Business*. Vol. 37, pp. 91-107.

García- Canal, E, and Guillén, M. (2008) "Risk and strategy of foreign location choice in regulated industries". *Strategic Management Journal*. Vol. 29, Iss. 10, pp. 1097-1115.

Gastanaga, V.M. Nugent, J.B. and Pashamova, B. (1998) "Host country reforms and FDI inflows: how much difference do they make". *World Development*. 26 (7) pp. 1299-1314.

Gastil Index of Democracy http://www.freedomhouse.org.

Ghosal, S. and Moran, P. (2005) "*Towards a good theory of management*". En J. Birkinshaw and G. Piramal, Editors, *Sumantra Ghoshal on management: A force for good*. pp. 1-27 London: Financial Times Prentice Hall.

Goldberg, V.B. (1976) "Regulation and administered contracts". *Bell Journal of Economics*. Vol. 7, pp. 426-448.

Granovetter, M. (1995) "Coase revisited: the problem of business groups in modern economy". *Industrial and Corporate Change* 4(1): pp. 93-130.

Green, R.T. and Cunningham, W.H. (1975) "The determinants os U.S. foreign investments: an empirical explanation". *Management International Review*. Vol. 3, Febrero. pp. 113-120.

Gupta, S. Davoodi, H. and Alonso-Terme, R. (1998) *"Does corruption affect income inequality and poverty?"*. International Monetary Fund Working Paper.

Habib, M. and Zurawicki, L. (2002) "Corruption and foreign direct investment". *Journal of International Business Studies*. Vol. 33, Iss. 2, pp. 291-307.

Hakkala, K. Norback, P.J. and Svaleryd, H. (2008) "Asymmetric effects of corruption on FDI: evidence from Swedish Multinational Firm". *Review of Economics and Statistics*. Vol. 90, Iss. 4, pp. 627-642.

Hallerber, M. and Basinger, S. (1998) "Internationalization and changes in tax policy in OECD countries: the importance of domestic veto players". *Comparative Political Studies*. Vol. 31, pp. 321-352.

Henisz, W.J. (1998) *"The institutional environment for international investment"*. Doctoral dissertation, Hass School of Business, University of California. Berkeley.

Henisz, W.J. (2000) "The institutional environment for economic growth". *Economics and Politics* Vol. 12pp. 1-31.

Henisz, W.J. (2003) "The power of the Buckley and Casson thesis: the ability to manage institutional idiosyncrasies". *Journal of International Business Studies*. Vol. 34, pp. 173-184.

Henisz, W.J. (2004) "Political institutions and policy volatility". *Economics and Politics*. Vol. 16, No. 1, pp. 1-27.

Henisz, W.J. and Delios, A. (2001) "Uncertainty, imitation and plant location: Japanese multinacional corporations." *Administrative Science Quarterly*. Vol. 46, Iss. 3. pp.443-475.

Henisz, W.J. (2004) "Political institutions and policy volatility". *Economics and Politics*. Vol. 16, No. 1, pp. 1-27.

Henisz, W.J. and Delios, A. (2001) "Uncertainty, imitation and plant location: Japanese multinational corporations." *Administrative Science Quarterly*. Vol. 46, Iss. 3. pp.443-475.

Henisz, W.J. and Mansfield, E.D. (2006) "Votes and vetoes: the political determinants of comercial openness". *International Studies Quarterly*. Vol. 50, Iss. 1, pp. 189-212.

Henisz, W.J. and Zelner, B.A. (1999) *"Political risk and infrastructure investment"*. Working Paper The Wharton School. University of Pennsylvania.

Henisz, W.J. and Zelner, B.A. (2001) "The institutional environment for telecommunications investment". *Journal of Economics and Management Strategy*. Vol. 10, Iss. 1, pp. 123-147.

Henisz, W.J. and Zelner, B.A. (2002) "The institutional environment for infrastructure investment". *Industrial and Corporate Change*. Vol. 11, No. 2, pp. 355-389.

Holburn, G.L.F. (2001) *"Regulatory institutions and firm strategy: Theory and evidence from the electric power industry"*. Doctoral Dissertation University of California at Berkeley.

Huang, Y. Morck, R. and Yeung, B. (2003). *"ASEAN Countries, External Threat and FTAA"*. Paper presented at FTAA and Transpacific Business Linkages, Tokyo.

Husted, B. W.; Allen. D. W. (2000) "Is it Ethical to use Ethics as a Strategy". Journal of Business Ethics. Vol. 27, pp. 21-31.

Jiménez, A. (2010) "Does political risk affect the scope of expansion abroad? Evidence from Spanish MNEs". *International Business Review*. Vol. 19, Iss. 6, pp. 619-633.

Jiménez, A. (in press) "Political risk as a determinant of Southern European FDI in neighbouring developing countries". *Emerging Markets Finance and Trade.* Forthcoming.

Jiménez, A. and Durán, J.J. (2009) "La responsabilidad social de la empresa multinacional española frente al riesgo político de los países de destino. ¿Amenaza u oportunidad?". *Revista de Responsabilidad Social de la Empresa.* No. 3, pp. 131-158.

Jiménez, A. Durán, J.J. and De la Fuente, J.M. (in press) "El riesgo político como determinante de la estrategia de localización de las empresas multinacionales españolas". *Revista Europea de Dirección y Economía de la Empresa*. Forthcoming.

Johanson, J. and Vahlne, J.E. (1977) "The internationalization process of the firm: A model of knowledge development and increasing foreign market commitments". *Journal of International Business Studies.* Vol. 8, pp. 23-32.

Johanson, J. and Vahlne, J.E. (1990) "The mechanism of internationalization". International Marketing Review. Vol. 7, Iss. 4, pp. 411-432.

Johanson, J. and Wiedersheim-Paul, F. (1975) "The internationalization of the firm: Four Swedish cases". *Journal of management studies.* Vol. 12, Iss.3, pp. 305-322.

Kaufman, D. Kraay, A. and Zoido-Lobaton, P. (1999) *"Aggregating governance indicators"*. World Bank Working Paper 2195.

Khanna, T. (2000) "Business groups and social welfare in emerging markets: existing evidence and unanswered questions". *European Economic Review.* Vol. 44. pp. 748-761.

Khanna, T. and Palepu, K. (1998b) "Policy shocks, market intermediaries and corporate strategy: evidence from Chile and India". *Journal of Economics and Management* Strategy. Vol. 8, Iss. 2, pp. 271-310.

Khanna, T. and Palepu, K. (1999) "The right way to restructure conglomerates in emerging markets". *Harvard Business Review* (July-August) pp. 125-134.

Knack, S. (2006) *"Measuring corruption in Eastern Europe and Central Asia: A critique of the cross-country indicators"*. World Bank Policy Research Working Paper No. 3968.

Knack, S. and Keefer, P. (1995) "Institutions and economic performance: Cross-country tests using alternative institutional measures". *Economics and Politics*. Vol. 7, pp. 207-227.

Kobrin, S.J. (1982) "*Managing political risk assessment*". University of California Press.

Lambsdorff, J. G. (2003) "How corruption affects persistent capital flows". *Economics of Governance.* Vol. 4, Iss. 3, pp. 229-243.

López_Duarte, C. and Vidal-Suárez, M. (2010) "External uncertainty and entry mode choice: cultural distance, political risk and language Diversity". *International Business Review.* Vol. 19, Iss. 6, pp. 575-588.

Loree, D.W. and Guisinger, S.E. (1995) "Policy and non-policy determinants of US equity foreign direct investment". *Journal of International Business Studies*. Vol. 26, Iss. 2, pp. 281-299.

Mahon, J. F. and MCGovan, R. A. (1998) "Modeling industry political dynamics". *Business and Society.* Vol. 37, Iss. 4, pp. 390-413.

Marois, B. (1981) "Comment les enterprises françaises gèrent le risque politique". *Revue Française de Gestion.* May-August, pp. 4-9.

McWilliams, A. and Siegel, D. (2001) "Corporate Social Responsibility: A Theory of the Firm Perspective". *Academy of Management Review.* Vol. 26, Iss. 1, pp. 117-127.

Molero, J. (1999) "Las ventajas tecnológicas relativas y la internacionalización de la economía española". *Papeles de Economía Española.* Vol. 8, pp. 58-73.

Nee, V. (1992) "Organizational dynamics of market transition: hybrid forms, property rights and mixed economy in China". *Administrative Science Quarterly*. Vol. 33, pp. 194-210.

North, D.C. (1990) "*Institutions, institutional change, and economic performance*". Cambridge University Press, New York.

Olson, M. (1965) "*The logic of collective action: public goods and the theory of groups*". Harvard University Press, Cambridge, MA.

Olson, M. (1982) "*The rise and decline of nations*". Yale University Press, New Haven, CT.

Olson, M. (1993) "Dictatorship, democracy and development". *American Political Science Review*. Vol. 87, pp. 567-576.

Peng. M. Wang, D. Y. L. and Jiang, Y. (2008) "An institution-based view of international business strategy". *Journal of International Business Studies*. Vol. 39, pp. 920-936.

Pla, J. (1999) "Filiales y entrada en los mercados internacionales. Factores determinantes". *Revista de Economia Aplicada*. Vol. 20, Iss. 8, pp. 29-51.

Rodriguez, P. Uhlenbruck, K. and Eden, L. (2005) "Government corruption and the entry strategy of multinationals". *Academy of Management Review*. Vol. 30, Iss. 2, pp. 383-396.

Root, F.R. (1968) "The expropriation of American companies: what happened to 38 companies". *Business Horizons* Vol.1, pp. 69-74.

Root, F.R. and Ahmed, A.A. (1978) "The influence of policy instruments on manufacturing direct foreign investment in developing countries". *Journal of International Business Studies*. Vol. 9. pp. 81-93.

Rummel, R.J. and Hennan, D.A. (1978) "How multinationals analyze political risk". *Harvard Business Review*. January-February, pp. 67-76.

Slangen, A. H. L. and Tulder, R.M.J. (2009) "Cultural distance, political risk or governance quality? Towards a more accurate conceptualization and measurement of external uncertainty in foreign entry mode research". *International Business Review*. Vol. 18, pp. 276-291.

Spiller, P.T. (1993) "Institutions and regulatory commitment in utilities' privatization". *Industrial and Corporate Change*. Vol. 2, pp. 387-450.

Smarzynska, B.K. and Wei, S.J. (2002) *"Corruption and cross-border investment: firm level evidence"*. William Davidson Working Paper No. 494.

Tanzi, V. (1995) *"Corruption: arm's-length relationships and markets"*. In: *The Economics of Organized Crime*, (Ed.) Gianluca Fiorentini and SamPeltzman Cambridge, England: Cambridge University Press.

Transparency International http://www.transparency.org.

Treisman, D. (2000) "Decentralization and inflation: commitment, collective action or continuity". *American Political Science Review*. Vol. 94. pp. 837-857.

Tsebelis, G. (1995) "Decision-making in political systems: veto players in presidentialism, parliamentarism, multicameralism and multipartyism". *British Journal of Political Science*. Vol. 25, Iss. 3, pp. 289-325.

Vernon, R. (1971) "*Sovereignty at Bay: the multinational spread of US enterprises*". Basic Books: New York.

Vernon, R. (1978) "The strain on national objectives: the developing countries" *Storm over the Multinationals: The Real Issues*. Pp. 139-173. Cambridge, MA: Harvard University.

Vial, J. (2003). "*Business Climate and Investment in Latin America*". Paper presented at FTAA and Transpacific Business Linkages, Tokyo.

Waddock, S. and Graves, S. (1997) "The corporate social performance – financial performance link". *Strategic Management Journal*. Vol. 18, Iss. 4, pp. 309-319.

Wan, W.P. (2005) "Country resource environments, firm capabilities, and corporate diversification strategies". *Journal of Management Studies*. Vol. 42, pp. 161-171.

Wei, S.J. (2000a) "How taxing is corruption on international investors". *Review of Economics and Statistics*. Vol. 82, Iss. 1, pp. 1-11.

Wei, S. J. (2000b) "Local corruption and global capital flows". *Brookings Papers on Economic Activity*. Vol. 2, pp. 303-354.

Welch, L. S. and Luostarinen, R. (1988) "Internationalization: evolution of a concept". *Journal of General Management*. Vol. 14, Iss. 2, pp. 34-55.

Williamson, O.E. (1975) *Markets and Hierarchies: Analysis and antitrust implications*. New York: Free Press.

Williamson, O.E. (1985) *The economic institutions of capitalism*. New York: Free Press.

Wittman, D. (1989) "Why democracies produce efficient results". *Journal of Political Economy*. Vol. 97, pp. 1395-1424.

World Bank (2001) http://www.worldbank.org/publicsector/anticorrupt/index.ctm.

Zelner, B.A. (1999) "*Political institutions, political competition and investment strategies in the electric utility industry: Domestic and cross-national applications*". Doctoral dissertation, University of California.

In: Foreign Investment
Editor: Torre DeSare and Daniele Caprioglio

ISBN 978-1-61470-358-7

Chapter 5

HANDS OFF MY INVESTMENT! A TIME-SERIES CROSS-SECTION ANALYSIS OF THE RELATIONSHIP BETWEEN A NEW MEASURE OF POLITICAL RISK AND FOREIGN DIRECT INVESTMENT

Jo Jakobsen*

Norwegian University of Science and Technology,
Department of Sociology and Political Science, Trondheim, Norway

ABSTRACT

Political risk still plagues foreign investors. Yet one particular kind of business thrives on such risks, namely the political risk assessment industry. The assessments and predictions on offer, however, generally suffer from a number of flaws, which the present chapter seeks to remedy. It does so by way of creating a composite, multidimensional political risk index – POLRISK – which covers 192 countries and territories, and which is based on a variety of publicly available sources. The chapter first presents a brief summary of the theoretical rationale for this multidimensional approach to political risk assessment, along with a description of the methodology employed. It then proceeds to test, by way of a carefully executed time-series cross-section analysis, whether or not multinational companies are influenced by political risk when making investment location decisions. And results show that they are: the relationship between POLRISK and inflows of foreign direct investment (FDI) is consistently positive and significant. Moreover, the new measure performs much better than one of the most widely used commercial political risk indexes, the International Country Risk Guide (ICRG). This perhaps suggests that the political risk assessment industry may not pay sufficient heed to the complexity and multidimensionality of the political risk phenomenon.

* Telephone: +47 73551141, Fax: +47 73591564, E-mail: jo.jakobsen@svt.ntnu.no

Introduction

Political risk – succinctly defined as the impact of non-market events, processes, and characteristics on international business – still plagues foreign investors. Yet one particular kind of business thrives on such risks, namely the political risk assessment industry. The assessments and predictions on offer, however, generally suffer from a number of flaws: they are expensive, and therefore out of reach of many academics and businesses; their coverage is restricted; they draw upon the subjective opinions of only a few country experts; and they are largely disconnected from the theoretical and empirical academic literature, causing them to disregard important dimensions of political risk (Henisz, 2000, p. 335; Oetzel, Bettis, and Zenner, 2001; Schroeder, 2008; Snider 2005, pp. 204–5).

The proposed chapter seeks to remedy some of these flaws. It does so by way of creating a composite, multidimensional political risk index – POLRISK – which covers 192 countries and territories, and which is based on a variety of publicly available sources. The chapter first presents a brief summary of the theoretical rationale for this multidimensional approach to political risk assessment, along with a description of the methodology employed in the creation of POLRISK. It then proceeds to test, by way of a carefully executed time-series cross-section analysis, whether or not multinational companies (MNCs) are influenced by political risk when making investment location decisions. And results show that they are: the relationship between POLRISK and inflows of foreign direct investment (FDI) is consistently positive and significant. Moreover, the new measure performs much better than one of the most widely used commercial political risk indexes, the International Country Risk Guide (ICRG). This perhaps suggests that the political risk assessment industry may not pay sufficient heed to the complexity and multidimensionality of the political risk phenomenon. The POLRISK index, for its part, may indeed have some valuable characteristics that help remedy some of the drawbacks of commercial risk assessments: the coverage of the index is extensive; it relies for its estimation on a variety of sources and methodologies; the index is well-rooted in the academic literature; it pays heed to the inherent multidimensionality of the phenomenon of political risk; and, not least, all the sources that I draw on to create POLRISK are publicly available at no cost, thereby making this index a useful and accessible measure of political risk for foreign direct investors.

Political Risk – Sources and Effects

The Causal Chain

Political risks in international business are those events, processes, and actions of a political content that have the potential to – directly or indirectly – seriously hamper the goals of foreign direct investors (Jakobsen, 2010). A list of such risks would necessarily be quite extensive and would include, among other acts and events, expropriations, terrorist attacks, bribe demands, and the imposition of price controls.

For political risk analysts, the basic challenge is one of prediction; ideally, the likelihood of political risk events and actions should be estimated well before they occur. For such prediction or forecasting to succeed, though, some sort of causal link between *sources* of political risks and political risk effects must be identified (Howell, 1998; Jakobsen, 2010; Robock, 1971). Academics' search for this causal link started for real in the 1970s (Green, 1974; Kobrin, 1979; Robock, 1971). In particular, the early literature identified *political instability* as a potent source of political risk effects (Thunell, 1977; Weston and Sorge, 1972). It was argued that such instability – which includes, among other things, terrorism activities, war, frequent government changes, and severe social unrest – could seriously deteriorate the investment climate of a country and thereby cause losses for the firms.

In recent years, a new wave of literature has contended that government intervention into the affairs of MNCs, which arguably constitutes the most common form of risk effects (Butler and Joaquin, 1998; Graham, 1996; Henisz, 2002; Jensen, 2006; O'Sullivan, 2005; Wells, 1998), is intimately linked to a country's institutional framework (Ahlquist, 2006; Blanton and Blanton, 2009; Guerin and Manzocchi, 2009; Henisz, 2002; Jakobsen, 2006; Jensen, 2006, 2008). It is often argued, for example, that authoritarian regimes without proper checks on the executive are more likely than democratic regimes with sound institutions to institute policy reversals, thereby creating for the MNCs the dreaded environment of *policy* instability.

Although political instability and political institutions certainly matter, they still only constitute half the story. Evidence from institutionally sound and politically stable countries serves to indicate that other forces are also at play. Consider the United States. Fairly recent, widely publicised cases of domestic opposition in the U.S. to acquisition deals include the takeover of by Dubai Ports World of the United Arab Emirates of PandO, a British port operator with investments in key U.S. cities;[1] the December 2004 takeover of IBM's personal-computer business by Chinese PC maker Lenovo (which caused a row among some senior Republican Congressmen, who claimed that IBM's facilities could then be used to spy for the Chinese armed forces);[2] the botched attempt by Chinese state-owned oil company CNOOC to buy Unocal for $18.5 billion;[3] and the (the slightly amusing but certainly predictable) uproar in 2008 over the bid by Belgium's Inbev for St. Louis-based brewer Anheuser-Busch.[4] These cases, and many more, can better be explained by reference to such forces as economic nationalism and the preferences and attitudes of political decision-makers (and of the public at large). Unfortunately, though, nationalism, ideology, preferences, and the like, which have long since been accepted as prominent sources of realized political risk (Boddewyn and Cracco, 1972; Moran, 1974; Robock, 1971), are not easily measured and operationalized. I therefore choose to include the economic policies themselves, along with an evaluation of countries' macroeconomic performance, in a comprehensive risk assessment framework. The assumption I thereby make is that nationalism, ideology, and state preferences are, to a great extent, reflected in economic policies and institutions (see, e.g., Jakobsen and Jakobsen, 2011). This means that a (recent) history of MNC-unfriendly economic policies, institutions, and performance also spells trouble for today's and tomorrow's foreign investors.

[1] The port debacle was only resolved when Dubai Ports World announced in March 2006 that it would sell its American port operations to a U.S. firm (Dubai seeks to calm the storm over ports. The Economist, 10 March 2006).

[2] Chinese firm buys IBM PC business. BBC News, 8 December 2004; Chinese companies abroad. The Economist, 30 June 2005.

[3] Bogus fears send the Chinese packing. The Economist, 2 August 2005.

[4] Love me, love me not. The Economist, 10 July 2008.

The Multifaceted Nature of Political Risk

The methodology presented in this chapter should be well suited to remedy some of the faults that bedevil commercial political risk indexes. First, all the sources that I draw on to create the POLRISK index are publicly available at no cost. Second, the coverage is extensive: 192 countries and territories are tracked for the period 1996–2003, 160 of which are assigned a composite POLRISK score for every year in this period. (Note that 2003 is the terminal year in my study given that data on the variable that serves as the basis for comparison – the International Country Risk Guide Index (ICRG) – was only available for the period up until that year.) Third, POLRISK is based on a useful mix of subjective assessments and objective, "hard" data; it relies for its estimation on a variety of sources (and thus different methodologies). Fourth, the index is well-rooted in the academic literature. Fifth, I also include in my framework an assessment of economic governance, implicitly acknowledging that it would be counterproductive to conduct a risk assessment without taking into account how last year's and this year's investors were treated.

The latter argument indicates that POLRISK is made up of assessments of both perceived sources of risk and political risk effects. The former generally constitute socio-political attributes of a country, or "correlates of future trouble" (e.g., ethnic tensions, authoritarianism, and low human development); the latter involves an assessment of the current investment-cum-economic regime (e.g., ownership restrictions, inflation, foreign exchange controls). According to Howell (1998), most risk assessment firms use one (but only one) of these two distinct strategies, and the majority settles for the former. However, the "conjunctural nature of social causation" (Ragin, 1987, p. 25) renders a unidimensional approach to political risk forecasting inappropriate. A certain political risk effect rarely has only one source. Therefore, neither of these strategies is sufficient, yet both are necessary.

Following this line of thought, one can expect that even if a country is perceived to be particularly risky on one specific dimension, this risk may be offset by other dimensions. Israel, for example, is riddled with problems of internal (potential and actual) political instability, and the country is entangled in seemingly ever-lasting diplomatic (and military) tensions with its closest neighbors. If only these issues were to be decisive in an evaluation of the country's investment climate, Israel would not receive much FDI. However, Israel's political institutions are solid, economic freedom prevails, and the economy is strong. In total, therefore, Israel may be considered relatively low-risk.

This logic also works the other way around; low risk on one dimension does not exclude high risk on any other dimension or in total. In the mid-1990s, sundry foreign investors in Indonesia were only too slow to acknowledge this. At the time, this South-East Asian nation was perceived as something of a haven for multinational companies; billions of dollars of FDI found its way to a fast-growing economy that was rich in terms of natural resources and cheap labor and whose authoritarian government had long been pursuing fairly liberal economic policies (Jeon and Ahn, 2004; Lecraw, 1996; Spar, 1996). Although apparently stable and therefore coveted by foreign investors and risk assessment companies alike, in reality Indonesia was "a powder keg waiting to explode" (Garten, 1997, p. 4). General Suharto's autocratic and human-rights-breaching regime was rife with less visible problems of corruption, cronyism, bureaucratic incompetence, financial mismanagement, poverty, and ethnic and religious tensions. These were problems by and large related to political institutions and socio-political grievances and not to the (economic) preferences and attitudes of the regime (MacIntyre, 2001). Not surprisingly, the powder keg *did* explode, in 1998. This followed months of widespread public unrest and urban riots, and it led to the resignation of Suharto, more socio-political unrest, the implementation of a harsher investment regime, and the (often belated) fleeing of foreign investors.

METHODOLOGY

POLRISK consists of three main dimensions selected under the guidance of the existing conceptual, theoretical, and empirical literature. The three dimensions include socio-political instability and grievances (SOCPOL), political institutions (POLINST), and economic governance (ECOGOV), the latter dimension being a measure of countries' economic institutions, policies, and performance. Each dimension, in turn, is made up of several sub-indicators drawn from a variety of sources, including the World Bank, the IMF, Freedom House, the Polity IV Project, and UNCTAD.

Earlier I have argued that the commercial risk assessment industry could be criticized on several grounds, as many indeed do (e.g., Henisz, 2000, p. 335; Oetzel, Bettis, and Zenner, 2001; Schroeder, 2008; Snider 2005, pp. 204–5). I firmly believe, as stated earlier, that the methodology employed herein is well suited to remedy many of these faults.

The main source upon which I draw to create POLRISK is the World Bank Governance Indicators (WBGI) dataset, estimated by Kaufmann, Kraay, and Mastruzzi (2005, 2009). Covering 209 countries and territories for the period 1996–2009, this dataset presents six dimensions of governance estimated on the basis of surveys of firms and individuals, assessments made by commercial risk rating firms, and information assembled by NGOs and multilateral aid agencies. The indicators reflect information from several hundred individual variables drawn from sundry sources produced by many different organizations.

General Research Methodology

To create the three main dimensions (SOCPOL, POLINST, and ECOGOV), the following general research methodology is employed. First, each sub-indicator is converted into a 0–1 scale, with 0 representing high risk and 1 representing low risk. (If the sub-indicator itself consists of several parts, each of the constituent elements is rescaled prior to the creation of the sub-indicator.) Following Gwartney and Lawson (2004), the following formulas are used in the rescaling process: $X = (V_i - V_{min}) / (V_{max} - V_{min})$ if the original variable's positive values represent low risk; $X = (V_{max} - V_i) / (V_{max} - V_{min})$ if the original variable is negatively correlated with the main dimension. Here, V_i equals a case's value on the original variable while V_{min} and V_{max} represent pre-selected cut-off points. Some sub-indicators have natural max and min values; for instance, Freedom House's *civil liberties* index runs from 1 (free) to 7 (not free). Most sub-indicators, though, have to be assigned some other appropriate cut-off points. For example, the min and max values for the World Bank's *political stability* variable (which has a mean of zero and a standard deviation of one) are set to that variable's 1st and 99th percentile values, respectively, for the year 2000 (i.e., the chosen base year for the index).

The next step, then, is to combine the sub-indicators into a composite 0–100 dimension by weighing each of them according to their perceived relevance. Thus I obtain three equally scaled dimensions of risk. The last step consists of combining these dimensions into a composite POLRISK index (which also ranges from 0 to 100).

The primary objective of this chapter is to create a multidimensional country-level political risk index based on publicly available information. A secondary, although by no means unimportant goal is to make this index as comprehensive as possible regarding the coverage of countries and years, yet without compromising on the quality of the information conveyed. To ensure comprehensiveness, and under the fairly reasonable assumption that most socio-political change only occur slowly (Kaufmann, Kraay, and Mastruzzi, 2009; North, 1990),[5] missing data on each sub-indicator are linearly interpolated if: (a) a sub-indicator only contains values for some years (this applies to the governance indicators, which, for the beginning of the period, are only available for every second year, and to UNDP's *human development index*); and (b) a country has a missing value on a sub-indicator but non-missing values for at least one of the previous and one of the later year(s). Third, to further secure the comprehensiveness of the index, a country is assigned a score on a main dimension for a specific year if it has at least *k*-1 non-missing values (after interpolation) for that same year, where *k* denotes the number of that dimension's constituent sub-indexes.[6] The other sub-indexes are then rescaled (for that country only), so that the country in question can be assigned a value in the 0–100 range.

Socio-Political Instability and Grievances

The first of the constituent dimensions of POLRISK involves a broad evaluation of the degree to which a country is plagued by potential or actual socio-political instability and grievances (SOCPOL). This main dimension consists of three sub-indicators: *political stability and absence of violence* (one of the World Bank Governance Indicators), Freedom House's *civil liberties index*,[7] and UNCTAD's *human development index*.[8]

Political stability and absence of violence is an indicator "measuring the likelihood of violent threats to, or changes in, government, including terrorism" (Kaufmann, Kraay, and Mastruzzi, 2005, p. 4). This indicator effectively covers most aspects of what the political risk literature refers to as political instability. A significant number of individual sources and variables have been used by the authors in the estimation process, including Political Risk Services' internal conflict, external conflict, and ethnic tensions, and The Economist Intelligence Unit's violent demonstrations, social unrest, and international tensions.

Of course, political instability itself has its more fundamental causes, including economic hardships which may cause rebellions and even outright war; racial disorders causing social

---

5 For example, the World Bank governance indicators' values for 2004 correlate between .810 (*political stability and absence of violence*) and .925 (*government effectiveness*) with their respective 1996 values.

6 Because the Polity IV Project – from which I draw two of the POLINST dimension's constituent variables, namely *executive constraints* and *regime durability* – only involves countries whose 2002 population exceeds five hundred thousand, and since these variables together only make up 20 percent of POLINST, I allow for countries to have missing values on both these two sub-indicators.

7 The *civil liberties* index is available for download at http://www.freedomhouse.org/.

8 The *human development index* is available for download at http://hdr.undp.org/en/statistics/.

unrest; grievances against MNCs' "exploitation" of the developing world leading to terrorist attacks against such companies; and consistent breaches of human rights which may help cause popular uprising against the regime. I therefore also include in my index two such measures of a country's general socio-political and economic attributes.

First, Freedom House's yearly *civil liberties* index rates countries from 1 to 7 according to the extent to which the regime provides for freedom of assembly, demonstration, and open public discussion, as well as protection from police terror, torture, and unjustified imprisonment. This is, in effect, a measure of human rights in a broad sense of the word. Apart from representing a possible source of political unrest, human rights abuses may also cause reputational risks – the "most significant new political risks since the 1990s" (Bray, 2003, p. 294) – to multinationals investing in repressive regimes.

Acknowledging that there is "a close correlation between human development [...] and country risk" (Bouchet, Clark, and Groslambert, 2003, p. 51), I also include UNDP's *human development index* (HDI) in the index. The HDI ranges from 0 to 1 and measures countries' achievements in terms of life expectancy, educational attainment, and real income per capita. The index is, for the period under study, only available for 1995, 2000, and 2002, so missing country-years are interpolated. This should not be a major problem, though, since the HDI's constituent parts change very slowly.

Thus, measures of political stability (weighted 60%), civil rights (20%), and human development (20%) make up the SOCPOL index.

Political Institutions

The second dimension, POLINST, measures the state of countries' political institutions – the formal and informal "rules of the game in a society" (North, 1990, p. 3).

The first constituent sub-indicator of POLINST is Freedom House's *political rights* index. Effectively a measure of democracy, this index includes an evaluation of, among other things, electoral freedom, the existence and power of the political opposition, and the accountability of the government to the electorate between elections.

Although some scholars have argued that authoritarianism *qua* authoritarianism has scant deterrent effects on foreign investors, especially in developing countries (Li and Resnick, 2003; O'Donnell, 1978), others stress that non-democratic nations have a number of characteristics that tend to make them politically riskier than their democratic counterparts: Autocratic regimes, although seemingly stable, may hide an underlying instability that eventually causes erratic and unpredictable change (Bremmer, 2005; Feng, 2001; Gates et al., 2006). Furthermore, a regime transition from autocracy to democracy may render old contracts worthless (Heradstveit, 2001). Others contend that investing in repressive host countries leads to reputational risks for multinationals and increases the likelihood of NGO (and shareholder) activism and costly litigation processes against the management (Blanton and Blanton, 2009; Bray, 2003; Kobrin, 2005b).[9] Still others argue that autocracy worsens the

---

[9] Deborah Spar (1999) argues that a marked shift in the sectoral pattern of FDI has ensured that less foreign direct investment finds its way to regimes that violate human and labor rights. Multinationals in manufacturing and services (the growth and spread of which account for much of the FDI boom of the 1990s) are less likely than extractive-sector companies to ally themselves with dictators and more likely to invest in countries with an abundance of skilled labor (and high labor standards) and a large pool of well-off consumers.

investment climate by increasing the ability of bureaucrats and local businesses to extract rents from administrative procedures, exploit political institutions often marred by cronyism, and constrain MNC operations (Jakobsen and de Soysa, 2006; Jakobsen and Jakobsen, 2011; Morisset and Neso, 2002). Lastly, many hold that autocracies, given the lack of a separation of powers and checks and balances on the executive, cannot make credible promises to protect investors' property rights (Henisz, 2002; Jakobsen, 2006; Jensen, 2006, 2008).

This latter point induces me to include, in addition to the more general *political rights* indicator, a specific measure of checks and balances or *executive constraints*. This measure "refers to the extent of institutionalized constraints on the decision-making powers of chief executives" (Marshall and Jaggers, 2002, p. 23) and ranges from 1 to 7. It is drawn from the Polity IV Project.[10]

From the same project I also extract a proxy for *regime durability* measured as the number of years since the last regime transition (i.e., a 3-point or greater shift in the main Polity index). I thereby acknowledge: (a) that a lack of democratic structures may, to a certain extent, be offset by a regime's apparent stability (as, one could argue, is the case in China); and (b) that investors in *fledgling* democracies do not enjoy the same level of predictability with regard to the political environment as MNCs setting up plants in established democracies (Gates et al., 2006).

The final three sub-dimensions of POLINST are all drawn from the World Bank governance indicators dataset. *Rule of law* is an index that measures crime, the efficiency of the judiciary, and the enforceability of contracts.

Sources used for its creation include Global Insight (e.g., losses and cost of crime, enforceability of government contracts), Political Risk Services (law and order), and World Markets Online (judicial independence, crime).

The fifth sub-indicator to be included in the POLINST dimension is *control of corruption*, which is an assessment of the extent to which public power is misused for private gain (Lambsdorff, 2003).

For a multinational company, such practice has several consequences: corruption in the judiciary undermines the rule of law and leads to arbitrary court decisions; "grease payments" may come back to haunt the investor if the media, NGOs, or opposition politicians find out; the practice of "petty" or bureaucratic corruption can be a permanent nuisance and a constant source of delays for the company; and graft also has less direct yet equally troubling effects on foreign investors in that it undermines the markets, diverts government money to unprofitable ventures, lowers investment, and thus also lowers growth (Cuervo-Cazurra, 2006; Meschi, 2009; Mauro, 1995; Shleifer and Vishny, 1993; Wei, 2000).

Finally, I include the sub-indicator *government effectiveness*. This is a proxy for the effectiveness of the bureaucracy and public service provision and the credibility of the government's commitment to policies. Among the sources used for its creation are The Economist Intelligence Unit's quality of bureaucracy and excessive bureaucracy/red tape, and World Economic Forum's quality of general infrastructure and public spending composition.

In summary, then, the POLINST dimension is made up of political rights (weighted 15%), executive constraints (10%), regime durability (10%), rule of law (25%), corruption (25%), and government effectiveness (15%).

---

[10] Polity IV data are available for download at http://www.systemicpeace.org/polity/polity4.htm.

Economic Governance

A measure of countries' economic institutions, policies, and performance, the last main dimension is ECOGOV. A number of empirical studies have suggested that, *ceteris paribus*, MNCs are drawn to nations that are open to trade (Bevan, Estrin, and Meyer, 2004; Jun and Singh, 1996; Morisset, 2000) and participate in bilateral, regional, and multilateral politico-economic institutions (Büthe and Milner, 2008); employ few controls on capital and profits (Click, 2005; Li and Resnick, 2003); ensure low inflation and a stable exchange rate (Li and Resnick, 2003; Treviño, Daniels, and Arbeláez, 2002); are reluctant to expropriate private property (Gastanaga, Nugent, and Pashamova, 1998); and generally allow private ownership of business (Bevan, Estrin, and Meyer, 2004; Treviño, Daniels, and Arbeláez, 2002). Reflecting economic freedom and state preferences for trade liberalization and capital inflows, such policies, moreover, constitute an increasingly common feature in developed and developing countries alike (Kobrin, 2005a; Simmons and Elkins, 2004; Simmons, Dobbin, and Garrett, 2006).

The latter observation notwithstanding, some scholars' early contention that nationalism causes problems for multinationals (Boddewyn and Cracco, 1972; Moran, 1974; Robock, 1971) still holds some truth. Moreover, nationalistic and anti-foreign capital sentiments do not seem to vanish with the level of development (Wells, 1998). In most countries, foreign ownership in specific industries is still restricted or at least met with considerable skepticism (Golub, 2003).

The first sub-indicator to be included in ECOGOV is the World Bank Governance Indicator *regulatory quality*, which purports to measure the policies themselves and which includes estimations of market-unfriendly policies, including poor supervision of banks and high levels of regulations in the economy (Kaufmann, Kraay, and Mastruzzi, 2009).

The indicator is based on sources and variables such as Heritage Foundation's government intervention, wage/prices, and banking, and Political Risk Services' investment profile.

What is not covered by *regulatory quality*, though, is macroeconomic performance. Such performance may have both direct and indirect effects on foreign investors. The effects are direct and negative when hyperinflation complicates pricing decisions, or when exchange rate changes either raises the cost of inputs (when the host country's currency appreciates) or lowers the value of repatriated profits (when the currency depreciates). The effects are indirect when negative growth, a depreciating currency, or steep inflation reduce the purchasing power of host-country consumers.

Thus, the next sub-indicator, *macroeconomic performance,* combines different and equally weighted elements of the macroeconomic environment, namely GDP per capita, economic growth, exchange rate volatility, and absolute consumer price changes.[11] Due to this variable being highly skewed, I take the natural logarithm of GDP per capita[12] before recoding it into a 0–1 scale on the basis of min and max values at the sample 1st and 99th

---

[11] A country is assigned a score on *macroeconomic performance* for a given year if it has non-missing values on at least three of the constituent variables for the same year, after missing values are interpolated according to the rules specified in the general methodology section. This decision rule also applies to the *FDI preferences and experience* sub-indicator.

[12] Data are in current US$ and are available for download from UNCTAD's website at http://www.unctad.org/Templates/Page.asp?intItemID=1584&lang=1.

percentile values, respectively, for the year 2000. The economic growth variable is measured as the average GDP growth rate for the last three years (with data from the IMF's World Economic Outlook).[13] Min and max values are set at the sample 5th and 95th percentiles for 2000.

Exchange rate volatility is the standardized absolute exchange rate deviation from the average exchange rate of local currency units vis-à-vis US dollars the last three years, and is also measured as a three-year average.

Max and min values are set at the sample 5th and 95th percentile values, respectively, for the base year. And finally, a variable measuring *absolute* consumer price changes (average for the last three years) is included. This indicator has max and min values at zero and at the sample 95th percentile value, respectively, for 2000. Data are from the IMF's World Economic Outlook database.

The third constituent part of ECOGOV is a proxy for countries' *FDI preferences and experience*.

This index consists of three separate variables: The Heritage Foundation/World Street Journal's *capital flows and foreign investment* (which makes up 50% of the sub-indicator); FDI divided by GDP, three-year average (weighted 25%); and FDI per capita, three year average (weighted 25%).

Min and max values for FDI/GDP are set at the sample 10th and 90th percentile values, respectively, for 2000, while FDI per capita uses cut-off points at the sample 5th and 95th percentile values. FDI data are from the UNCTAD database. The *capital flows and foreign investment* variable, from the Heritage Foundation, ranges from one to five and evaluates nations' FDI policies.[14]

The fourth component of ECOGOV is an index of *international economic linkages*. Here, country-years receive .25 points for membership in each of the following international economic organizations: OECD, WTO/GATT, the International Centre for Settlement of Investment Disputes (ICSID), and the Multilateral Investment Guarantee Agency (MIGA). The basic assumption is that memberships in such organizations increase investor confidence in the host's commitment to economic freedom (Büthe and Milner, 2008).

In sum, the third main dimension, ECOGOV, is made up of regulatory quality (weighted 40%), macroeconomic performance (20%), FDI preferences and experience (20%), and international economic linkages (20%).

The composite POLRISK index is calculated in the following way: POLRISK = [SOCPOL + (1.5 * POLINST) + ECOGOV] / 3.5. The POLINST dimension is given greater weight because of the large number of sub-indicators it contains. Moreover, some of its sub-indicators – not least, *control of corruption* – can be expected to affect the other two dimensions as well.

Table 1 exhibits information on the main dimensions, their respective sub-indicators, and each sub-indicator's relative significance in the make-up of POLRISK.

---

13 Economic growth data can be downloaded from the World Economic Outlook database at http://www.imf.org/external/pubs/ft/weo/2005/01/data/index.htm.

14 The *index of economic freedom* (and its constituent sub-indexes) can be downloaded at http://www.heritage.org/research/features/index/downloads.cfm.

Table 1. The relative contribution of POLRISK's sub-indicators

Main dimension	Sub-indicator	Source	Contribution to POLRISK (%)
	Political Instability	World Bank Governance Ind.	17.14
SOCPOL	Civil Liberties	Freedom House	5.71
	Human Development Index	UNDP	5.71
	Political Rights	Freedom House	6.43
	Executive Constraints	Polity IV Project	4.29
POLINST	Regime Durability	Polity IV Project	4.29
	Law and Order	World Bank Governance Ind.	10.71
	Control of Corruption	World Bank Governance Ind.	10.71
	Government Effectiveness	World Bank Governance Ind.	6.43
	Regulatory Quality	World Bank Governance Ind.	11.43
	Economic Performance	UNCTAD, IMF	5.71
	GDP per capita		
	GDP growth		
	Exchange rate volatility		
	Inflation		
ECOGOV	FDI Preferences	Heritage, UNCTAD	5.71
	Capital Flows index		
	FDI per capita		
	FDI/GDP		
	International Economic Linkages		5.71
	OECD membership		
	WTO/GATT membership		
	ICSID membership		
	MIGA membership		
			100 %

Data and Methods

Political Risk as a Determinant of FDI

By and large, the empirical literature is inconclusive with regard to the impact of proxies of political risk on FDI. Starting with Thunell (1977) and Schneider and Frey (1985), political instability (i.e., event counts of political assassinations, coups, strikes, etc.) has been shown to deter investors, but results are far from strong. Moreover, recent research has found such event counts to vary greatly in their prediction of FDI (Brunetti and Weder, 1997; Campos and Nugent, 1998; Le and Zak, 2006; Li and Resnick, 2003; Sethi et al., 2003). Indexes constructed by commercial risk assessment companies, like ICRG and BERI, have also been employed in empirical analyses. Here, too, results are inconclusive (Altomonte 2000; Gastanaga, Nugent, and Pashamova, 1998; Loree and Guisinger 1995; Treviño and Mixon 2004). In recent years, several scholars have tried to estimate the effects of the institutional environment on FDI. This literature generally points in one general direction: sound institutions tend to promote FDI (Ahlquist 2006; Blanton and Blanton 2009; Guerin and

Manzocchi 2009; Henisz 2002; Jensen 2006, 2008). Taken as a whole, though, results on the effects of political risk on FDI are relatively weak. A significant part of the problem, I surmise, is the fact that many of these studies fail to include a proxy for political risk that fully acknowledges the multidimensionality and complexity of a concept that is, admittedly, difficult to gauge.

Variables

The present study's dependent variable is FDI inflows, logged to reduce skewness and avoid problems of undue "influence" and heteroskedasticity.[15] The main independent variable of interest is POLRISK. For the important sake of comparison, in some of the model specifications I employ the International Country Risk Guide's composite risk index (ICRG) in lieu of POLRISK (ICRG data are from the World Bank (2004)). ICRG is a risk assessment company that lets expert consultants rank countries on 22 risk-related indicators. These scores are then aggregated so that each country receives a composite risk score ranging between 0 and 100.[16]

Of course, in an analysis of the determinants of FDI a number of variables relating to host-country potential have to be controlled. In the empirical literature, a consistent finding is that market size matters greatly (Chakrabarti, 2001; Flores and Aguilera, 2007), as does economic growth (Büthe and Milner, 2008; Flores and Aguilera, 2007; Jensen, 2003). I therefore include GDP (logged) and GROWTH in the model, with data from UNCTAD and IMF's World Economic Outlook, respectively. Denoting host-country potential for export-oriented MNCs and, possibly, signaling host-government commitment to liberal trade policies, trade openness is, in most studies, also found to be a potent predictor of FDI (Bevan, Estrin, and Meyer, 2004; Büthe and Milner, 2008; Jun and Singh, 1996; Morisset, 2000). TRADE (i.e., the sum of imports and exports, divided by GDP and logged) is therefore included, with data from the World Bank (2004). In addition, GDP per capita (GDPPC, logged) will also be controlled, even though this variable is often found to have little statistical effect on FDI inflows (Jakobsen and Jakobsen, 2011; Jensen, 2003; Li and Resnick, 2003; Loree and Gusinger, 1995). Data are from UNCTAD.

A possibly significant omission from most studies of the determinants of FDI, natural resources should also be controlled. Here, a measure of minerals and metals exports (MINMET, logged) is included, with data from UNCTAD.[17] I also control for estimated oil reserves (OIL, logged) and natural gas production (GAS, logged).[18] Due to the high correlation (.86) between these two variables, and because preliminary analyses revealed potential problems of multicollinearity (and since these variables evidently do not have a

[15] Transforming variables presents a few minor problems, such as how to treat negative values. In this model, such values are set to a very small number (i.e., .01 million US$) relative to the lowest absolute annual values. This transformation, however, only affects about 5 per cent of total country-years in our sample. FDI data can be downloaded from UNCTAD's website at http://www.unctad.org/Templates/Page.asp?intItemID=1923&lang=1.

[16] For a description of ICRG's methodology, see http://www.icrgonline.com/.

[17] Data on exports of minerals and metals can be downloaded at http://r0.unctad.org/infocomm/Handbook/pdfs/tab2004%201-1.pdf.

[18] Data on world oil reserves and natural gas production are made available to the public by the U.S. Energy Information Administration at http://www.eia.doe.gov/emeu/international/reserves.html.

strong impact on the dependent measure), in most model specifications I prefer to use a petroleum dummy (DPETRO), where observations are coded 1 if estimated oil reserves exceed two billion barrels *or* if natural gas production exceeds 1,000 billion cubic feet per year.

Another troublesome omission from most empirical analyses – at least from those that do not have any information on the source or home country of the FDI flows – is some sort of control for geographical distance between the potential host country and major sources of capital. I therefore include a variable denoting the FDI outflow-weighted summed surface distance between host countries and four major centers of capital: Brussels (a proxy for Western Europe), Washington D.C. (a proxy for USA and Canada), Tokyo (Japan), and Hong Kong (a proxy for Hong Kong, Taiwan, and mainland China).[19] The variable (WDIST) is logged to reduce skewness.

Finally, I acknowledge that FDI, by sheer definition, exhibits a significant degree of stickiness and I therefore also include a measure of accumulated FDI (i.e., FDI stock), divided by GDP (STOCK), as recommended by others (Barry, Görg, and Strobl, 2003; Bobonis and Shatz, 2007).

The data have a time-series cross-section structure, containing information on each country (*i*) for each year (*t*) over the period 1996–2003, which is why I apply a time-series cross-section (TSCS) design. The dataset is cross-sectionally dominant, meaning that the cross-section units (far) outnumber the temporal units ($N>T$) (Stimson, 1985). It is worth noting that all independent variables, except WDIST, are lagged one year,[20] under the assumption that it takes some time for changes in the explanatory variables to affect FDI.

RESULTS

The Base Model

Table 2 depicts results from the base model, which should function as a useful reference points for later models. In column 1, all variables are significant, and all but one are significant at the .01 level of confidence (OIL being the exception). I do not include STOCK in the model, though, possibly leading to an overestimation of POLRISK's impact on FDI. According to this specification, a one-point increase in POLRISK, other thing being equal, induces a 5.02 percent increase in FDI inflows, while a ten-point improvement in POLRISK is associated with a 63.23 percent increase in FDI.

Not surprisingly, GDP has a strong impact on the dependent measure; the estimated elasticity of FDI with respect to GDP is .853. Also, GROWTH, TRADE, WDIST, MINMET, and GAS are highly significant with the expected signs. The same is not true for OIL, however. One possible reason why this variable turns out with a negative sign is that indigenous control over the petroleum sector is often regarded as a matter of national prestige

---

[19] Data on distances between world capitals can be obtained from http://www.chemical-ecology.net/java/capitals.htm. Data on FDI outflows are from UNCTAD.

[20] MINMET is lagged two years because we did not have data on that variable for 2002. This, however, should not be a major problem as MINMET correlates .967 both with MINMET lagged one year and MINMET lagged two years.

(Bray, 2003; Vernon, 1971). Domestic technology and skills permitting, many countries have therefore chosen to nationalize this industry (either partly or fully), thus actively *discouraging* FDI. Also note that GDPPC is negative and significant. On the one hand, this may suggest that when all dimensions of risk and potential are properly controlled for, MNCs prefer to invest in low-wage countries. On the other hand, GDPPC is highly correlated with both GDP and POLRISK, leading to possible problems of multicollinearity and, therefore, unreliable parameter estimates (Hamilton, 1992, p. 82).

Table 2. Determinants of FDI, 1996–2003, base model

lnFDI	(1)	(2)	(3)	(4)	(5)
POLRISK	.049***		.022***		.013***
	(.005)		(.005)		(.003)
ICRG		.006		.006	
		(.009)		(.008)	
lnSTOCK			.516***	.574***	.545***
			(.037)	(.038)	(.036)
lnGDP	.853***	.978***	.871***	.877***	.841***
	(.051)	(.056)	(.043)	(.047)	(.041)
GROWTH	.046***	.058***	.039***	.046***	.041***
	(.012)	(.014)	(.011)	(.012)	(.011)
lnTRADE	.483***	.633***	.070	-.024	.005
	(.117)	(.128)	(.112)	(.123)	(.109)
lnGDPPC	-.498***	-.092	-.167**	.058	
	(.071)	(.073)	(.067)	(.065)	
lnWDIST	-.429***	-.228*	-.557***	-.388***	-.510***
	(.119)	(.134)	(.111)	(.120)	(.110)
lnMINMET	.049***	.085***	.046***	.054***	.042**
	(.018)	(.024)	(.017)	(.021)	(.017)
lnOIL	-.031*	-.115***			
	(.018)	(.018)			
lnGAS	.046***	.060***			
	(.017)	(.019)			
DPETRO			-.421***	-.718***	-.497***
			(.135)	(.132)	(.132)
Constant	-.427	-5.408***	.134	-2.035	-.521
	(1.434)	(1.535)	(1.305)	(1.392)	(1.282)
Countries	156	128	156	128	156
Observations	990	849	990	849	990
R^2	.651	.612	.709	.701	.707

Notes: OLS standard errors in parentheses; *significant at the 10% level; **significant at the 5% level; ***significant at the 1% level.

This latter interpretation is not implausible given the VIF and tolerance scores for the model; tolerance scores for GDPPC, GDP, POLRISK, OIL, and GAS are all hovering around

.20, suggesting that it may be appropriate to drop one or more variables (Hamilton, 1992, p. 134).

Turning to column 2, we can note that ICRG's political risk index is insignificant. While we should not place too much confidence in these OLS regression results (on account of likely problems of heteroskedasticity and autocorrelation), perhaps they could be taken as preliminary evidence that POLRISK, in terms of predictive qualities, might have something to offer which ICRG does not. In Columns 3–4, I include DPETRO in lieu of OIL and GAS, the former being a petroleum dummy variable that turns out negative and significant. In addition, I include STOCK, which is positive and highly significant. ICRG remains insignificant. POLRISK, however, is still positive and significant, although the value of its *b* coefficient drops markedly. Also note that the inclusion of STOCK makes TRADE insignificant, perhaps indicating that the relationship between the latter variable and FDI is spurious. That is, MNCs' location decisions may not be significantly influenced by countries' level of trade openness; rather, parent companies are inclined to move capital to its existing subsidiaries, and MNC subsidiaries are known to be engines of world trade.

Paying heed to tolerance scores, in column 5 I choose to drop GDPPC. This does have some impact on the main variable of interest, POLRISK, whose standard error drops from .005 to .003 but whose *b* coefficient also drops noticeably compared to columns 1 and 3. Significance levels for all variables (barring MINMET, which drops from .01 to .05) remain unaffected, though. Importantly, VIF and tolerance scores improve substantially when GDPPC is dropped from the model (and when DPETRO takes the place of OIL and GAS). Keeping in mind that other empirical studies have shown that GDP per capita has little effect on FDI inflows, I therefore choose to drop GDPPC from most reported specifications.

Applying ordinary least squares to pooled data does not come without its problems. OLS "simply ignores the pooled structure of the data" (Stimson, 1985, p. 918), treating each observation (i.e., country-year) as independent from the others. With pooled TSCS data, Gauss-Markov and other regression assumptions cannot be expected to be met (Kittel, 1999, p. 245). In particular, pooling data induces problems of heteroskedasticity and autocorrelation which, in turn, make OLS estimates inefficient and biased (Sayrs, 1989, p. 20). A quick examination of the residuals from the specification in *Table 2*, column 5 reveals that my model is indeed troubled by heteroskedasticity. A Breusch-Pagan/Cook-Weisberg test tells us that we can reject the null hypothesis of constant error variance (and a Ramsey RESET test for omitted variables is highly significant).

With time-series cross-section data, a possible solution to the constant coefficients model's omitted variable problem is to estimate a fixed-effects model. However, it is doubtful that including country dummies is an expedient strategy. Of course, the inclusion of *time dummies* on the right-hand side is justified by the data; FDI levels vary greatly from year to year, suggesting that there may be large unit-invariant differences between time periods. The inclusion of *N*-1 country dummies, on the other hand, is harder to justify. This would seriously drain the model of degrees of freedom, introduce problems with multicollinearity, and render redundant the variables that are relatively invariant, like STOCK and DPETRO (Beck, 2001, p. 285; Wooldridge, 2003, pp. 466–7). To be sure, I am not only interested in explaining changes in FDI levels *within* countries over time; I also wish to account for differences *between* nations. Some sort of control for time-invariant omitted variables should be included nonetheless. Following Jun and Singh (1996), therefore, in most of the model specifications I employ nine *regional dummies* to control for region-specific factors (developed countries constitute a region of their own).[21]

In *Table 3*, column 1, I include region dummies along with time dummies in a specification that otherwise consists of the same variables that was employed in *Table 2*, column 5 (due to space considerations, none of the dummy variables are reported). POLRISK still exhibits significant influence on FDI. The other independent variables do not change much with the inclusion of time and region controls. However, TRADE now becomes significant (but only at the .10 level), while MINMET loses significance.

Table 3. Determinants of FDI, 1996–2003, with time and region dummies

lnFDI	(1) Regular SEs	(2) Robust SEs	(3) Robust SEs
POLRISK	.015***	.013**	.015*
	(.004)	(.006)	(.008)
lnSTOCK	.525***	.545***	.525***
	(.035)	(.080)	(.079)
lnGDP	.928***	.841***	.928***
	(.045)	(.070)	(.059)
GROWTH	..042***	.041***	.042***
	(.010)	(.015)	(.015)
lnTRADE	.190*	.005	.190
	(.111)	(.200)	(.194)
lnWDIST	-.719***	-.510**	-.719***
	(.156)	(.198)	(.241)
lnMINMET	.014	.042*	.014
	(.016)	(.023)	(.026)
DPETRO	-.405***	-.497*	-.405
	(.132)	(.281)	(.271)
Constant	-.039	-.521	-.039
	(1.592)	(.2564)	(2.437)
Country dummies	No	No	No
Time dummies	Yes	No	Yes
Region dummies	Yes	No	Yes
Countries	156	156	156
Observations	990	990	990
R^2	.746	.707	.746

Notes: Column 1 reports OLS standard errors in parentheses; columns 2-3 report robust standard errors in parentheses; *significant at the 10% level; **significant at the 5% level; ***significant at the 1% level.

[21] Following UNCTAD's (2004) classification, dummies for the following regions are created: Developed countries; North Africa; Other Africa (omitted category); South America; Other Latin America and the Caribbean; West Asia; Central Asia; South, East and South-East Asia; The Pacific; Central and Eastern Europe.

Following Beck and Katz (1995, 1996), I choose to estimate the regression parameters by OLS, which should yield consistent, albeit inefficient results. The standard errors, on the other hand, are probably distorted. The recommended estimation method in Stata, especially when the sample size is large, is regress cluster (Wiggins, 1999; Wooldridge, 2003, p. 261), that is, OLS regression with Huber-White's heteroskedastic-consistent robust estimates of the standard errors and, perforce, robust estimates also of the *t* statistics. In *Table 3*, column 2, I use robust standard errors in a regression devoid of time and region dummies, noting that the parameter estimates are the same but that standard errors are substantially larger than in the reference model specification depicted in *Table 2*, column 5. In *Table 3*, column 3, I proceed to include dummies for time and region. It is worth noting that POLRISK is only significant at the .10 level. This entices me to perform further tests to make sure that earlier results were not predominantly caused by deflated standard errors.[22]

Even though the data only cover the period from 1996 to 2003, serial correlation in the errors could still be a problem (as could contemporaneous correlation, i.e. correlation between the errors of different units). A TSCS version of the Lagrange-multiplier (LM) test reveals that the model is, in fact, seriously plagued by first-order serial correlation. Following Beck and Katz (1995, 1996), who argue that an explicit measure of the stickiness of the data is often warranted when we are dealing with TSCS data, I choose to include a lagged dependent variable (LDV) on the right-hand side of the equation. By doing so, I basically treat the LDV as an explanatory variable in its own right, expecting it to represent germane omitted historical factors and thus to account for a large part of the variance in FDI (Kittel, 1999, p. 230; Wooldridge, 2003, p. 300). In addition, I reckon that the inclusion of the LDV will rid the model of autocorrelation. Another test of the effects of the lagged residuals on the residuals, this time also controlling for lagged FDI, reveals that the autocorrelation problem is close to being fixed. The autoregression coefficient decreases significantly (and even becomes negative) with the inclusion of the LDV.

A Fully Specified Model of the Effects of POLRISK on FDI

In *Table 4*, final versions of the model are exhibited. Here, I have dropped TRADE and MINMET, both of which have generally proven to be insignificant in the presence of region and time dummies and when robust standard errors are employed. Excluding these two variables substantially reduces the model's residual problems of multicollinearity, as evidenced by VIF and tolerance scores. DPETRO, on the other hand, is retained in the model; its effects on FDI have proven to be inconsistent, yet sometimes significant. All specifications include time and region dummies.

---

[22] A series of diagnostic tests for outliers and observations with large leverage values – including avplots, standardized and studentized residuals, and DFBETA values – revealed that Indonesia (because of a significant drop in the country's POLRISK score in the late 1990s coinciding with sudden and substantial foreign capital *outflows*) and Angola (due to its sizable oil-related FDI inflows in the period) might exert some influence on our model as a whole and, in particular, on POLRISK's coefficient. Although including dummies for these countries lowers the standard error and thus increases the level of significance of our main variable of interest, the results do not change so much as to justify the inclusion of any country dummies in the specifications to follow.

Table 4. Determinants of FDI, 1996–2003, accounting for autocorrelation

lnFDI	(1) Robust SEs	(2) Robust SEs	(3) Robust SEs	(4) Robust SEs	(5) PCSEs/AR1	(6) PCSEs/AR1
LDV			.540***	.546***		
			(.061)	(.063)		
POLRISK	.021***		.010***		.024***	
	(.007)		(.004)		(.004)	
ICRG		.024*		.012*		.025**
		(.014)		(.007)		(.010)
lnSTOCK	.558***	.572***	.202***	.207***	.448***	.474***
	(.079)	(.080)	(.070)	(.072)	(.117)	(.120)
lnGDP	.883***	.909***	.402***	.413***	.866***	.898***
	(.040)	(.050)	(.059)	(.062)	(.043)	(.041)
GROWTH	.039**	.043***	.024**	.023**	.024**	.025**
	(.015)	(.016)	(.009)	(.010)	(.010)	(.011)
lnWDIST	-.708***	-.616***	-.356***	-.303**	-.606***	-.498***
	(.216)	(.230)	(.110)	(.116)	(.089)	(.103)
DPETRO	-.311	-.454	-.207	-.279*	-.317**	-.488***
	(.284)	(.320)	(.146)	(.160)	(.151)	(.142)
Constant	.322	-.874	.798	.110	-.114	-1.861**
	(1.917)	(1.871)	(1.053)	(1.055)	(1.029)	(.818)
Time dummies	Yes	Yes	Yes	Yes	Yes	Yes
Region dummies	Yes	Yes	Yes	Yes	Yes	Yes
Countries	163	131	161	131	163	131
Observations	1057	893	1047	889	1057	893
R^2	.779	.730	.804	.803	.618	.628

Note: Columns 1–4 report robust standard errors in parentheses; parameters in Columns 5–6 are estimated by Prais-Winsten FGLS assuming a common AR1 process in the disturbances, with panel-corrected standard errors in parentheses; *significant at the 10% level; **significant at the 5% level; ***significant at the 1% level.

Providing us with a useful benchmark, in *Table 4*, columns 1–2, I estimate the model without a lagged dependent variable. As one would expect, POLRISK is highly significant, although its effects on FDI are not overwhelming; a one-point increase in the POLRISK index yields a 2.11 percent increase in FDI inflows, *ceteris paribus*, while a ten-point POLRISK improvement is associated with a 23.22 percent increase in FDI.

In column 2, I note that ICRG, which also ranges from 0 to 100, exhibits much a similar effect, though its coefficient (.024) is slightly larger than POLRISK's (.021). The standard error of ICRG's coefficient is substantial, though, thereby rendering the variable significant only at the .10 level.

Moving on to Columns 3–4, where I have included an LDV to remedy the autocorrelation problem, we note that the levels of significance of both POLRISK and ICRG remain unaffected despite that both variables' *b* coefficients decrease. Of course, adding an LDV makes for a strong test of the statistical relationships between the other regressors and FDI. This is so because the lagged dependent variable tends to soak up variance and mask or reduce other possible causal effects of the independent variables (Kittel, 1999, p. 230). It therefore seems reasonable to put some faith in the results exhibited in Columns 3–4. I therefore tentatively conclude that POLRISK is positively and significantly related to FDI.

Also noteworthy is the conspicuous stability of most of the other variables in the model; STOCK, GDP, GROWTH, and WDIST have all proven to have a highly significant effect on FDI in all model specifications.

Investment location decisions of multinational companies seem to be unequivocally influenced by the size and growth rate of the host country market, by the distance between the MNC headquarter and the host country, by previous levels of FDI, and – as is the focal point of the present analysis – by political risk, broadly defined.

In *Table 4*, Columns 5–6, I replace the robust standard errors with panel-corrected standard errors (PCSEs) and employ the AR(1) correction for first-order autocorrelation. Keeping in mind that Beck and Katz (1995) argue that this method is ideal only when *T* is relatively large, I merely use these results as a robustness check. I nonetheless take some comfort from the fact that the results, compared to Columns 1–4, by and large stay the same.

Sensitivity Analysis

In *Table 5*, I perform a brief sensitivity analysis, using the same independent variables as in *Table 4* (including time and region dummies and a lagged dependent variable) and reporting robust standard errors. In Columns 1–2, I use FDI per capita logged (FDIPC) as the dependent variable, as some empirical studies do (Busse, 2004; Jakobsen and Jakobsen, 2011).

This change of dependent variable also induces me to re-introduce GDPPC among the regressors, suspecting that omitting it from a model where FDI is measured relative to population size will lead to a significant overestimation of the impact of POLRISK. (Of course, then I also re-introduce problems of multicollinearity.)

In Columns 3–4, I once again change the dependent variable, this time into FDI divided by GDP and logged (FDIGDP), as some scholars seem to favor (e.g., Asiedu and Lien, 2004; Büthe and Milner, 2008).

Notwithstanding that using FDIGDP as the dependent variable makes the analysis conceptually different (Li and Resnick, 2003, p. 200), the main results of interest stay roughly the same: POLRISK is positive and significant at the .05 level, and ICRG is rendered insignificant.

Table 5. Determinants of FDI, 1996–2003, sensitivity analysis

	(1) lnFDIPC	(2) lnFDIPC	(3) lnFDIGDP	(4) lnFDIGDP
LDV	.478***	.490***	.427***	.443***
	(.078)	(.082)	(.083)	(.093)
POLRISK	.013**		.012**	
	(.007)		(.005)	
ICRG		.007	.456**	.009
		(.012)	(.187)	(.011)
lnSTOCK	.321**	.332**	.456**	.464**
	(.321)	(.129)	(.187)	(.197)
lnGDP	-.019	-.000	.033	.072
	(.034)	(.040)	(.051)	(.061)
GROWTH	.034***	.039***	.036**	.043**
	(.012)	(.014)	(.016)	(.018)
lnGDPPC	.504***	.576***		
	(.102)	(.128)		
lnWDIST	-.409***	-.349**	-.402**	-.320*
	(.145)	(.151)	(.159)	(.158)
DPETRO	-.411**	-.516**	-.514**	-.617**
	(.206)	(.221)	(.216)	(.238)
Constant	-3.386*	-4.058**	1.663	.848
	(1.802)	(1.736)	(1.660)	(1.627)
Time dummies	Yes	Yes	Yes	Yes
Region dummies	Yes	Yes	Yes	Yes
Countries	161	131	161	131
Observations	1047	889	1047	889
R^2	.681	.700	.477	.512

Note: Robust standard errors in parentheses; *significant at the 10% level; **significant at the 5% level; ***significant at the 1% level.

CONCLUSION

It is not particularly surprising that the POLRISK index has proven to be consistently significant under sundry conditions, while ICRG's results have been less convincing overall. POLRISK should indeed have some valuable characteristics that help remedy some of the drawbacks of commercial risk assessments: the coverage of the index is extensive; it relies for its estimation on a variety of sources and methodologies; the index is well-rooted in the academic literature; it pays heed to the inherent multidimensionality of the concept of political risk; and, not least, all the sources that I draw on to create POLRISK are publicly available at no cost, thereby making this index a very useful and accessible measure of political risk.

Extensive testing of the relationship between political risk and multinationals' investment location decisions contributes to validating these claims. Controlling for host-country potential and taking into account problems of heteroskedasticity, autocorrelation, and multicollinearity, political risk – when broadly defined and properly measured – significantly affects the behavior of foreign direct investors.

One possible reason why the empirical literature is inconclusive with regard to the impact of political risk on FDI is that most proxies of political risk tend to be unidimensional. For example, if we only liken political risk to political *instability* we could be induced to build our plant in relatively stable North-Korea, disregarding the fact that this country's political institutions are a shambles, that Kim Jong-il's erratic regime has a preference for Marxist economic policies, and that other foreign investors wisely stay away. The academic literature, taken as a whole, teaches us that political risk might be – and, one could argue, really *is* and should thus always be treated as – a multidimensional phenomenon. Of course, political stability or instability *does* matter; investing in places like Somalia, Afghanistan, and Iraq is not for the faint-hearted. However, political institutions and economic governance also matter and may either reinforce the picture of an unstable and investor-unfriendly nation (as is the case in Somalia), or help improve the image of a turbulent country (as in Israel and Colombia), or – as in North-Korea – work to inform investors that seeming stability is, at best, only one-third of the story.

A word of caution is nonetheless warranted. The index, and thus also the analysis, starts as late as in 1996, the first year for which decent data on such important political risk sub-indicators as corruption, rule of law, and government economic policies are available. Unfortunately, a small T means that I cannot effectively estimate a fixed-effects model; hence, I cannot rid the model of all unobserved "noise" stemming from country-specific (often historical) factors. On the other hand, the model does include a set of region dummies which should help alleviate some of these concerns. Yet it is important to stress that the observed effects of POLRISK on FDI are not large enough to justify any definitive conclusions.

Perhaps the most valuable result of this study is the tentative evidence that political risk still matters greatly to international investors. Of course, the official story tells us that in the last couple of decades host governments have become more receptive toward multinational companies. And let there be no doubt: much has changed since the turbulent period of the 1960s and 1970s – the "expropriation era." But multinationals still seem to run into trouble abroad. A global wave of (often) half-hearted liberalism does not, by any means, deter neither rational nor irrational host governments from exploiting the opportunities provided to them by the inherent irreversibility of large fixed-asset investments. Neither does the growth of international capital flows make non-governmental organizations applaud the positive effects of MNCs, nor does it restrain international or domestic terrorists and rebel groups. The risks may have changed, but they have not disappeared.

References

Ahlquist, J. (2006). Economic Policy, Institutions, and Capital Flows: Portfolio and Direct Investment Flows in Developing Countries. *International Studies Quarterly, 50*(3), 681-704.

Altomonte, C. (2000). Economic Determinants and Institutional Frameworks: FDI in Economies of Transition. *Transnational Corporations*, *9*(2), 75-106.

Asiedu, E., and Lien, D. (2004). Capital Controls and Foreign Direct Investment. *World Development*, *32*(3), 479-90.

Barry, F., Görg, H., and Strobl, E. (2003). Foreign Direct Investment, Agglomerations, and Demonstration Effects: An Empirical Investigation. *Review of World Economics*. *139*(4), 583-600.

Beck, N. (2001). Time-Series–Cross-Section Data: What Have We Learned in the Past Few Years? *Annual Review of Political Science, 4*(1), 271-293.

Beck, N., and Katz, J. N. (1995). What To Do (and Not To Do) With Time-Series Cross-Section Data. *American Political Science Review, 89*(3), 634-647.

Beck, N., and Katz, J. N. (1996). Nuisance vs. Substance: Specifying and Estimating Time Series–Cross-Section Models. *Political Analysis, 6*(1), 1-36.

Bevan, A., Estrin, S., and Meyer, K. (2004). Foreign Investment Location and Institutional Development in Transition Economies. *International Business Review, 13*(1), 43-64.

Blanton, S. L., and Blanton, R. G. (2009). A Sectoral Analysis of Human Rights and FDI: Does Industry Type Matter? *International Studies Quarterly*, *53*(2), 469-493.

Bobonis, G. J., and Shatz, H. J. (2007). Agglomeration, Adjustment, and State Policies in the Location of Foreign Direct Investment in the United States. *Review of Economics and Statistics*, *89*(1), 30-43.

Boddewyn, J. J., and Cracco, E. F. (1972). The Political Game in World Business. *Columbia Journal of World Business*, *7*(1), 45–56.

Bouchet, M. H., Clark, E. and Groslambert, B. (2003). *Country Risk Assessment: A Guide to Global Investment Strategy*. Chichester: Wiley.

Bray, J. (2003). Attracting Reputable Companies to Risky Environments: Petroleum and Mining Companies. In I. Bannon, and P. Collier (Eds.), *Natural Resources and Violent Conflict: Options and Actions* (pp. 287-352). Washington, D.C.: World Bank.

Bremmer, I. (2005). Managing Risk in an Unstable World. *Harvard Business Review*, *82*(June), 51-60.

Brunetti, A., and Weder, B. (1997). Investment and Institutional Uncertainty: A Comparative Study of Different Uncertainty Measures. Technical Paper No. 4. Washington, D.C.: World Bank.

Busse, M. (2004). Transnational Corporations and Repression of Political Rights and Civil Liberties: An Emprical Analysis. *Kyklos, 57*(1), 45-66.

Büthe, T., and Milner, H. V. (2008). The Politics of Foreign Direct Investment into Developing Countries: Increasing FDI through International Trade Agreements? *American Journal of Political Science*, *52*(4), 741-762.

Butler, K. C., and Joaquin, D. J. (1998). A Note on Political Risk and the Required Return on Foreign Direct Investment. *Journal of International Business Studies*, *29*(3), 599-607.

Campos, N. F., and Nugent, J. B. (1998). Investment and Instability. CERGE-EI Working Paper No. 128.

Chakrabarti, A. (2001). The Determinants of Foreign Direct Investments: Sensitivity Analyses of Cross-Country Regressions. *Kyklos*, *54*(1), 89-114.

Click, R. W. (2005). Financial and Political Risks in US Direct Foreign Investment. *Journal of International Business Studies*, *36*(5), 559-575.

Cuervo-Cazurra, A. (2006). Who Cares about Corruption? *Journal of International Business Studies*, *37(*6), 807-822.

Feng, Y. (2001). Political Freedom, Political Instability, and Policy Uncertainty: A Study of Political Institutions and Private Investment in Developing Countries. *International Studies Quarterly*, *45*(2), 271-294.

Flores, R. G., and Aguilera, R. V. (2007). Globalization and Location Choice: An Analysis of US Multinational Firms in 1980 and 2000. *Journal of International Business Studies, 38*(7), 1187-1210.

Garten, J. E. (1997). Troubles ahead in Emerging Markets. *Harvard Business Review, 75*(3), 38-49.

Gastanaga, V. M., Nugent, J. B., and Pashamova, B. (1998). Host Country Reforms and FDI Inflows: How Much Difference Do They Make? *World Development, 26*(7), 1299-1314.

Gates, S., Hegre, H., Jones, M. P., and Strand, H. (2006). Institutional Inconsistency and Political Instability: Polity Duration, 1800–2000. *American Journal of Political Science, 50*(4), 893-908.

Golub, S. S. (2003). Measures of Restrictions on Inward Foreign Direct Investment for OECD Countries. *OECD Economic Studies, 36*(1), 85-116.

Graham, E. M. (1996). *Global Corporations and National Governments.* Washington, D.C.: Institute for International Economics.

Green, R. T. (1974). Political Structures as a Predictor of Radical Political Change. *Columbia Journal of World Business, 9*(1), 28-36.

Guerin, S. S., and Manzocchi, S. (2009). Political Regime and FDI from Advanced to Emerging Countries. *Review of World Economics, 145*(1), 75-91.

Gwartney, J., and Lawson, R. (2004). *Economic Freedom of the World: 2004 Annual Report.* Vancouver: Fraser Institute.

Hamilton, L. C. (1992). *Regression with Graphics.* Belmont, CA: Wadsworth.

Henisz, W. J. (2000). The Institutional Environment for Multilateral Investment. *Journal of Law, Economics and Organization, 16*(2), 334-364.

Henisz, W. J. (2002). *Politics and International Investment: Measuring Risks and Protecting Profits.* Cheltenham: Edward Elgar.

Heradstveit, D. (2001). *Democracy and Oil: The Case of Azerbaijan.* Wiesbaden: Reichert.

Howell, L. D. (1998). An Introduction to Country and Political Risk Analysis. In L. D. Howell (Ed.), *The Handbook of Country and Political Risk Analysis* (pp. 3-9). New York: PRS Group.

Jakobsen, J. (2006). Does Democracy Moderate the Obsolescing Bargain mechanism? – An Empirical Analysis, 1983–2001. *Transnational Corporations,15*(3), 65-104.

Jakobsen, J. (2010). Old Problems Remain, New Ones Crop Up: Political Risk in the 21st Century. *Business Horizons, 53*(5), 481-490.

Jakobsen, J., and de Soysa, I. (2006). Do Foreign Investors Punish Democracy? Theory and Empirics, 1984–2001. *Kyklos, 59*(3), 383-410.

Jakobsen, J., and Jakobsen, T. G. (2011). Economic Nationalism and FDI: The Impact of Public Opinion on Foreign Direct Investment in Emerging Markets, 1990–2005. *Society and Business Review, 6*(1), 61-76.

Jensen, N. M. (2003). Democratic Governance and Multinational Corporations: Political Regimes and Inflows of Foreign Direct Investment. *International Organization, 57*(3), 587-616.

Jensen, N. M. (2006). *Nation-States and the Multinational Corporation.* Princeton, NJ: Princeton University Press.

Jensen, N. M. (2008). Political Risk, Democratic Institutions, and Foreign Direct Investment. *Journal of Politics, 70*(4), 1040-1052.

Jeon, B. N., and Ahn, S. Y. (2004). Multinational Corporations and Host Country Receptivity: Perceptions from Three Asian Countries. *Multinational Business Review, 12*(2), 17-36.

Jun, K. H., and Singh, H. (1996). The Determinants of Foreign Direct Investment in Developing Countries. *Transnational Corporations, 5*(2), 67-105.

Kaufmann, D., Kraay, A., and Mastruzzi, M. (2005). Governance Matters IV: Governance Indicators for 1996–2004. Washington, D.C.: World Bank (http://info.worldbank.org/governance/wgi/resources.htm, last consulted 19 January, 2011).

Kaufmann, D., Kraay, A., and Mastruzzi, M. (2009). Governance Matters VIII: Governance Indicators for 1996–2008. Washington, D.C.: World Bank (http://info.worldbank.org/governance/wgi/resources.htm, last consulted 19 January, 2011).

Kittel, B. (1999). Sense and Sensitivity in Pooled Analysis of Political Data. *European Journal of Political Research, 35*(2), 225-253.

Kobrin, S. J. (1979). Political Risk: A Review and Reconsideration. *Journal of International Business Studies, 10*(1), 67-80.

Kobrin, S. J. (2005a). The Determinants of Liberalization of FDI Policy in Developing Countries: A Cross-Sectional Analysis, 1992–2001. *Transnational Corporations, 14*(1), 67-104.

Kobrin, S. J. (2005b). Multinational Enterprise, Public Authority, and Public Responsibility: The Case of Talisman Energy and Human Rights in Sudan. In R. Grosse (Ed.), *International Business and Government Relations in the 21st Century* (pp. 191-216). Cambridge: Cambridge University Press.

Le, Q. V., and Zak, P. J. (2006). Political Risk and Capital Flight. *Journal of International Money and Finance, 25*(2), 308-329.

Lecraw, D. J. (1996). Indonesia: The Critical Role of Government. In J. H. Dunning, and R. Narula (Eds.), *Foreign Direct Investment and Governments: Catalysts for Economic Restructuring* (pp. 316-347). London: Routledge.

Li, Q., and Resnick, A. (2003). Reversal of Fortunes: Democratic Institutions and Foreign Direct Investment Inflows to Developing Countries. *International Organization, 57*(1), 175-211.

Loree, D. W., and Guisinger, S. E. (1995). Policy and Non-Policy Determinants of U.S. Equity Foreign Direct Investment. *Journal of International Business Studies, 26*(2), 281-299.

MacIntyre, A. (2001). Institutions and Investors: The Politics of the Economic Crisis in Southeast Asia. *International Organization, 55*(1), 81-122.

Marshall, M. G., and Jaggers, K. (2002). Political Regime Characteristics and Transitions, 1800–2002. Dataset Users Manual. Center for International Development and Conflict Management (CIDCM), University of Maryland, College Park (http://www.cidcm.umd.edu/inscr/polity, last consulted November 12, 2010).

Mauro, P. (1995). Corruption and Growth. *Quarterly Journal of Economics, 110*(3), 681-712.

Meschi, P. X. (2009). Government Corruption and Foreign Stakes in International Joint Ventures in Emerging Economies. *Asia Pacific Journal of Management, 26*(2), 241-261.

Moran, T. H. (1974). *Multinational Corporations and the Politics of Dependence: Copper in Chile*. Princeton, NJ: Princeton University Press.

Morisset, J. (2000). FDI in Africa: Policies also Matter. *Transnational Corporations, 9*(2), 107-126.

Morisset, J. P., and Neso, O. L. (2002). Administrative Barriers to Foreign Investment in Developing Countries. *Transnational Corporations*, *11*(2), 99-121.

North, D. C. (1990). *Institutions, Institutional Change and Economic Performance*. Cambridge: Cambridge University Press.

O'Donnell, G. (1978). Reflections on the Patterns of Change in the Bureaucratic Authoritarian State. *Latin American Research Review*, *13*(1), 3-38.

Oetzel, J. M., Bettis, R. A., and Zenner, M. (2001). Country Risk Measures: How Risky Are They? *Journal of World Business, 36*(2), 128-145.

O'Sullivan, R. C. (2005). Learning from OPIC's Experience with Claims and Arbitration. In T. H. Moran, and G. T. West (Eds.), *International Political Risk Management: Looking to the Future* (pp. 30-74). Washington D.C.: World Bank.

Ragin, C. C. (1987). *The Comparative Method: Moving beyond Qualitative and Quantitative Strategies*. Berkeley, CA: University of California Press.

Robock, S. H. (1971). Political Risk: Identification and Assessment. *Columbia Journal of World Business, 6*(4), 6-20.

Sayrs, L. W. (1989). Pooled Time Series Analysis. Sage University paper series on quantitative applications in the social sciences, 07-001. Beverly Hills, CA: Sage.

Schneider, F., and Frey, B. S. (1985). Economic and Political Determinants of Foreign Direct Investment. *World Development, 13*(2), 161-175.

Schroeder, S. K. (2008). The Underpinnings of Country Risk Assessment. *Journal of Economic Surveys*, *22*(3), 498-535.

Sethi, D., Guisinger, S. E., Phelan, S. E., and Berg, D. M. (2003). Trends in Foreign Direct Investment Flows: A Theoretical and Empirical Analysis. *Journal of International Business Studies, 34*(4), 315-326.

Shleifer, A., and Vishny, R. W. (1993). Corruption. *Quarterly Journal of Economics*, *108*(3), 599-617.

Simmons, B. A., and Elkins, Z. (2004). The Globalization of Liberalization: Policy Diffusion in the International Political Economy. *American Political Science Review*, *98*(1), 171-189.

Simmons, B. A., Dobbin, F., and Garrett, G. (2006). The International Diffusion of Liberalism. *International Organization*, *60*(4), 781-810.

Snider, L. (2005). Political Risk: The Institutional Dimension. *International Interactions, 31*(3): 203-222.

Spar, D. (1996). Trade, Investment, and Labor: The Case of Indonesia. *Columbia Journal of World Business*, *31*(4), 30-39.

Spar, D. (1999). Foreign Investment and Human Rights. *Challenge*, *42*(1), 55-80.

Stimson, J. A. (1985). Regression in Time and Space: A Statistical Essay. *American Journal of Political Science, 29*(4), 914-947.

Thunell, L. H. (1977). *Political Risks in International Business: Investment Behavior of Multinational Corporations*. New York: Praeger.

Treviño, L. J., and Mixon, F. G. (2004). Strategic Factors Affecting Foreign Direct Investment Decisions by Multi-national Enterprises in Latin America. *Journal of World Business, 39*(3), 233-243.

Treviño, L. J., Daniels, J. D., and Arbeláez, H. (2002). Market Reform and FDI in Latin America: An Empirical Investigation. *Transnational Corporations*, *11*(1), 29-48.

UNCTAD (United Nations Conference on Trade and Development) (2004). *World Investment Report 2004: The Shift towards Services.* New York/Geneva: United Nations.

Vernon, R. (1971). *Sovereignty at Bay: The Multinational Spread of U.S. Enterprises.* London: Longman.

Wei, S. J. (2000). How Taxing is Corruption on International Investors? *Review of Economics and Statistics*, *82*(1), 1-11.

Wells, L. T. (1998). God and Fair Competition: Does the Foreign Direct Investor Face Still Other Risks in Emerging Markets? In T. H. Moran (Ed.), *Managing International Political Risk* (pp. 15-43). Malden, MA: Blackwell.

Weston, J. F., and Sorge, B. W. (1972). *International Managerial Finance.* Homewood, IL: R. D. Irwin.

Wiggins, V. (1999). Comparing XTGLS with Regress Cluster (). Stata Corporation (http://www.stata.com/support/faqs/stat/xtgls_rob.html, last consulted 4 August, 2009).

World Bank (2004). World Development Indicators, CD ROM. Washington, DC: World Bank.

Wooldridge, J. M. (2003). *Introductory Econometrics: A Modern Approach.* (2nd edition.) Mason, OH: Thomson South-Western.

In: Foreign Investment
Editor: Torre DeSare and Daniele Caprioglio

ISBN 978-1-61470-358-7

Chapter 6

THE EFFECT OF INWARD FDI ON ECONOMIC GROWTH: AN EMPIRICAL INVESTIGATION FOR THE LEAGUE OF ARAB STATES

Pascal L. Ghazalian*
Department of Economics,
University of Lethbridge,
Lethbridge, Alberta, Canada

ABSTRACT

This study estimates the effect of inward FDI on economic growth for the League of Arab States (LAS) countries over the period 1990-2007. The empirical investigation relies on a dynamic specification using GMM estimation techniques. The empirical results show moderate effect of inward FDI on economic growth where a 10% increase in inward FDI as a share of GDP accelerates economic growth by 0.22% in the short run and 1.07% in the long run. Estimating the effect for different LAS sub-regions reveals positive effect for the *Maghreb* and *Mashreq* countries but not for the Arab Gulf countries and for the Arab LDCs. Finally, the empirical results emphasize the positive effect of human capital in realizing larger benefits from inward FDI in terms of economic growth. However, trade openness and the level of development in financial markets are found not to have such effects.

INTRODUCTION

Inward Foreign Direct Investment (FDI) is considered as a potential factor that promotes economic growth in the host countries. These growth effects are realized through externalities in the form of innovation and technology transfer from foreign affiliates of Multinational Enterprises (MNEs) to domestic firms (Solow, 1956, Findlay, 1978; Wang 1990; Romer, 1993). When foreign affiliates of MNEs introduce new technologies or products, domestic

* Email: pascal.ghazalian@uleth.ca

firms could realize benefits through the diffusion effect. The latter occurs by exposure or employment turnovers from foreign affiliates to domestic firms. Furthermore, the presence of foreign affiliates would increase the level of competition in the domestic host country. This situation would impel domestic firms to use resources more efficiently and to develop new technologies and products (Blomström and Kokko, 1998). The positive implications of inward FDI for economic growth can also be channelled through vertical industrial linkages between foreign affiliates and domestic suppliers (Rodriguez-Clare, 1996; Markusen and Venables, 1999; Alfaro and Rodriguez-Clare, 2004; Javorcik, 2004). These vertical implications occur through technology spillover from foreign affiliates to the domestic suppliers of primary and intermediate products. They can also occur by inducing these domestic suppliers to upgrade their managerial operations and production processes in order to meet the more stringent requirements of the foreign affiliates.

The occurrence of inward FDI in the host country may not be sufficient to result in higher returns in terms of economic growth. Many empirical studies emphasized the role of the absorptive capacity and human capital stock of the host country in order to realize higher benefits from inward FDI (Borensztein et al., 1998; Xu, 2000). Other empirical studies outlined that the economic growth effects of inward FDI are enhanced when host countries are characterized by developed financial systems that improve capital allocation (Alfaro et al., 2004; Durham, 2004) and by open trade regimes (Balasubramanyam et al., 1996).

This study aims at estimating the effect of inward FDI on economic growth for the League of Arab States (LAS) region. The LAS organization is composed of 22 Arab countries that are hosts of a growing FDI stock.[1] Data from the United Nations Conference on Trade and Development's (UNCTAD's) FDI Database indicate that the aggregate inward FDI stock in the LAS region increased from 56.7 billion USD in 1990 to 351.8 billion USD in 2007. In 2007, the inward FDI stock was the highest in Saudi Arabia reaching 76.1 billion USD, followed by United Arab Emirates (54.8 billion USD) and Egypt (50.5 billion USD). The ratio of inward FDI stock to Gross Domestic Product (GDP) in the LAS region currently corresponds to regions with similar levels of income per capita. For instance, in 2007, the ratio of inward FDI stock to GDP in the South American Mercado Común del Sur (MERCOSUR) was 0.24 compared to 0.23 in the LAS region. However, there is a significant variation in the ratio of inward FDI stock to GDP among the LAS member countries. In 2007, the ratio of inward FDI stock to GDP in Lebanon and Jordan was above 0.83 whereas this ratio remained below 0.12 in Kuwait and Qatar. Many authors (e.g., Sekkat and Veganzones, 2004; Chan and Gemayel, 2004; Henry and Springborg, 2010) noted that inward FDI flow to Arab countries is still falling below the potentials and attributed these limitations to, among other factors, inadequate foreign exchange liberalization policies, unstable macroeconomic and political conditions, and lack of economic transparency.

The LAS member countries are characterized by a significant level of diversity in terms of macroeconomic factors, economic policies, and openness to trade and international business. Many LAS members are oil-producing countries (e.g., Saudi Arabia, United Arab

[1] The main objective of the LAS is to "draw closer the relations between member States and co-ordinate collaboration between them, to safeguard their independence and sovereignty, and to consider in a general way the affairs and interests of the Arab countries" (League of Arab States, 1945). The LAS member countries are: Algeria, Bahrain, Comoros, Djibouti, Egypt, Iraq, Jordan, Kuwait, Lebanon, Libya, Mauritania, Morocco, Oman, Palestinian Territories, Qatar, Saudi Arabia, Somalia, Sudan, Syria, Tunisia, United Arab Emirates, and Yemen.

Emirates), enjoying income per capita above 13,000 USD (2007 estimates). Meanwhile, some other LAS member countries (e.g., Djibouti, Egypt, Sudan) have income per capita below 1,500 USD (2007 estimates). Also, there is a substantial variation in the education indicators, being higher in some LAS countries (e.g., Lebanon, Tunisia) and significantly lower in other LAS countries (e.g., Djibouti, Mauritania).[2] Furthermore, there are important differences in the economic policies and openness to trade and international business since some LAS countries (e.g., United Arab Emirates, Bahrain) adopt relatively open policies whereas some other LAS countries (e.g., Algeria, Morocco, Syria) implement more restrictive international policies.[3] These factors, among others, are expected to influence the extent of the effect of inward FDI on economic growth. The diversity among the LAS member countries provides us the opportunity to carry out a comprehensive study that investigates the effect of inward FDI on economic growth and the factors influencing the magnitude of this effect.

Despite the fact that some LAS countries (e.g., Egypt, Morocco, Tunisia) have implemented reforms in FDI legislations, there is still a long way to reach the potentials of inward FDI. Some LAS countries still maintain restrictive regulatory policies vis-à-vis inward FDI compared to other LAS countries. For example, statistical indicators from the annual surveys entitled *Economic Freedom of the World* produced by the Fraser Institute show that the degree of freedom in foreign ownership of capital for Algeria, Kuwait, and Syria has a score of 4.8, 3.8, and 4.9, respectively, over a scale of 10. Comparatively, the corresponding scores for Bahrain, Jordan, Tunisia, and the United Arab Emirates are 8.5, 7.5, 7.6, and 7.0, respectively. Also, many LAS countries are falling behind with regulations limiting the freedom in credit, labour and business markets. In this category, the scores for Algeria, Egypt, and Morocco are 5.0, 4.9, and 5.2, respectively, compared to the scores for Bahrain, Kuwait, and Oman of 8.2, 7.8, and 7.6, respectively. Hence, the potentials of inward FDI can be reached through liberalized inward FDI and international business policies. These policies should complement the essential international business requirements of (economic and institutional) transparency and (political and macroeconomic) stability, as emphasized in many studies (e.g., Sekkat and Veganzones, 2004; Chan and Gemayel, 2004; Henry and Springborg, 2010).

The objective of this study is two-fold. First, we empirically assess the effect of inward FDI on economic growth in the LAS member countries. This effect is also disentangled for different geo-economic sub-regions of the LAS zone. Second, we determine the factors that influence the magnitude of the effect of inward FDI on economic growth (e.g., absorptive capacity, trade openness, financial markets). The empirical investigation relies on a dynamic framework using Generalized Method of Moments (GMM) estimation techniques for a panel data covering the LAS member countries and spanning over the period 1990-2007. The empirical results will provide insights on the effect of inward FDI on economic growth and the factors influencing its magnitude. The empirical results will also serve to develop long term FDI policies by the LAS member countries and also by the LAS organization. In the

[2] World Bank's Tertiary School Enrolment Data reveals higher enrolments of 49% and 32% in Lebanon and Tunisia, respectively, but significantly lower enrolments of 3% and 4% in Djibouti and Mauritania, respectively.

[3] Data from the annual surveys entitled *Economic Freedom of the World* that are produced by the Fraser Institute show an index of freedom to trade internationally for Algeria, Morocco, and Syria of 6.1, 6.0, and 5.6 (out of 10) in 2007, respectively. Meanwhile, this index is significantly higher for United Arab Emirates (8.6) and Bahrain (7.7).

case of positive evidence of inward FDI effect on economic growth, LAS organization and individual member countries will be invited to step forward in liberalizing FDI, credit, and business regulations and to enhance foreign exchange and economic transparency. In the case of insignificant or negative effect of inward FDI on economic growth, caution should be exercised regarding current and potential tax breaks and subsidies that are aimed to attract inward FDI.

The remainder of this chapter is organized as follows. The next section provides a review of the empirical literature that estimates the effect of inward FDI on economic growth. This is followed by a section that presents and discusses the empirical specification and the econometric method used to estimate the effect of inward FDI on economic growth and the factors influencing the magnitude of this effect. The next section presents and discusses the benchmark empirical results. This section also presents the results for different geo-economic sub-regions of the LAS zone. The final section provides concluding remarks.

Review of the Empirical Literature

The empirical literature has found mixed results regarding the effect of inward FDI on economic growth. Balasubramanyam et al. (1996) estimated the effect of inward FDI on economic growth across developing countries with different trade policy regimes. More specifically, they tested the hypothesis of Bhagwati (1978) that export promoting strategy is likely to attract more efficiently benefits from inward FDI than import substituting strategy. Their empirical results lent support to this hypothesis. Borensztein et al. (1998) investigated the effect of inward FDI on economic growth using a cross-section dataset covering FDI flows from developed countries to developing countries. Borensztein et al. (1998) found positive effects that are only expressed when the level of human capital, represented by the educational attainment, surpasses a minimum threshold. Xu (2000) investigated whether the activities of United States (US) MNEs abroad has promoted economic growth in developing countries and Least Developing Countries (LDCs) using a panel dataset covering the period 1966-1994. Xu (2000) found positive effects in the case of developing countries that generally meet minimum requirements of human capital but not in the case of LDCs with human capital levels falling below the required threshold. Khawar (2005) carried out an empirical analysis aiming at estimating the effect of inward FDI on real income per capita. Khawar (2005) found positive effects irrespective of any level of human capital requirement. Khawar (2005) outlined that the endogeneity between inward FDI and real income per capita remains essential in deriving robust inferences on the direction of causality.

The role of financial markets in enhancing positive effects of inward FDI on economic growth is examined in many empirical studies. Hermes and Lensink (2003) studied the effect of developed financial markets in realizing higher benefits from inward FDI on economic growth using a dataset covering 67 developing countries over the period 1970-1995. Hermes and Lensink (2003) found that 37 countries have sufficiently developed financial markets to allow for positive effects. Alfaro et al. (2004) found that inward FDI alone has ambiguous effect on economic growth using a dataset from 71 developed and developing countries between 1975 and 1995. However, Alfaro et al. (2004) detected that countries with well developed financial markets have their economic growth promoted by inward FDI. Also,

Durham (2004) derived equivalent outcomes using a dataset covering 80 countries from 1979 through 1998. Durham (2004) found that the effect of inward FDI on economic growth is contingent on the level of development of financial markets.

Carkovic and Levine (2005) used the Generalized Method of Moment (GMM) panel estimator to assess the effects of inward FDI on economic growth for a five year averaged datasets over the period 1960-1995 covering 64 developed and developing countries. After controlling for endogeneity in the dataset and other growth determinants, Carkovic and Levine (2005) found little evidence supporting the claim of enhancing effect of inward FDI on economic growth. Furthermore, they found that the interaction terms between inward FDI and variables depicting the level of human capital, the level of development in financial markets, and the degree of trade openness have no statistically significant effects. Ghosh and Wang (2009) estimated the effect of both inward and outward FDI on economic growth for the Organization for Economic Cooperation and Development (OECD) countries using a panel dataset covering the period 1980-2004. Ghosh and Wang (2009) found positive but moderate effects of inward FDI on economic growth. Furthermore, Ghosh and Wang (2009) reported that the human capital stock does not exert significant influence on the magnitude of the inward FDI effect on economic growth. They explained this outcome by the fact that the dataset mainly includes developed OECD countries where stocks of human capital have already exceeded the minimum requirement threshold to realize the growth potentials from inward FDI.

EMPIRICAL SPECIFICATION AND ESTIMATION METHOD

In this section, we present the empirical specification to characterize the effect of inward FDI on economic growth for a panel dataset comprising 20 LAS countries and spanning over the period 1990-2007.[4] Following the empirical literature on economic growth (e.g, Eichengreen and Leblang, 2003; Carkovic and Levine, 2005), we adopt the following dynamic empirical specification:

$$\ln RGDPC_{it} - \ln RGDPC_{it-1} = \alpha + (\beta - 1)\ln RGDPC_{it-1} + \gamma \ln FDI_{it} + \Lambda \mathbf{CV}_{it} + \eta_i + \varepsilon_{it} \quad (1)$$

where $RGDPC_{it}$ represents the real GDP per capita of country i at time t, FDI_{it} depicts the value of inward FDI stock as a share of GDP and is treated as endogenous variable, $\mathbf{CV}_{it}$ is a vector of growth determinant control variables, and $\eta_i \sim IID(0, \sigma_\eta^2)$ and $\varepsilon_{it} \sim IID(0, \sigma_\varepsilon^2)$ are assumed to be independent of each other and among themselves. Rearranging, the basic autoregressive model is specified as:

$$\ln RGDPC_{it} = \alpha + \beta \ln RGDPC_{it-1} + \gamma \ln FDI_{it-k} + \Lambda \mathbf{CV}_{it} + \eta_i + \varepsilon_{it} \quad (2)$$

[4] Observations pertaining to the Palestinian Territories and Somalia are not included in the dataset because of extensively missing observations.

Arellano and Bond (1991) implemented a difference generalized method of moments (GMM) estimator to estimate dynamic panel equations where differencing wipes out unobserved country-specific effects. The moment conditions exploit the orthogonality conditions between the differenced errors and lagged values of the dependent variable. Blundell and Bond (1998) argued that lagged levels are weak instruments to the first differenced equations when individual series are persistent over time and when there is a relatively small number of time-series observations. In a follow-up paper, Blundell and Bond (2000) demonstrated that the first-differenced GMM estimator has a large finite sample bias and limited precision. Blundell and Bond (2000) showed that these potential problems are lessened by considering the adjustments suggested by Arellano and Bover (1995) and by Blundell and Bond (1998). These adjustments consist of complementing the differenced equations with the original set of equations in levels where lagged differences are employed as instruments. The system is then estimated as a whole.

The GMM estimator with heteroskedasticity-robust standard errors is considered to estimate the empirical equation. The GMM estimator is associated with two essential tests proposed by Arellano and Bond (1991), Arellano and Bover (1995), and Blundell and Bond (1998). The first test is the Sargan/Hansen test of over-identifying restrictions with the null hypothesis being the inability to reject the over-identification restrictions. The second test is to detect the presence of serial correlation. While first-order autocorrelation in differenced residuals maintains the consistency of estimates, second-order autocorrelation does not. Therefore, the second test diagnoses second-order serial autocorrelation. Failure to reject the null hypothesis implies that the original error term is serially uncorrelated.

The dataset used in the empirical investigation is assembled from different sources. Values of real GDP per capita at current USD are derived from the Penn World Table 6.3. Values of inward FDI stock are collected from the UNCTAD's FDI Database. The vector of growth determinant control variables includes government size, the level of development of the financial markets, trade openness, and inflation.[5] These variables are sourced from the World Bank Database. Government size is represented by government spending as a share of GDP. Government spending can promote economic growth through the provision of public goods such as education and infrastructure. However, government spending can slow down economic growth by diverting resources from productive sectors to the government. The level of development of financial markets is represented by the credit to the private sector by domestic financial intermediaries as a share of GDP. Developed financial markets facilitate the efficient allocation of resources over time, the diversification and the hedging of risk, and the exchange of goods and services. Hence, developed financial markets are expected to have a positive effect on economic growth. The degree of trade openness is represented by the summation of exports and imports as a share of GDP. Trade openness is expected to enhance economic growth by allowing countries to specialize on the basis of their comparative advantages and by transferring technology from higher-productivity trading partners. Inflation is measured as annual growth rate of GDP deflator in the empirical application. Persistent and high inflation rates are expected to result in negative externalities on economic activities. For instance, higher inflation rates would foster more conservative investment strategies, make

[5] The effects of the Gulf war (1990-1991) and Iraq invasion (2003-2004) are controlled by dummy variables. The empirical regressions are also carried out when dropping the corresponding observations. The results remain robust.

exports relatively more expensive, and intensify frictions in the credit markets that make hard for banks to adjust nominal interest rates. Summary statistics of these variables are presented in Table 1.

Table 1. Summary Statistics

Variable	Mean	Standard Deviation	Minimum	Maximum
Real GDP per capita (Current USD)	10,014.9	12,727.9	629.8	104,707.5
Inward FDI Stock (Million of Current USD)	5,891.4	9,176.3	0	76,146.1
Inward FDI stock (as a Share of GDP)	0.21	0.22	0	1.04
Government Spending (as a Share of GDP)	0.25	0.14	0.07	2.10
Inflation Rate (Annual Percentage)	9.9	18.3	-29.3	159.3
Openness to Trade (Import and Export as a Share of GDP)	0.68	0.32	0.08	1.77
Private Credit (as a Share of GDP)	0.36	0.24	0.01	0.98
School Enrollment, Tertiary (Gross Percentage)	16.6	11.9	0	59.0

Estimation Results

Table 2 displays the results from the GMM estimation of the basic empirical model. Table 2 also reports the Arellano-Bond test of AR(1) and AR(2), and the Sargan/Hansen test of over-identifying restrictions. The outcomes from both tests are satisfactory. The former test indicates the consistency of the GMM estimator and the latter test implies failure to reject the null hypothesis of over-identification restrictions. Column (i) of Table 2 presents the results for a preliminary empirical specification with the control variables being excluded. The estimated coefficient on the inward FDI variable is positive and significant at the 1% level. Column (ii) of Table 2 reports the results when the empirical specification includes the macroeconomic control variables listed in the previous section. The estimated coefficient on the inward FDI variable is slightly reduced but remains positive and significant at the 1% level. Column (iii) presents the results of an augmented empirical specification that adds a variable depicting the level of human capital. The latter is represented by the tertiary school enrolment as a gross percentage of the population and is sourced from the World Bank's World Development Indicator database. Compared to the results in column (ii), the estimated coefficients of the inward FDI variable and of the macroeconomic control variables exhibit little changes.

The results in column (iii) indicate that a 10% increase in the stock value of inward FDI as a share of GDP induces 0.22% economic growth in the short run and 1.07% in the long run. The estimated coefficients on the government expenditure and inflation variables are negative and significant at the 5% and 10% levels, respectively. Also, the results show that the level of development of financial markets has no significant effect on economic growth whereas trade openness promotes economic growth. More specifically, a 10% increase in the sum of import and export values as a share of GDP promotes economic growth by 0.11% in the short run and 5.49% in the long run. The estimated coefficient on the schooling variable is positive and significant at the 5% level, indicating that a 10% increase in the human capital stock depicted by the tertiary school enrolment promotes economic growth by 0.42% in the short run and 2.03% in the long run. Column (iv) implements the GMM estimation when using one-period lagged FDI variable which is treated as a predetermined variable in the estimation procedure. The results remain quantitatively and qualitatively robust.[6]

Table 2. Effect of Inward FDI on Economic Growth in the LAS Countries (GMM Estimation)

	(i)	(ii)	(iii)	(iv)
Ln(Real GDP per Capita)$_{it-1}$	0.876a (0.051)	0.812a (0.073)	0.794a (0.077)	0.901a (0.079)
Ln(FDI)$_{it}$	0.030a (0.008)	0.024a (0.007)	0.022a (0.007)	0.025a (0.007)
Ln(Government Size)$_{it}$		-0.159b (0.078)	-0.148b (0.072)	-0.155b (0.074)
Ln(Private Credit)$_{it}$		0.017 (0.020)	0.026 (0.023)	0.023 (0.022)
Inflation$_{it}$		-0.0009c (0.0005)	-0.0008c (0.0005)	-0.0009c (0.0005)
Ln(Openness to Trade)$_{it}$		0.125a (0.045)	0.113a (0.043)	0.120a (0.042)
Ln(Schooling)$_{it}$			0.042b (0.018)	0.046b (0.019)
Observations	320	320	320	320
Sargan/Hansen test (*p*-value)	0.41	0.29	0.31	0.32
Arellano-Bond test AR(1) (*p*-value)	0.00	0.00	0.00	0.00
Arellano-Bond test AR(2) (*p*-value)	0.33	0.26	0.28	0.28

Notes: Standard errors are in parentheses with "a", "b", and "c" denoting significance at the 1%, 5%, and 10% level, respectively.

Table 3 presents the results of the effect of inward FDI on economic growth for different LAS geo-economic sub-regions. The LAS sub-regions are categorized into the *Maghreb* sub-region (Algeria, Libya, Morocco, and Tunisia), *Mashreq* sub-region (Egypt, Iraq, Jordan, Lebanon, and Syria), Gulf Cooperation Council (GCC) region (Bahrain, Kuwait, Oman, Qatar, Saudi Arabia, and the United Arab Emirates), and Arab LDCs (Comoros, Djibouti, Mauritania, and Yemen). As in Table (2), column (i) presents the results from a preliminary empirical specification with macroeconomic control variables being excluded. Column (ii) presents the results when including the macroeconomic control variables in the empirical specification. Column (iii) shows the results when adding the tertiary schooling variable to the empirical specification. The estimated coefficients on the inward FDI variables are

[6] Equivalent empirical results are obtained when using larger time lags.

slightly modified and qualitatively equivalent across columns. Interestingly, these estimated coefficients show significant variation across different LAS sub-regions.

Table 3. Effect of Inward FDI on Economic Growth in Different LAS Geo-Economic Sub-Regions (GMM Estimation)

	(i)	(ii)	(iii)	(iv)
Ln(Real GDP per Capita)$_{it-1}$	0.848a (0.073)	0.807a (0.076)	0.781a (0.079)	0.776a (0.081)
Ln(FDI)$_{it}$ (*Maghreb* Countries)	0.072a (0.024)	0.067a (0.026)	0.069a (0.027)	0.067b (0.028)
Ln(FDI)$_{it}$ (*Mashreq* Countries)	0.033a (0.010)	0.029a (0.011)	0.027a (0.010)	0.026a (0.010)
Ln(FDI)$_{it}$ (Gulf Cooperation Council Countries)	0.020 (0.022)	0.014 (0.018)	0.016 (0.019)	0.016 (0.018)
Ln(FDI)$_{it}$ (Arab Least Developing Countries)	0.015 (0.014)	0.017 (0.013)	0.012 (0.012)	0.014 (0.012)
Ln(Government Size)$_{it}$		-0.136c (0.072)	-0.125c (0.069)	-0.119 (0.067)
Ln(Private Credit)$_{it}$		0.019 (0.022)	0.025 (0.023)	0.027 (0.024)
Ln(Inflation)$_{it}$		-0.0010c (0.0006)	-0.0009c (0.0005)	-0.0008 (0.0005)
Ln(Openness to Trade)$_{it}$		0.122a (0.043)	0.131a (0.044)	0.136a (0.044)
Ln(Schooling)$_{it}$			0.047b (0.021)	0.049b (0.022)
Observations	320	320	320	320
Sargan/Hansen test (*p*-value)	0.39	0.28	0.32	0.33
Arellano-Bond test AR(1) (*p*-value)	0.00	0.00	0.00	0.00
Arellano-Bond test AR(2) (*p*-value)	0.31	0.24	0.25	0.26

Notes: Standard errors are in parentheses with "a", "b", and "c" denoting significance at the 1%, 5%, and 10% level, respectively.

From Column (iii) of Table 3, the estimated coefficients on inward FDI for the *Maghreb* and *Mashreq* sub-regions are positive and significant at the 1% level. These estimated coefficients indicate that a 10% increase in inward FDI stock as a share of GDP in the *Maghreb* and *Mashreq* sub-regions enhances economic growth by 0.69% and 0.27% in the short run and by 3.15% and 1.23% in the long run, respectively. However, the estimated coefficient on the inward FDI variable for the GCC sub-region is not significant. This outcome could be associated with the fact that most GCC countries are oil exporting countries where economic growth is mainly derived from increases in oil demand and prices and where there is a significant proportion of inward FDI that is associated with the oil industry. The estimated coefficient on the inward FDI variable for the Arab LDCs is also not significant. This outcome could reflect the implications of inadequate levels of human capital stock in these countries. For instance, the percentage of enrolment in tertiary school is still below 4% in 2007 for Comoros, Djibouti and Yemen. Finally, column (iv) shows that the results are not altered when representing the inward FDI variable as a lagged and predetermined variable.

Table 4. Implications of Schooling, Trade Openness, and Level of Financial Development for the Magnitude of the Effect of Inward FDI on Economic Growth in the LAS Countries (GMM Estimation)

	(i)	(ii)	(iii)	(iv)	(v)	(vi)
Ln(Real GDP per Capita)$_{it-1}$	0.767a (0.084)	0.791a (0.075)	0.798a (0.080)	0.759a (0.085)	0.785a (0.079)	0.794a (0.082)
Ln(FDI)$_{it}$	-0.010 (0.026)	0.026b (0.011)	0.024a (0.007)	-0.008 (0.027)	0.022b (0.011)	0.023a (0.007)
Ln(FDI)$_{it}$× Ln(Schooling)$_{it}$	0.018a (0.007)			0.017a (0.007)		
Ln(FDI)$_{it}$× Ln(Openness to Trade)$_{it}$		-0.007 (0.038)			-0.005 (0.040)	
Ln(FDI)$_{it}$× Ln(Private Credit)$_{it}$			-0.003 (0.004)			-0.002 (0.004)
Ln(Government Size)$_{it}$	-0.162a (0.068)	-0.151b (0.073)	-0.139b (0.070)	-0.166a (0.069)	-0.144b (0.070)	-0.143b (0.072)
Ln(Private Credit)$_{it}$	0.021 (0.022)	0.024 (0.023)	0.017 (0.025)	0.019 (0.023)	0.026 (0.024)	0.019 (0.027)
Inflation$_{it}$	-0.0009 (0.0006)	-0.0009c (0.0005)	-0.0008c (0.0005)	-0.0009c (0.0005)	-0.0009c (0.0005)	-0.0008c (0.0005)
Ln(Openness to Trade)$_{it}$	0.137a (0.050)	0.120a (0.046)	0.119a (0.046)	0.141a (0.052)	0.125a (0.049)	0.114b (0.047)
Ln(Schooling)$_{it}$	0.052b (0.023)	0.043b (0.019)	0.044b (0.019)	0.049b (0.025)	0.046b (0.020)	0.041b (0.018)
Observations	320	320	320	320	320	320
Sargan/Hansen test (*p*-value)	0.38	0.41	0.39	0.39	0.42	0.40
Arellano-Bond test AR(1) (*p*-value)	0.00	0.00	0.00	0.00	0.00	0.00
Arellano-Bond test AR(2) (*p*-value)	0.35	0.37	0.35	0.36	0.37	0.35

Notes: Standard errors are in parentheses with "a", "b", and "c" denoting significance at the 1%, 5%, and 10% level, respectively.

Table 4 presents the results from augmented empirical specifications that examine the role of human capital stock, development in financial markets, and trade openness in realizing larger positive effects of inward FDI on economic growth. Column (i) shows the results from the empirical specification that includes the interaction between inward FDI and tertiary schooling variables. The estimated coefficient on inward FDI becomes statistically not significant whereas the estimated coefficient on the interaction term between inward FDI and tertiary schooling variables is positive and significant at the 1% level. These results highlight the positive role of human capital in realizing higher benefits from inward FDI in the LAS countries. For example, in 2007, Lebanon and Libya had the highest percentage enrolment in tertiary school among LAS member countries of 49% and 59%, respectively. This means that a 10% increase in inward FDI stock as a share of GDP has an increasing effect on economic growth in both countries of around 0.7% in the short run and 7.7% in the long run. These estimates are significantly higher than the average effect displayed in Table 2. Also, there have been significant increases in tertiary school enrolment in many LAS countries. Based on the empirical results, these increases are expected to magnify the benefit from inward FDI in terms of economic growth. For example, the enrolment in tertiary school in Tunisia was 7.9% in 1990 but reached 31.6% in 2007. Hence, a 10% increase in inward FDI stock to GDP ratio promoted economic growth by 0.37% in the short run and 1.58% in the long run in 1990 but reached 0.62% in the short run and 2.67% in the long run in 2007. These results are consistent with many empirical findings (e.g., Borensztein et al., 1998; Xu, 2000) that human capital stock has positive and significant implications on the magnitude of the effect of inward FDI on economic growth.

Column (ii) of Table 4 includes the interaction between inward FDI and trade openness variables to the empirical specification. The estimated coefficient on the inward FDI variable is positive and significant at the 5% level and is slightly higher than the estimated coefficient reported in Table 2. However, the coefficient on the interaction term is not significant, implying limited effect of trade openness on the magnitude of the inward FDI effect on economic growth. Column (iii) includes the interaction between inward FDI and private credit variables to the empirical specification. The estimated coefficient on the inward FDI variable is quantitatively and qualitatively equivalent to the estimated coefficient reported in Table 2 whereas the estimated coefficient on the interaction term is not significant. The latter implies that the level of development in financial markets has no implications for the magnitude of the inward FDI effect on economic growth in the LAS countries. Columns (iv) through (vi) present the results from the empirical specification where the inward FDI variable enters as a lagged and predetermined variable. The results remain quantitatively and qualitatively robust.

CONCLUSION

Inward FDI is commonly considered as a factor that enhances economic growth of the host countries. These effects are channelled through innovation and technology transfer from foreign affiliates of MNEs to domestic firms, or through vertical industrial linkages between foreign affiliates and domestic firms. Previous empirical studies found mixed evidence on the occurrence of these positive effects. This paper considers a dynamic empirical specification to estimate the effect of inward FDI on economic growth for the LAS countries over the period 1990-2007 using a GMM estimator. The empirical results support, in general, the hypothesis of moderate and positive effect of inward FDI on economic growth. They indicate that a 10% increase in inward FDI as a share of GDP accelerates economic growth by 0.22% in the short run and 1.07% in the long run. Other results highlight the positive effect of trade openness and human capital stock and the negative effect of government expenditure and inflation on economic growth.

When estimating the effect of inward FDI on economic growth for various LAS geo-economic sub-regions, the empirical results reveal significant differences. The effect is the highest for the *Maghreb* region where a 10% increase in inward FDI as a share of GDP enhances economic growth by 0.69% in the short run and by 3.15% in the long run. Also, this effect is positive and significant for the *Mashreq* region standing at 0.27% in the short run and 1.23% in the long run. However, the effects of inward FDI on economic growth for the GCC countries and for Arab LDCs are not statistically significant. Also, the empirical results emphasize the positive effect of human capital stock in realizing larger benefits from inward FDI in terms of economic growth. Meanwhile, the empirical results show that developed financial markets and higher levels of trade openness have not magnified the positive effect of inward FDI on economic growth.

Based on the empirical findings of this study, the LAS member countries are invited to adopt liberalization policy when formulating and modifying FDI legislations. Also, the LAS member countries can offer incentives to attract inward FDI by removing barriers on the foreign ownership of capital and by providing tax-cuts on foreign earnings. Finally, it is important to emphasize that stable macroeconomic conditions, enhanced economic transparency, and liberalized foreign exchange are essential determinants of an adequate environment for inward FDI.

REFERENCES

Alfaro L., A. Chanda, S. Kalemli-Ozcan and S. Sayek. 2004. "FDI and Economic Growth: The Role of Local Financial Markets". *Journal of International Economics* **64(1)**: 89-112.

Alfaro, L. and A. Rodriguez-Clare. 2004. "Multinationals and Linkages: Evidence from Latin America". *Economia* 4(2): 113-170.

Arellano, M. and S. Bond. 1991. "Some Tests of Specification for Panel Data: Monte Carlo Evidence and an Application to Employment Equations". *Review of Economic Studies* 58(2): 277-297.

Arellano, M. and O. Bover. 1995. "Another Look at the Instrumental Variable Estimation of Error Component Models". *Journal of Econometrics* 68(1): 29-51.

Balasubramanyam, V.N., M. Salisu and D. Sapsford. 1996. "Foreign Direct Investment and Growth in EP and IS Countries". *The Economic Journal* 106(434): 92-105.

Bhagwati, J.N. (1978). *Anatomy and Consequences of Exchange Control Regimes*. National Bureau of Economic Research (NBER), New York, NY.

Blomström, M. and A. Kokko. 1998. "Multinational Corporations and Spillovers." *Journal of Economic Surveys* 12(2): 1-31.

Blundell, R.W. and S.R. Bond. 1998. "Initial Conditions and Moment Restrictions in Dynamic Panel Data Models". *Journal of Econometrics* 87(1): 115-143.

Blundell, R.W. and S.R. Bond. 2000. "GMM Estimation with Persistent Panel Data: An Application to Production Functions". *Econometric Reviews* 19(3): 321-340.

Borensztein, E., J. De Gregorio and J.-W. Lee. 1998. "How Does Foreign Direct Investment Affect Growth?". *Journal of International Economics* 45(1): 115-135.

Durham, K.B. 2004. "Absorptive Capacity and the Effects of Foreign Direct Investment and Equity Foreign Portfolio Investment on Economic Growth". *European Economic Review* 48(2): 285-306.

Carkovic M. and R. Levine. 2005. "Does Foreign Direct Investment Accelerate Economic Growth?" in H. T. Moran, E. Graham and M. Blomstrom (Eds.), *Does FDI Promote Development?* Institute for International Economics, Washington, DC.

Chan, K. and E. Gemayel. 2004. "Risk Instability and the Pattern of Foreign Direct Investment in the Middle East and North Africa Region". International Monetary Fund (IMF) Working Paper No.04/139, IMF, Washington, DC.

Eichengreen, B. and D. Leblang. 2003. "Capital Account Liberalization and Growth: Was Mr. Mahathir Right?". *International Journal of Finance and Economics* 8(3): 205-224.

Findlay, R. 1978. "Relative Backwardness, Direct Foreign Investment, and the Transfer of Technology: a Simple Dynamic Model". *Quarterly Journal of Economics* **92**(1): 1-16.

Ghosh, M. and W. Wang. 2010. "Does FDI Accelerate Economic Growth? The OECD Experience Based on Panel Data Estimates for the Period 1980-2004". *Global Economy Journal* 9(4), Article 1: 1-21.

Javorcik, B.S. 2004. "Does Foreign Direct Investment Increase the Productivity of Domestic Firms? In Search of Spillovers through Backward Linkages". *American Economic Review* 94(3): 605-627.

Henry, C.M. and R. Springborg. 2010. *Globalization and the Politics of Development in the Middle East*. Cambridge University Press, Cambridge, New York, NY.

Hermes, N. and R. Lensink, 2003. "Foreign Direct Investment, Financial Development and Economic Growth". *Journal of Development Studies* 40(1): 142-163.

Khawar, M. 2005. "Foreign Direct Investment and Economic Growth: A Cross Country Analysis". *Global Economy Journal* 5(1): 1-11.

League of Arab States. 1945. *Pact of the League of Arab States*. Available at: http://avalon.law.yale.edu/20th_century/arableag.asp. Accessed November 17, 2010.

Markusen, J. and A.J. Venables. 1999. "Foreign Direct Investment as a Catalyst for Industrial Development". *European Economic Review* 43(2): 335-338.

Rodriguez-Clare, A. 1996. "Multinationals, Linkages and Economic Development". *American Economic Review* 86(4): 852-873.

Romer, P. 1993. "Idea Gaps and Object Gaps in Economic Development". *Journal of Monetary Economics* 32(3): 543-573.

Sekkat, K. and M.-A. Veganzones. 2004. "Trade and Foreign Exchange Liberalization, Investment Climate and FDI in the MENA Countries". Working Papers No. CEB 04-023, Free University of Brussels, Brussels, Belgium.

Solow, R.M. 1956. "A Contribution to the Theory of Economic Growth". *Quarterly Journal of Economics* 70(1): 65-94.

Wang, J.-Y. 1990. "Growth, Technology Transfer, and the Long-Run Theory of International Capital Movements". *Journal of International Economics* 29(3-4): 255-271.

Xu, B. 2000. "Multinational Enterprises, Technology Diffusion, and Host Country Productivity Growth". *Journal of Development Economics* 62(2): 477-493.

In: Foreign Investment
Editor: Torre DeSare and Daniele Caprioglio
ISBN 978-1-61470-358-7

Chapter 7

Do Political Freedoms Attract or Discourage Foreign Direct Investment? Evidence from Central and Eastern Europe and Former Soviet Union

Jac C. Heckelman
Wake Forest University, North Carolina, U. S.

Abstract

The evidence on the relationship between political freedoms and foreign direct investment (FDI) is mixed. Part of the problem in interpreting results is that past cross-country studies have generally used a large sample of diverse nations and broad measures of political freedoms which do not vary much over time. In this chapter the relationship between political freedoms and FDI in the Central and Eastern European and Former Soviet Union nations is analyzed using recently developed political freedom indexes by Freedom House specific to the transition economies, over the period 1999-2008. By focusing on a specific region of the world which has undergone recent dramatic change in its political institutions, both in terms of positive reforms in certain nations and increased repression in others, a better estimation of the true impact of political freedom can be determined. It is found that greater political freedoms in general discourage FDI. However, not all types of political freedoms significantly hinder FDI. In particular, freedoms related to judicial framework, civil society, and corruption significantly limit FDI, while freedoms related to electoral process and governance do not. Finally, the results for media independence are dependent on specification.

Introduction

Developing nations often rely upon foreign direct investment (FDI) to help finance their current account deficits. FDI is also a method of importing technology and is expected to have spillover benefits to other firms in the host country. For these and other reasons, governments openly court FDI to stabilize their current accounts and promote development of their economies. Structural reforms may even be undertaken to make their economies more attractive to foreign investors. Reforms can sometimes include the political landscape as well.

Previous studies have found contrasting results on whether political freedoms in the domestic country help or harm FDI levels. Feng (2003) reports that a broad measure of political freedoms created by Freedom House, representing both political rights and civil liberties, is negatively correlated with FDI, in marked contrast to the typically positive correlation he finds between political freedoms and private domestic investment. Harms and Ursprung (2002) find that the overall level of political rights and civil liberties, either considered individually or combined into a single value, is beneficial to FDI inflows. In contrast, Adam and Filippaios (2007) find that civil liberties have a negative return to FDI whereas political rights have a positive return. Li and Resnick (2003) find that political freedoms increase property rights, but once controlling for property rights that political freedoms have a direct negative effect on FDI.

Part of the problem in interpreting these results is that past cross-country studies have generally used a large sample of diverse nations and broad measures of political freedoms which do not vary much over time. In this chapter, I follow the lead of several other studies which have conducted region-specific analysis of cross-country FDI inflows, such as Asiedu (2006) for Sub-Saharan Africa, Chan and Gemayel (2004) for North Africa and the Middle East, and Bengoa and Sanchez-Robles (2003) for Latin America. None of these studies considered political freedoms as a potential determinant. Here, the focus will be on the transition nations of Central and Eastern Europe and Former Soviet Union (CEEFSU), where FDI has climbed dramatically in recent years from an average of just under 4% of GDP to over 9% of GDP in 2007. By focusing on a specific region of the world which has undergone recent dramatic change in its political institutions, both in terms of positive reforms in certain nations and increased repression in others, a better estimation of the true impact of political freedoms can be determined. Furthermore, a new index of political freedoms specific to the transition nations allows for a more nuanced approach because each nation is rated on six separate areas of political freedom. Regression analysis supports Feng's (2003) finding that greater political freedoms in general discourage FDI when using an aggregated measure of political freedoms, but further analysis reveals that statistical significance is limited to only three of the six categories of political freedoms which comprise the aggregated index.

Measuring Political Freedoms

Freedom House developed the *Nations in Transit* series of political freedom indicators beginning in 1997. This series covers six broad areas of political freedoms. The civil society index assesses the growth of nongovernmental organizations, their organizational capacity and financial sustainability, and the legal and political environment in which they function; the development of free trade unions; and interest group participation in the policy process. The judicial index highlights constitutional reform, human rights protections, criminal code reform, judicial independence, the status of ethnic minority rights, guarantees of equality before the law, treatment of suspects and prisoners, and compliance with judicial decisions. The media index addresses the current state of press freedom, including libel laws, harassment of journalists, editorial independence, the emergence of a financially viable private press, and Internet access for private citizens. The corruption index looks at public perceptions of corruption, the business interests of top policy makers, laws on financial disclosure and conflict of interest, and the efficacy of anticorruption initiatives. The electoral index examines national executive and legislative elections, electoral processes, the development of multiparty systems, and popular participation in the political process. The governance index considers the stability of the governmental system; the authority of legislative bodies; decentralization of power; the responsibilities, election, and management of local governmental bodies; and legislative and executive transparency.

Each index ranges from 1 to 7, where 1 represents the highest level of freedom possible. The aggregated index score is simply the average of the six category rankings. Trends for the sample nations from 1999 – 2008 are presented in Table 1. Turkmenistan was rated the worst for political freedoms at the start and became even more repressive over time. Turkmenistan also garnered the worst rating at the midpoint, and again at the end of the sample period. Poland was initially rated the best in 1999, but slipped somewhat over time, to the point where by 2008 it was rated less free than six other nations. Yet, even the most politically free nation in 2008 (Estonia) was not as free as Poland was in 1999. Overall the average political freedom rating has become successively worse. Only six nations were given better ratings in both 2004 and 2008 than they had in 1999, whereas ten were rated successively worse in both 2004 and 2008. Meanwhile, Lithuania and Slovakia saw new reforms achieved by 2004 partially reversed by 2008. As repressed as Tajikistan already was in 1999, it allotted even less political freedom in 2008 despite a slight improvement by 2004. Overall, Bosnia experienced the greatest improvement between 1999 to 2008; its almost one and half point change representing more than a 25% rating adjustment. Conversely, Russia scored a 30% worse rating in 2008 compared to its 1999 rating of 4.58.

Although the tendency of many studies has been to rely on the broadest freedom measures possible, there is reason to believe different types of political freedoms can have different effects on FDI. The civil society, judicial, and media categories of the *Nations in Transit* series describe various civil liberties whereas the corruption, electoral, and governance categories better represent political rights.[1] As noted earlier, Adam and Filipanos (2007) found contrasting results from broad indexes of civil liberties and political rights. Even within this taxonomy, alternative measures can have contrasting effects because they work through different channels. For example, corruption and judicial framework directly affect business transactions and the potential for investment, whereas media independence and electoral process work more indirectly as potential oversight mechanisms.

Each type of political freedom considered here can either help or hinder FDI inflows. On the one hand, greater civil society may promote free trade and foreign investment but interest groups and other nongovernmental organizations may just as likely try to block globalization and resist rapid change which can upset the status quo, especially in the newly independent Eurasian nations. An independent judiciary is better suited to the protection of property rights which would attract FDI, but also more likely to hold investors accountable for human rights violations and other illegal operations, which may scare them off. While foreign investors recognize that media independence can serve as a useful conduit for unbiased information, they may also fear exposure of their own unpopular or unlawful activities and therefore shy away from countries where the media are more independent.

---

[1] See Heckelman (2010) for a detailed comparison.

Table 1. Aggregated Political Freedom Rating

	Level			Change		
	1999	2004	2008	1999-2004	2004-2008	1999-2008
Albania	4.75	4.13	3.88	-0.63	-0.25	-0.88
Armenia	4.79	5.00	5.19	0.21	0.19	0.40
Azerbaijan	5.58	5.63	6.00	0.04	0.38	0.42
Belarus	6.25	6.54	6.69	0.29	0.15	0.44
Bosnia	5.42	4.29	3.98	-1.13	-0.31	-1.44
Bulgaria	3.58	3.25	2.83	-0.33	-0.42	-0.75
Croatia	4.46	3.83	3.67	-0.63	-0.17	-0.79
Estonia	2.25	1.92	1.85	-0.33	-0.06	-0.40
Georgia	4.17	4.83	4.65	0.67	-0.19	0.48
Hungary	1.88	1.96	2.13	0.08	0.17	0.25
Kazakhstan	5.50	6.25	6.38	0.75	0.13	0.88
Kyrgyzstan	5.08	5.67	5.79	0.58	0.13	0.71
Latvia	2.29	2.17	2.06	-0.13	-0.10	-0.23
Lithuania	2.29	2.13	2.21	-0.17	0.08	-0.08
Macedonia	3.83	4.00	3.85	0.17	-0.15	0.02
Moldova	4.25	4.88	4.88	0.63	0.00	0.63
Poland	1.58	1.75	2.31	0.17	0.56	0.73
Romania	3.54	3.58	3.35	0.04	-0.23	-0.19
Russia	4.58	5.25	5.96	0.67	0.71	1.38
Slovakia	2.71	2.08	2.27	-0.63	0.19	-0.44
Slovenia	1.88	1.75	1.88	-0.13	0.13	0.00
Tajikistan	5.75	5.71	5.98	-0.04	0.27	0.23
Turkmenistan	6.75	6.88	6.94	0.13	0.06	0.19
Ukraine	4.63	4.88	4.13	0.25	-0.75	-0.50
Uzbekistan	6.38	6.46	6.85	0.08	0.40	0.48
average	4.17	4.19	4.23	0.03	0.04	0.06
std deviation	1.54	1.68	1.75	0.46	0.32	0.64

Foreign investors also may be hindered by rampant corruption and therefore seek countries where corruption is more limited, yet corruption can also be beneficial to investors in order to circumvent inefficient policies and bureaucratic red tape. Greater electoral control by the general public in determining leadership should in theory make the government more responsive to the public's needs. However, this also increases the likelihood of governmental party, and therefore policy, change. Roland (2002) believes this to be especially problematic for democracy in the transition nations where fundamental economic alterations could temporarily lead to recession during the adjustment period. Voters might not support reform candidates or quickly look to reverse economic policy at the first sign of distress. Foreign investors may prefer dealing with a stable autocrat rather than the uncertainty of the changing whims of the general public. Finally, greater decentralization of governance can result in an environment better able to adapt to local conditions but overlapping jurisdictions can also result in conflicting policies and greater bureaucracy.

Thus it is an empirical question as to whether or not each type of political freedom on net benefits or limits FDI inflows.

For these reasons, the regression analysis will consider each measure separately, in addition to the overall average effect. Previously, the most extensively analyzed component has been corruption, although that is not normally interpreted specifically as a political freedom.

Egger and Winner (2005) find that corruption attracts FDI among a mixed sample of OECD and developing economies. In constrast, Asiedu (2006) finds corruption limits FDI inflows to Africa while Méon and Sekkat (2004) find no significant effect of corruption on FDI inflows into the Middle East.

In an analysis of bilateral FDI inflows between 183 home economies to 106 host economies, Cuervo-Cazurra (2006) finds that greater levels of corruption in the host country attracts more FDI from nations that are relatively corrupt themselves, but reduces FDI stemming from nations that have laws prohibiting engaging in bribery abroad. The net effect of corruption is found to be negative.

Specification

The sample consists of pooled cross-sectional data on 25 transition countries in Central and Eastern Europe and Former Soviet Union over two time periods for a total of 50 observations. Data span from 1999 – 2008, as determined by the availability of the Freedom House *Nations in Transit* political freedoms data.[2]

The specifications take the form of:

$$FDI_{it} = \alpha + \beta INCOME_{it} + \gamma INFLATION_{it} + \lambda TRANSITION_{it} + \delta FREEDOM_{it} + e_{it}$$

where for each for country i in period t:

FDI_{it} = log ratio of foreign direct investment rate to GDP;
$INCOME_{it}$ = log of initial real per capita income;
$INFLATION_{it}$ = log of standard deviation of the inflation rate;
$TRANSITION_{it}$ = value of the EBRD transition index;
$FREEDOM_{it}$ = value of the Freedom House index.

The dependent variable, *FDI*, is measured as the log of average FDI to GDP ratio over each five year period, from 1999-2003 and 2004-2008.

[2] Beginning in 2005, governance is measured by separate indexes for national and local governance. These are averaged together for consistency with the earlier years.

Initial income is included for a convergence effect. Poorer economies would need greater levels of investment to stimulate higher growth to be able to eventually catch-up to the wealthier nations.[3] A negative coefficient on *INCOME* would be consistent with such long-run income convergence. The importance of uncertainty [Brunetti and Weder (1998)] is captured by the log value of the standard deviation of inflation. Greater variance in prices would be expected to be inversely correlated with FDI inflows. Data for these variables are taken from the World Bank World Development Indicators on-line database.

The European Bank of Reconstruction and Development (EBRD) Transition Index is included as a proxy for market distortions. The index runs from 1 to 4.33, where lower values indicate a control economy and higher values indicate the economy more closely resembles open policies as administered in the developed nations. Scores are determined by the EBRD's Office of the Chief Economist on 13 categories comprised of: large-scale privatization; small-scale privatization; enterprise restructuring; price liberalization; trade and foreign exchange; competition policy; banking reform and interest rate liberalization; securities markets and other financial institutions; water and waste water; electric power; railways; roads; and telecommunications. It is expected for FDI to be greater where the markets are more open.

Finally, and most important for this chapter, the score representing the extent of political freedoms is included. As described above, ratings for the Freedom House *Nations in Transit* index range from 1 to 7, with lower values representing a greater degree of political freedom. To avoid confusion on interpreting the coefficients, each political freedom category index is inverted and standardized to a 0 – 1 scale so that higher values represent greater freedom. The aggregated index value is then the average of the normalized six component scores. Because each type of freedom can have different effects, additional regressions are also run using the normalized score of each political freedom category index separately.

For the first set of regressions, the indexes representing the EBRD transition scores and the Freedom House political freedom scores are computed using the average values during the respective five year periods. This helps to avoid problems associated with single-year anomalies stemming from a sudden but not lasting change. Yet, this introduces a different potential problem in that index values may be endogenous if policy reforms respond to economic conditions. For example, Li and Reuveny (2003) find that FDI inflows have an initial positive influence on democratization which then weakens over time. Robertson and Watson (2004) find that greater changes (either increases or decreases) to FDI result in larger levels of corruption. Dutta and Roy (2009) find FDI is positively correlated with an index of media freedom. In addition, some scholars have also questioned if the organizations creating such subjective indexes are influenced in their perceptions by economic performance [Bollen (1993), Koelble and Lipuma (2008)]. Due to potential endogeneity concerns, a second set of regressions are presented using only the initial year values for these variables. Results are very similar, with one exception detailed below.

The sample consists of the countries included in the Freedom House *Nations in Transit* index. Yugoslavia is rated until the 2004 index, when separate scores begin for Serbia,

[3] There is debate, however, as to the benefit of FDI in particular, as opposed to gross fixed investment, for generating greater growth. Campos and Kinoshita (2002) find a positive correlation between FDI and growth for their sample of 25 CEEFSU nations from 1990-1998 but Mecinger (2003) sharply criticizes the study as being irrelevant for including years in which FDI was not allowed for some countries. Mecinger limits his sample to only eight European Union candidate countries with more developed economies (relative to the FSU) and finds a significantly inverse relationship between FDI and growth.

Montenegro, and Kosovo, so these nations are not included. In addition, the Czech Republic graduated from the EBRD and is no longer part of their Transition index. The remaining 25 CEEFSU countries listed in Table 1 constitute the regression sample.

Table 2. Summary Statistics

Variable	Mean	Std Dev	Minimum	Maximum
FDI ratio	5.93	4.55	0.66	24.30
FDI ratio logged	1.54	0.70	-0.40	3.19
GDP per capita	2476.61	2435.39	130.28	11421.10
GDP per capita logged	7.34	1.03	4.86	9.34
Inflation Std Dev	6.94	17.03	0.38	119.99
Inflation Std Dev logged	1.18	1.04	-0.94	4.78
Transition Index averages	2.78	0.64	1.21	3.89
Transition Index initial values	2.68	0.64	1.19	3.83
Political Freedoms – averages				
Aggregated Index	0.47	0.28	0.00	0.91
Civil Society	0.56	0.27	0.00	0.95
Judicial Framework	0.44	0.26	0.01	0.90
Media Independence	0.46	0.29	0.00	0.91
Corruption	0.44	0.26	0.01	0.86
Electoral Process	0.51	0.32	0.00	0.95
Governance	0.43	0.26	0.00	0.85
Political Freedoms – initial values				
Aggregated Index	0.47	0.28	0.00	0.91
Civil Society	0.56	0.27	0.00	0.95
Judicial Framework	0.44	0.26	0.00	0.87
Media Independence	0.47	0.29	0.00	0.91
Corruption	0.44	0.26	0.00	0.87
Electoral Process	0.51	0.31	0.00	0.95
Governance	0.44	0.25	0.00	0.87

Descriptive statistics for all variables are listed in Table 2. Among the various political freedoms, the highest average rating is assigned to civil society. Only civil society and electoral process have average values exceeding 0.5 on the converted normalized scale. Clearly, there is plenty of room for improvement in these political freedoms. In the next section, it is determined if further political reforms would be expected to attract or deter FDI inflows.

EMPIRICAL ANALYSIS

Regression results using the average values over each five year period for the transition and political freedom indexes are presented in Table 3. Regression results using initial year values (1998 and 2004) for the transition and political freedom indexes are presented in Table 4. For both tables, the first column uses the aggregated political freedom index comprised of the average value for all six categories, and the remaining columns use the value for each listed political freedom category individually. All regressions are estimated by Ordinary Least Squares (OLS) using White-robust standard errors.

Table 3. Effect of Political Freedoms on FDI, Average Concurrent Values

	Aggregated	Civil	Judicial	Media	Corruption	Electoral	Governance
constant	0.95	1.37*	0.41	1.09	0.33	1.31	0.42
	(0.82)	(0.77)	(0.84)	(0.86)	(0.89)	(0.85)	(0.92)
	[0.26]	[0.08]	[0.62]	[0.21]	[0.71]	[0.13]	[0.65]
GDP Per capita	-0.13	-0.18	-0.061	-0.13	-0.057	-0.16	-0.070
	(0.12)	(0.12)	(0.13)	(0.13)	(0.13)	(0.13)	(0.13)
	[0.29]	[0.15]	[0.64]	[0.30]	[0.66]	[0.23]	[0.60]
Inflation Std Dev	-0.16*	-0.16**	-0.17**	-0.17**	-0.16**	-0.16*	-0.16*
	(0.085)	(0.082)	(0.076)	(0.083)	(0.077)	(0.084)	(0.079)
	[0.07]	[0.05]	[0.03]	[0.04]	[0.04]	[0.07]	[0.05]
Transition Index	0.79**	0.76*	0.89**	0.73**	0.92**	0.67*	0.89**
	(0.38)	(0.44)	(0.34)	(0.36)	(0.36)	(0.38)	(0.37)
	[0.04]	[0.09]	[0.01]	[0.05]	[0.01]	[0.08]	[0.02]
Political Freedom	-0.97*	-0.76	-1.58**	-0.83	-1.66**	-0.51	-1.52**
	(0.54)	(0.98)	(0.58)	(0.55)	(0.61)	(0.54)	(0.61)
	[0.08]	[0.44]	[0.01]	[0.14]	[0.01]	[0.35]	[0.02]
R^2	0.25	0.23	0.28	0.24	0.29	0.23	0.28

White-robust standard errors in parentheses.
p-values in brackets.
* indicates significance at the 10 percent level.
** indicates significance at the 5 percent level.

The control variables all have the expected sign, although GDP per capita is not statistically significant. Thus, conditional convergence through FDI among the CEEFSU nations is not supported. Lack of significance for national income is consistent with Feng (2003), although he also controlled for population size rendering his GDP per capita variable akin to a total GDP interpretation. Price uncertainty in terms of the standard deviation of inflation is significantly inversely correlated with FDI. Neither Brunetti and Weder (1998) nor Coates et al. (2010) found this to significantly reduce total investment levels. The contrasting result here suggests foreign investors may be more concerned with variation in domestic prices in the host country than domestic investors, at least in this region. The positive and significant coefficient on the transition index indicates that the more the host country has policies which mimic other developed economies, the more FDI it attracts. Foreign investors, which are often dominated by developed economy actors, appear to be more comfortable investing in environments which more closely resemble their own. Greater market distortions, indicated by lower values of the index, appear to discourage foreign direct investment. These results are robust across all the reported regressions.

The aggregated political freedom index is inversely correlated with FDI; as shown in the first column of Table 3, this is at borderline significance level. In general, it appears that greater political freedoms will result in less foreign direct investment. The remaining columns reveal why statistical significance of the aggregated index is weak. Although each of the political freedom indexes generate a negative coefficient, half of them are statistically significant while the other half are not. In particular, a more independent judicial framework, more freedom from corruption, and greater decentralization of power in governance significantly reduce FDI. However, freedoms pertaining to civil society, media independence, and electoral process do not significantly impact FDI levels.

Table 4. Effect of Political Freedoms on FDI, Initial Year Values

	Aggregated	Civil	Judicial	Media	Corruption	Electoral	Governance
constant	0.85	1.22*	0.11	1.10	0.11	1.23	0.11
	(0.73)	(0.70)	(0.78)	(0.78)	(0.78)	(0.76)	(0.78)
	[0.25]	[0.09]	[0.89]	[0.17]	[0.89]	[0.11]	[0.89]
GDP	-0.14	-0.18	-0.043	-0.14	-0.043	-0.17	-0.043
Per capita	(0.12)	(0.12)	(0.13)	(0.13)	(0.13)	(0.13)	(0.13)
	[0.26]	[0.15]	[0.73]	[0.26]	[0.73]	[0.21]	[0.73]
Inflation	-0.15*	-0.16**	-0.14**	-0.16**	-0.14**	-0.15*	-0.14**
Std Dev	(0.078)	(0.075)	(0.070)	(0.079)	(0.070)	(0.077)	(0.070)
	[0.07]	[0.04]	[0.05]	[0.05]	[0.05]	[0.07]	[0.05]
Transition	0.91**	0.91**	1.06**	0.80**	1.06**	0.77**	1.06**
Index	(0.32)	(0.36)	(0.29)	(0.30)	(0.29)	(0.30)	(0.29)
	[0.01]	[0.02]	[0.00]	[0.01]	[0.00]	[0.02]	[0.00]
Political	-1.21**	-1.12	-2.06**	-0.92**	-2.06**	-0.69	-2.06**
Freedom	(0.47)	(0.94)	(0.57)	(0.45)	(0.57)	(0.45)	(0.57)
	[0.01]	[0.24]	[0.00]	[0.05]	[0.00]	[0.14]	[0.00]
R^2	0.28	0.26	0.35	0.27	0.35	0.26	0.35

White-robust standard errors in parentheses.
p-values in brackets.
* indicates significance at the 10 percent level.
** indicates significance at the 5 percent level.

Using the initial values for the transition index and political freedoms variables in Table 4 results in both larger magnitudes and stronger p-values across the board for these coefficients compared to in Table 3 which used the average values over each five year period. None of the results for the other variables are appreciably affected by this change. For the political freedom variables, this comparison suggests that if the contemporaneous averages are endogenously determined, the OLS estimates presented in Table 3 were biased toward zero. This could be the case if as an economy develops from increased FDI, greater political freedom reforms are enacted [Li and Reuveny (2003)], or if the government is perceived to be granting more freedom by the subjective evaluators [Bollen (1993)]. Thus, the extent of the harm to FDI from increasing political freedom was somewhat masked by using the concurrent endogenous averages instead of purely exogenous initial values.

For example, the magnitude of the aggregated index increases by over 20% and the p-value indicates it is now statistically significant at the 1% level. In addition, the importance of media independence is now revealed as well. Using the concurrent five-year average political freedom value, the coefficient on media freedom was negative but not statistically significant. Using the initial value, the coefficient on media freedom is more negative and statistically significant at the 5% level. Freedoms related to judicial, corruption, and governance, are significant at even higher levels than before. While freedoms related to civil society and electoral process have much stronger p-values in Table 4 than in Table 3, these variables would still not be considered statistically significant at conventional levels.

Conclusion

Political freedoms are often assumed to be a positive force for growth, but several studies have tended to undermine this connection. Mobarak (2005) find political rights are not significantly related to growth. Baum and Lake (2003) reject a direct connection between political freedoms and growth. Stroup and Heckelman (2001) find the significance of political rights depends on econometric specification and regional sample. Using extreme bound analysis, de Haan and Siermann (1995) conclude the relationship between political freedoms and growth is not robust. Although political freedoms are positively correlated with many of the determinants of growth (such as human capital [Baum and Lake (2003)], economic freedom [de Haan and Sturm (2003)], and trade [Mobark (2005)]) this chapter uncovers a potential off-setting relationship between political freedoms and FDI, which Lee and Tcha (2003) have identified as a particularly important contributor to growth and development among the European transition economies. Previous studies which have investigated the relationship between political freedoms and FDI have produced conflicting results [Harms and Ursprung (2002), Feng (2003), Li and Resnick (2003), Adam and Filippaios (2007)] for various diverse samples of countries. Here, the analysis is specific to transition nations in Central and Eastern Europe and Former Soviet Union.

Using data from the Freedom House Nations in Transit index which has a specific focus on the CEEFSU nations, it is found that greater political freedoms in general result in less FDI (as a percent of GDP). In particular, this relationship is strongest for freedoms related to judicial framework, corruption, and governance. The finding related to corruption in particular supports Egger and Winner's (2005) analysis on a large sample that did not include any FSU nations. No significant relationship was found for civil society or electoral process. Freedom of media was not significant using concurrent values, but was significantly negative using initial values. These results suggest that the enactment of further political reforms in CEEFSU nations will generally have an off-setting cost from reductions in FDI. Political reforms specific to civil society and electoral process will not significantly reduce FDI.

A secondary finding is that using concurrent values of the political freedom indexes may bias estimates toward zero, suggesting political freedoms may be endogenously determined. Government leaders may grant greater political freedoms as the nation develops ([Helliwell (1994), Barro (1996)]), and the extent of FDI may be such an indicator. It is important to note that many of these political freedoms are also inter-related. Heckelman (2010) finds several political freedoms Granger-cause another political freedom. Alternatively, FDI may also be used to directly or indirectly impact political institutions. For example, investment in non-governmental organizations (NGOs) can strengthen civil society. Recognizing the importance of human rights and involvement in the political process for increased worker productivity, activity by such NGOs may lead to improvement in judicial independence, electoral process and governance transparency. Foreign investors may also directly invest in media corporations and thereby push for greater autonomy. Finally, foreign investors may also be more resistant to corruption and use funds to ferret out existing corruption which hampers their business interests. These explanations are speculative and cannot be tested using the framework developed here. Further work in this area would be beneficial to systematically test if and how FDI has helped improve various political freedoms among the CEEFSU nations and elsewhere.

REFERENCES

Adam, A., and Filippaios, F. (2007). Foreign direct investment and civil liberties: A new perspective. *European Journal of Political Economy*, 23, 1038–1052.

Asiedu, E. (2006). Foreign direct investment in Africa: The role of natural resources, market size, government policy, institutions and political instability. World Economy, 29, 63–77.

Barro, R.J. (1996). Democracy and growth. *Journal of Economic Growth*, 1, 1-27.

Baum, M.A., and Lake, D.A. (2003). The *political* economy of growth: Democracy and human capital. *American Journal of Political Science*, 47, 333-347.

Bengoa, M., and Sanchez-Robles, B. (2003). Foreign direct investment, economic freedom and growth: New evidence from Latin America. *European Journal of Political Economy*, 19, 529–545.

Bollen, K. (1993). Liberal democracy: Validity and method factors in cross-national measures. *American Journal of Political Science*, 37, 1207-1230.

Brunetti, A., and Weder, B. (1998). Investment and institutional uncertainty: A comparative study of different uncertainty measures. *Weltwirtschaftliches Archiv*, 134, 513–533.

Campos , N.F. and Kinoshita, Y. (2002). Foreign direct investment as technology transferred: Some panel evidence from the transition economies. *The Manchester School,* 70, 398-419.

Chan K.K. and Gemayel E R. (2004). Risk instability and the pattern of FDI in the MENA region. IMF Working Paper Series WP/04/139.

Coates, D., Heckelman, J. C., and Wilson, B. (2010). The political economy of investment: Sclerotic effects from interest groups. *European Journal of Political Economy*, 26, 208-221.

Cuervo-Cazurra, A. (2006). Who cares about corruption? *Journal of International Business Studies*, 37, 807-822.

de Haan, J. and Siermann, C.L.J. (1995). A sensitivity analysis of the impact of democracy on economic growth. *Empirical Economics*, 20, 197-215.

Dutta, N. and Roy, S. (2009). The impact of foreign direct investment on press freedom. *Kyklos*, 62, 239-257.

Egger, P., and Winner, H. (2005). Evidence on corruption as an incentive for foreign direct investment. *European Journal of Political Economy*, 21, 932–952.

Feng, Y. (2003). Democracy, Governance, and Economic Performance: Theory and Evidence. Cambridge, MA: MIT Press.

Harms, P., and Ursprung, H.W. (2002). Do civil and political repression really boost foreign direct investment? *Economic Inquiry*, 40, 651–663.

Heckelman, J. (2010). Relationships among democratic freedoms in the former Soviet Republics: A causality analysis. *Constitutional Political Economy*, 21, 80-96.

Helliwell, J.F. (1993). Empirical linkages between democracy and economic growth. *British Journal of Political Science*, 24, 225-248.

Koelble, T.A. and Lipuma, E. (2008). Democratizing democracy: A postcolonial critique of conventional approaches to the 'measurement of democracy'. *Democratization*, 15, 1-28.

Lee, M. and Tcha, M.J. (2007). The color of money: The effects of foreign direct investment on economic growth in transition economies. *Review of World Economics*, 140, 211-229.

Li, Q., and Resnick, A. (2003). Reversal of fortunes: democratic institutions and foreign direct investment inflows to developing countries. *International Organization*, 57, 175–211.

Li, Q. and Reuveny, R. (2003). Economic globalization and democracy: An empirical analysis. *British Journal of Political Science*, 33, 29-54.

Mecinger, J. (2003). Does foreign direct investment always enhance economic growth? *Kyklos*, 56, 491-508.

Méon, P.-G. and Sekkat, K. (2004), Does the quality of institutions limit the MENA's integration in the world economy? World Economy, 27, 1475–98.

Mobarak, A. (2005). Democracy, volatility and development. *The Review of Economics and Statistics*, 87, 348–361.

Robertson, C.J. and Watson, A. (2004). Corruption and change: The impact of foreign direct investment. *Strategic Management Journal*, 25, 385-396.

Roland, G. (2002) The political economy of transition. *Journal of Economic Perspectives* 16, 29-50.

Stroup, M.D. and Heckelman, J.C. (2001). Size of the military sector and economic growth: A panel data analysis of Africa and Latin America. *Journal of Applied Economics*, 2, 329 360.

In: Foreign Investment
Editor: Torre DeSare and Daniele Caprioglio
ISBN 978-1-61470-358-7

Chapter 8

CORRUPTION, FOREIGN DIRECT INVESTMENT AND THE COST OF DOING BUSINESS IN VIETNAM

Tom Arnold[1*] ***and Bonnie Buchanan***[2]
The Robins School of Business, Department of Finance,
1 Gateway Road, Richmond, VA, U. S.
Department of Finance, Moore School of Business,
University of South Carolina, Columbia, SC, U. S.

ABSTRACT

Corruption is a key impediment to: foreign direct investment, an accurate measurement of political risk, and a barrier to effective corporate governance. By examining the political structure of Vietnam and the impediments created by corruption, this paper defines some of the difficulties with investing in Vietnam. However, with regard to the sugar industry, some solutions have emerged with companies taking direct control of contracting, offering credit, and the building of infrastructure.

Keywords: Corruption, political risk, emerging markets, foreign direct investment.

1. INTRODUCTION

Corruption is one of the most challenging governance problems confronting multinational enterprises today. The World Bank estimates that US$1 trillion – or approximately 3 percent of global gross domestic product (GDP) – is lost to corruption in the form of bribes annually (Rose-Ackerman (2004)). The Asian Development Bank defines corruption as "*the misuse of public or private office for personal gain*", and this is the definition that is utilized in this paper. In contrast, good corporate governance can be defined to be the extent to which companies are run in an honest and transparent manner, and is regarded as vital for overall

* E-mail address: tarnold@richmond.edu. Ph: (804) 287-6399

market confidence because it promotes efficiency of international capital allocation as well as a nation's overall wealth and welfare.

Shleifer and Vishny (1993) regard the structure of government institutions and of the political process as very important determinants of a country's corruption level. These authors find the illegality of corruption and the need for secrecy to promote the corruption make its impact much more costly than taxation. Mauro (1995) argues that corruption lowers investment thereby lowering growth and suggests there is evidence that bureaucratic efficiency may be at least as important a determinant of investment and growth as the political stability of a nation. According to Tanzi and Davoodi (1997), corruption combined with large public investments is likely to reduce an economy's growth.

Bardhan (1997) considers the damaging features of corruption and pursues the question of why corruption is perceptibly so varied in different societies. Bardhan examines cases where a great deal of corruption in dispensing licenses or loans, or mining and land concessions has historically been associated with the emergence of an entrepreneurial class in a developing market. Campos, Lien and Pradhan (2001) follow a similar line of reasoning that different corruption regimes have different effects on foreign direct investment. These authors find that corrupt regimes that are more predictable in the sense that those seeking favors from government do obtain those favors have less negative impact on investment than those that are less predictable. In a sense, corruption can be viewed as a transitional state (i.e. the emergence of an entrepreneurial class) that is interwoven within the structure of the government and becomes less detrimental as corruption is more organized and predictable.

However, corruption is still costly in that it can introduce inefficiencies that reduce competitiveness at the firm, industry and country level. Tanzi and Davoodi (1997) state that more corrupt countries spend relatively less on operations and maintenance and have an overall lower quality infrastructure. Wei (2000) shows that an increase in either the tax rate on multinational firms or the corruption level in host governments will reduce foreign direct investment substantially. Corruption reduces foreign direct investment by limiting the number of bidders or favoring those with inside connections over the most efficient candidates. Other associated effects of corruption include the introduction of added transactions costs to an investment project, reduced rates of return, loss of export markets, reduced shareholder protection, and foregone future investments by foreign firms.

The bottom line is that corruption is costly to any society. According to Shleifer and Vishny (1993) the first step in reducing corruption should be the creation of an accounting system that prevents theft from the government. Mauro (1995) finds that a one standard deviation improvement in a country's corruption index is associated with an increase in the investment rate of about 3 percent of gross domestic product (GDP). Vinod (1999) estimates that a one dollar (U.S.) reduction in corruption will benefit a developing country by at least U.S.$1.67.

In this study, the focus is on the country of Vietnam because of the paradox of the "East Asian Puzzle". In the aftermath of the 1997-1998 Asian financial crisis, combating corruption became a top priority for many countries in the region[1]. However, in a number of East Asian countries (Vietnam included), high rates of growth had been sustained over a long period

[1] There are competing views as to what triggered the Asian financial crisis and poor corporate governance in the form of "crony capitalism" has been identified as one of the root causes. Crony capitalism is the absence of effective discipline on corporate managers largely due to the complicated, opaque relationships between corporations, their owners and their financiers.

despite high levels of corruption. This observation is known as the "East Asian Puzzle" and poses a real challenge to the received wisdom that corruption impedes economic performance. The East Asian Puzzle is inconsistent with the theory that weak institutions of governance, of which corruption is a concrete manifestation, discourages investment and thus constricts growth.

In the 1990s, Vietnam was touted as the newest Asian tiger in the region. Between 1992 and 1997, GDP growth in Vietnam did not fall below 8 % per annum[2] and in order to sustain a rapid economic growth, Vietnam relied heavily on foreign investment. By the mid 1990s, flows of foreign investment averaged US$2 billion a year. However, a lack of transparency in the country's governance structure coupled with widespread bureaucratic procedures contributed to significant levels of corruption throughout Vietnam. To illustrate the magnitude of corruption, in 1998 nearly one third of Vietnam's public investment expenditure – equivalent to 5 % of GDP – was lost to fraud and corruption. Eventually, the slow pace of reforms and escalating problems of corruption dampened foreign direct investment in Vietnam for the remainder of the 1990s.

Bardhan (1997) describes Vietnam as a "thin" market – one that presents an ideal opportunity for officials to "milk the process of granting monopoly rights and transfers". A perfect example of foreign direct investment and associated problems with corruption and the costs of doing business in an emerging market is the "One Million Tonne Sugar Program" sponsored by the government of Vietnam during the mid-1990s (a "tonne" is a metric ton). The specific goal of the program was to develop a sugar industry within Vietnam capable of producing one million tonnes of refined sugar by the year 2000. The production goal was met, however, due to the inability of the government to allocate resources efficiently and police its borders from smugglers (a high tariff on sugar meant to aid the domestic producers encouraged large amounts of smuggling that could not effectively be stopped) led to large financial losses (see Arnold, Buchanan, and Lo (2006) for details). By 2001, the sugar project was imposing an annual cost of US $80-$120 million on the Vietnamese economy. This is a trend that is also observed in other industries in Vietnam including gold, diamonds, timber, ivory and Internet cards – these are items smuggled into the country in large volume because of the differences in prices between international markets and local markets.

In this paper we investigate the Vietnamese legal system (section two), the process for foreign direct investment (section 3), and how two sugar companies have successfully managed to deal with these issues (section 4).

2. Vietnamese Legal System and Corruption

Historically, Vietnam has a multilayered political and legal system. The legal framework is based on the Confucian, French and Socialist traditions[3]. Sidel (1997) describes Vietnam as a weak state in terms of the mobility of the central authorities to impose their will upon the lower administrative levels. Figure 1 provides an outline of the complex Vietnamese political and legal system.

[2] Source: Economist Intelligence Unit (2003).

[3] Legal influence varies according to the region of the country

Vietnam is a one-party state collectively run by the Communist Party General Secretary, the Prime Minister and the President. The Vietnamese political system can be described as follows: – the Party that "leads", a State that "manages" and numerous organizations that "represent". The Politbureau, or Communist Party Executive, comprises 15 members that leads the party on a day-to-day basis, and has the power to set government policy and vet all major appointments. The central government is chaired by the Prime Minister and contains 17 ministries, 5 ministry-level organizations and 26 other agencies.

Vietnam's judicial system is centralized and decision making authority ultimately rests with the National Assembly which comprises approximately 400 members. The National Assembly adopts laws and ordinances for national implementation, oversees governmental institutions and the court system, and also has a role in budgetary issues throughout the country. As indicated in Figure 1, the Vietnamese court system is subordinate to the National Assembly. The Supreme People's Court is responsible for the judicial work of the provincial and district courts. Sidel (1997) states that Vietnamese judges are still subject to pressure from local officials in economic, civil and criminal matters, and from national officials in larger-scale economic civil, criminal or political issues. The State Committee for Cooperation and Investment (SCCI) participates in legislative, regulatory and policy-drafting processes relating to foreign investment and has the responsibility for vetting significant investment projects. The Supreme People's Procuracy (SPP) deals with specialized tribunals for criminal, civil and economic cases.

Vietnam's local administrative system is divided into a further three levels: provinces (61 units), districts (600 units) and communes (10,330 units). At all three levels each locality has a representative body, people's council, and an executive body (the People's Committee) and these correspond to the National Assembly and the government at the central level. Party committees exist at every level of the bureaucracy and efforts have been made to establish a party presence in private enterprises throughout the country.

Four state-owned banks have traditionally dominated the Vietnamese banking system. After June 1991, foreign and joint venture banks were permitted into Vietnam. Throughout the 1990s, the country also pledged to reduce bad loans at state-controlled financial institutions. By the end of 2001 the State Bank of Vietnam estimated that bad debts in the banking system accounted for approximately 8.1 percent of outstanding loans in the country.

Attempts have been made to improve the country's legal framework by the creation of a modern tax structure and improvements to bankruptcy law, the labor code, mining law and domestic investment law. In 1992, rather than adopting a planned economy, Vietnam started to move towards a more market driven economy. In February 1999, the government scrapped the pegged exchange rate system in favor of a crawling peg system. The early 1990s were characterized by intense struggles over issues such as who would control foreign aid or foreign investment. Areas such as contract dispute resolution still require further development because the Vietnamese legal system has not yet developed the predictability and quality of decision making needed to support a market based system.

In terms of financial markets, Vietnam's stock exchange opened in 2000 and in 2003 was capitalized at US$140 million. Foreign ownership of up to 20 percent is permitted for the 17 currently listed companies on the exchange. In terms of debt market participation, international investors can buy up to 40 percent of local currency bonds. In September 2001, Vietnam pledged to privatize 2,500 of the 5,600 state-owned enterprises but privatization took place at a rather slow pace leading to a moratorium in 2001 on the creation of new state-owned enterprises (SOEs).

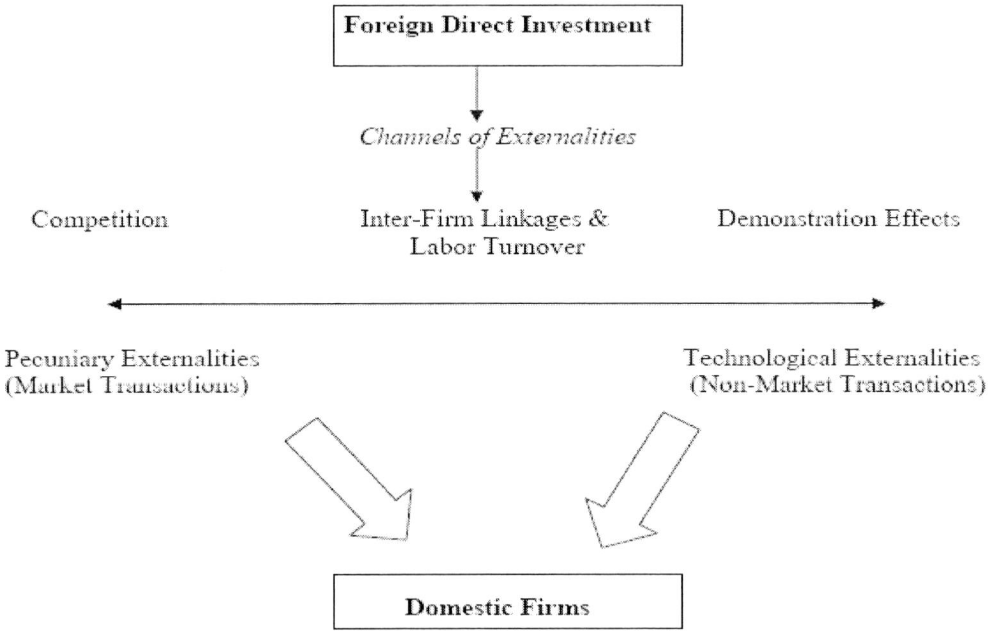

Figure 1. Vietnam: Political and Legal System.

Fforde (1997) finds that these SOEs tend to operate according to local and limited private interests, rather being public in nature. SOEs presence has declined from 40.5% in 1997 to 38.3% in 2002 (Nguyen et al. 2004).

Institutional weaknesses continue to impede business ventures in the country. A lack of transparency coupled with widespread bureaucratic procedures has led to significant levels of corruption throughout Vietnam. In 2002, the Transparency International Corruption Perceptions Index (CPI) ranked Vietnam 85 out of 102 countries surveyed and assigned a score of 2.4 out of 10.[4] Between 1997 and 2006, the CPI score assigned to Vietnam has consistently been low and has shown little indication of improvement over time.

Historically, corruption has thrived in Vietnam because of complicated and unclear administrative procedures, excessive regulations, the opaque nature of decision making, lack of public information, bureaucratic discretion on the part of middle level officials and long delays.[5] The Economist Intelligence Unit also cites low salaries, light punishments and a bureaucratic administration in which opportunities for bribes are widespread all contribute to permit a culture of corruption throughout the country.

---

[4] According to a World Bank 2000 report, a "complaints hotline" established in 1998, received 50,000 calls in the first year alleging corruption and government inefficiency.

[5] Le Monde (Feb 2000) provides an interesting statistic…of the 24,000 cars imported in 1996, one third were smuggled into Vietnam. Two years later, the Mekong car plant closed down, while Ford and BMW were facing serious difficulties.

Table 1. World Bank Governance Indicators for Vietnam 1996 – 2004

Top of Form Country Bottom of Form	Income Category	Dataset	Voice and Accountability					Political Stability				
			Percentile Rank (0-100)	Standard Deviation	Number of surveys/ Polls	Regional Average	Income Category Average	Percentile Rank (0-100)	Standard Deviation	Number of surveys/ polls	Regiona l Average	Income Category Average
VIETNAM	Low Income	2004	7.3	0.14	10	50	27.8	51.9	0.2	10	55.3	26.7
		2002	10.6	0.17	8	50.2	27.5	62.2	0.2	9	54.2	29.5
		2000	6.8	0.22	5	49	29.1	62.4	0.24	7	53	29.9
		1998	4.2	0.23	4	49.4	31	69.1	0.24	6	55.3	30.9
		1996	11.5	0.21	4	51.5	31.1	60.4	0.27	6	55	33.3
Top of Form Country Bottom of Form	Income Category	Dataset	Regulatory Quality					Government Effectiveness				
			Percentile Rank (0-100)	Standard Deviation	Number of surveys/ Polls	Regional Average	Income Category Average	Percentile Rank (0-100)	Standard Deviation	Number of surveys/ polls	Regiona l Average	Income Category Average
VIETNAM	Low Income	2004	27.6	0.19	10	50.6	25.1	44.2	0.15	12	46	21.5
		2002	24.5	0.18	9	42.3	25.4	47.3	0.15	11	50.4	24.5
		2000	21.9	0.26	6	43.3	29.4	43	0.18	8	51.8	28.5
		1998	24.5	0.25	5	40.3	28.8	49.2	0.22	6	50.3	30.6
		1996	25.4	0.24	6	48.3	26.8	57	0.21	6	57	27.5
Top of Form Country Bottom of Form	Income Category	Dataset	Rule of Law					Control of Corruption				
			Percentile Rank (0-100)	Standard Deviation	Number of surveys/ Polls	Regional Average	Income Category Average	Percentile Rank (0-100)	Standard Deviation	Number of surveys/ polls	Regiona l Average	Income Category Average
VIETNAM	Low Income	2004	35.7	0.12	15	53.3	23	27.1	0.12	13	45.3	23.5
		2002	42.3	0.13	13	51.1	25.2	34.2	0.13	12	44.3	26.6
		2000	25.1	0.15	11	49.2	25.9	27.4	0.14	10	44.4	27.6
		1998	20.5	0.18	9	45.8	26.7	29.5	0.15	8	47.9	27.1
		1996	34.3	0.16	8	53.6	26.4	30.7	0.22	6	52.4	28.3

Source: D, Kaufman, A. Kraay and M. Mastruzzi 2005. Governance Matters IV: Governance Indicators for 1996-2004. World Bank Policy research Working Paper. No. 3630.

This table presents the percentile ranking for Vietnam in 1996-2004 for six various governance indicators as well as regional and income category averages.

A World Bank study that measures six governance indicators is presented in Table 1. In governance categories such as "rule of law" and "control of corruption", Vietnam performs below the Asian regional average on both measures.

In the next section we outline the foreign direct investment process in Vietnam.

3. Foreign Investment Process in Vietnam

In 1986 a reform program of economic renovation, known as "*doi moi*" was formally adopted in Vietnam. The 1987 Foreign Investment Law set out the basic framework for foreign investment in Vietnam and the law was subsequently amended in 1990, 1992, 1996 and 2000. In the 1990s Vietnam relied heavily on a continued inflow of foreign investment in order to sustain rapid economic growth. From time to time, imports of cement, certain types of steel and cars have been banned in order to boost these industries in Vietnam.

Foreign invested enterprises, including both joint ventures and 100 percent foreign owned subsidiaries, grew at a rate of 20 percent annually between 1996 and 2001, making it the fastest growing part of the industrial economy. The leading investors (by country) in Vietnam were Singapore, Taiwan, South Korea and Japan (in terms of number of projects and capital invested).[64]

New foreign direct investment commitments declined after the Asian financial crisis of 1997, plummeting 40 percent. In 2001, foreign invested enterprises accounted for 35 percent of the country's industrial output. As of 2003, Vietnam was estimated to be spending almost US$5 in investment for every US$1 of additional annual output[65] , suggesting that much of its investment is not efficient.

The most important government body regulating foreign investment in Vietnam is the State Committee for Cooperation and Investment (SCCI), which was originally intended to be a one-stop venue for foreign investors. However, other government authorities, ministries and local People's Committees increasingly played a significant role in the assessment of foreign investment projects. The Prime Minister, Phan Van Khai, has acknowledged that "*Our administrative procedures are still cumbersome. You can get approval at the central level, but you still have problems at the local level with issues like land*".[66]

There are four avenues through which foreign investment can be made in Vietnam: a joint venture enterprise, a foreign wholly owned enterprise, a business co-operation contract and a build, operate, transfer (or BOT) arrangement. The most popular foreign investment avenue is the joint venture enterprise. Under Vietnamese law, joint ventures can be approved for a maximum term of 50 years and are considered to be legal entities with limited liability with each partner's liability limited to paid-in capital. There is a minimum foreign ownership requirement for joint venture companies of 30 percent, but no maximum limit is imposed. Typically, the local Vietnamese entity will require a 25 percent to 30 percent share of the joint venture. The Vietnamese authorities also tend to favor the joint venture as an effective way of involving local partners in the development of their country.

Joint ventures are used in the following:

---

[64] Economic Development Review (1998)

[65] Source: Economist Intelligence Unit

[66] Meyer and Nguyen (2005)

- construction and operation of telecom networks
- exploration of oil, natural gas, and other precious and rare resources
- construction and operation of industrial zones
- air, rail and sea transport
- cement production, steel and iron
- production of industrial explosives
- reforestation and planting of perennial crops
- tourism, sports, and entertainment

As a minimum requirement for foreign investment approval, the SCCI requires a joint venture agreement, feasibility study, and a joint venture charter. In negotiations, the key matters the SCCI considers are the investor's legal status, financial standing, business capacity, joint venture objectives, socio-economic effects including the environmental impact of the project, technology, and compliance of the project to Vietnamese law. Typically, foreign investors are eager that the agreement contain provisions for dispute resolution and control of a company's board of directors.

Other government agencies will usually be involved in the joint venture approval process. The Prime Minister's Office is required to approve large scale and sensitive investments. The key matters the People's Committee will consider are the suitability of the project to development of the respective sector and locality, local status and financial standing of the parties, labor supply, materials, water, power, transport, evaluation of the Vietnamese partner's assets contributed to the business, and the suitability of the project's location to local land planning. The Ministry of Science, Technology and Commerce reviews the technical aspects of foreign investment proposals.

Most foreign investments will also be subject to a number of different taxes, such as: profits tax, turnover tax, various withholding taxes, import duties, personal income tax for employees, social security, and health insurance premiums for employees. The basic profits tax rate for foreign invested entities in Vietnam is 25%.

Maitland (2002) analyses the conditions that promote corrupt activity targeted at multinational enterprises in Vietnam. First, public officials – particularly those at the provincial and local levels possess high degrees of autonomy and discretionary decision making powers over the operations of multinational enterprises. Secondly, official wages are very low, averaging US$25 per month. Finally, introduction of economic reforms constitute a significant threat to the beneficiaries of the previous system. This point is also reflected in the work of Rose-Ackerman (2004).

4. A Success Story

The One Million Tonne Sugar Program referenced in the beginning of the paper illustrates the problem with corruption and governmental inefficiency in Vietnam (see Arnold, Buchanan, and Lo (2006) for more specific details). The goal of the program was to convert large areas of poorer sections of the country for the production of sugarcane with the expectation of Vietnam becoming a net exporter of sugar. New sugar mills were to be built with a guaranteed supply of sugar available from local farmers. To protect the domestic supply of sugar, a large import tariff was placed upon foreign sugar.

What eventually emerged were a number of new small inefficient mills that were approved by local governing bodies instead of the central government in addition to some new large mills (the intended goal of the program), rampant sugar smuggling across the border (100,000 to 200,000 tonnes annually according to Arnold, Buchanan, and Lo (2006)), and a large portion of government promised infrastructure that never materialized (see Center for International Economics Report (2001)). Consequently, many foreign investors lost a tremendous amount of money (a drop in the market price of sugar in the late 1990s escalated problems). However, not all of the sugar mills lost money. Viewing the success of two particular mills allows one to see strategies that can surmount the problems of government inefficiency and corruption.

Two mills: Bourbon Tay Ninh Cane and Sugar Company (owned by Bourbon France) and locally owned Soc Trang Cane and Sugar Company, were both operating profitably in 2004 (Kiet; Saigon Times Weekly (March, 19, 2005)). Both mills employed similar strategies:

- Develop steady long-term relationships with clients through long-term contracts
- Have the firm build the infrastructure instead of waiting for the government
- Develop long-term relationships with suppliers
    - Insulate suppliers from price drops in the world market for sugar (i.e. increase the price paid to suppliers when the market price of sugar rises and do not decrease the price paid to suppliers when the market price of sugar decreases)
    - Provide credit to suppliers to develop better farming techniques and to increase the size and efficiency of farms

In viewing the strategy, one notices that the government and the state bank are almost eliminated from the investment process. Credit, infrastructure, and contracting with suppliers are controlled by the firm instead of relying on any state resources. Because wages are low, allowing the supplier some of the benefit of an escalating market price of sugar with protection from low market prices generates loyalty. Essentially, the strategy of these two mills is to not rely on the government and to have direct relationships with its suppliers. In other words, circumvent the government and establish direct relationships within the country.

Conclusion

The governmental structure of Vietnam is heavily bureaucratic with a central government that is not in control at the local level. Consequently, the opportunity for corruption and inefficiency are somewhat instituted through the structural dynamics of the government, judiciary, and banking system. When tariffs are imposed to promote domestic industry, smuggling across the border becomes rampant particularly when the local price of an item is much higher than the true market price of the item. In the case of the sugar industry, large stockpiles of unsold domestic sugar emerged in the early 2000s because "smuggled sugar" was much cheaper in price and readily available (see Arnold, Buchanan, and Lo (2006)).

This is not to say that foreign investment in Vietnam does not have any potential. The strategy of successful firms appears to be one of establishing direct relationships within the country. This relationship may include building infrastructure, providing credit, and a system for insulating local suppliers from short-term price fluctuations. In other words, the better a firm is at providing for its stakeholders within Vietnam including resources that are supposed to supplied by the government, the higher the probability of success. If a firm chooses to invest in Vietnam, the additional costs of this successful strategy should be incorporated as part of the decision-making process. These additional costs are the result of corruption and inefficiency which hopefully will dissipate over time.

REFERENCES

Arnold, T. Buchanan, B., and Lo, J. (2006), The Subtlety of Political Risk with Foreign Direct Investment: The Case of the Vietnamese Sugar Industry, *Journal of Financial Case Research*, Vol 8, No 2. pp. 9-20.

Bardhan, P. (1997) Corruption and Development: A Review of Issues, *Journal of Economic Literature*. 35, pp. 1320-1346.

Campos, J.E., Lien, D. and Pradhan, S. (2001), *Corruption and Its Implications for Investments*. Chapter 1.

Centre for International Economics (December, 2001), *Vietnam Sugar Program, Where Next?* (report prepared for the World bank), *http://www.thecie.com.au/publications/CIE-vietnam_sugar.pdf.*

Fforde, A (2004), Vietnam in 2003: The Road to Ungovernability? *Asian Survey*. 44, 1 pp 121-129.

http://www.transparency.org/policy_research/surveys_indices/cpi.

Kiet, P.V. (March 19, 2005) *Sugar: A Sweet Taste of Profit*, Saigon Times Weekly.

Maitland, E (2002) *Corruption and the Outsider*: Multinational Enterprises in Vietnam.

Mauro, P. (1995) Corruption and Growth, *Quarterly Journal of Economics*. 110. pp. 681-712.

Meyer, K.E. and Nguyen, H. V (2005), Foreign Investment Strategies and Sub-national Institutions in Emerging Markets: Evidence from Vietnam, *Journal of Management Studies*. 42(1), pp. 63-93.

LeMonde (February, 2000), Party versus State in Vietnam. Translated by Malcolm Greenwood.

Nguyen, T.H., Nguyen, H.V and Meyer, K.E. (2004) FDI in Vietnam, in Estrin, S and Meyer, K. E. (eds) *Investment Strategies in Emerging Economies*. Cheltenham Elgar.

Rose-Ackerman, S. (2004), The Challenge of Poor Governance and Corruption, Copenhagen Consensus Project, *Working Paper*.

Shleifer, A and Vishny, R.W. (1993). Corruption, *Quarterly Journal of Economics*. 108: 599-617.

Sidel, M. (1997), Vietnam: *The Ambiguities of State-Directed Legal Reform*, in Tan (ed.) Asian Legal Systems: Law, Society and East Asia. Butterworths, pp 356-389.

Tanzi, V. and Davoodi, H. (1997), Corruption, Public Investment and Growth, *IMF Working Paper*, 97/139, Washington D.C. International Monetary Fund.

Transparency International Corruption Perceptions Index 2002

Vinod, H.D. (1999), Statistical Analysis of Corruption Data and Using the Internet to Reduce Corruption, *Journal of Asian Economics*, 10, 591-603.

Wei, S.J. (2000), How Taxing is Corruption on International Investors? *Review of Economics and Statistics*, Vol 82, pp. 1-11.

INDEX

D

E

F

G

H

I

S

T

U

V

W

Y